The
Jesus
Who
Never
Lived

H. WAYNE HOUSE

HARVEST HOUSE PUBLISHERS

EUGENE, OREGON

Cover by Koechel Peterson & Associates, Inc., Minneapolis, Minnesota

The Jesus Who Never Lived
Copyright © 2008 by H. Wayne House
Published by Harvest House Publishers
Eugene, Oregon 97402
www.harvesthousepublishers.com

Library of Congress Cataloging-in-Publication Data

House, H. Wayne.
The Jesus who never lived / H. Wayne House.
    p. cm.
Includes bibliographical references and indexes.
ISBN-13: 978-0-7369-2321-7 (pbk.)
ISBN-10: 0-7369-2321-7 (pbk.)
1. Jesus Christ—Historicity. 2. Jesus Christ—Biography—Sources. I. Title.
BT303.2.H68 2008
232.9—dc22

                                                            2008012050

Printed in the United States of America

08 09 10 11 12 13 14 15 16 / LB-NI / 10 9 8 7 6 5 4 3 2 1

"This book stands unique in the current literature about Jesus. It is not another book defending the biblical Jesus as the historical Jesus, though it does that. It is not another book defending the biblical Jesus against cultic distortions, though it does that. No, *The Jesus Who Never Lived* is a readable, engaging treatment of the myriad ways—some true, most distorted—that Jesus has been viewed, from his family and early disciples, through the early Church Fathers and their creeds, up to the current depictions of Jesus that have multiplied like rabbits.

"Anyone who wants to see what all the fuss has been about will want to read this book, and anyone who wants a clear presentation of the real Jesus could not find a better source. I highly recommend it."

J.P. MORELAND
Distinguished Professor of Philosophy, Talbot School of Theology,
and author of *Kingdom Triangle*

"Jesus' life has always evoked alternative interpretations, as indicated by Jesus' question regarding his own contemporaries—'Who do people say the Son of Man is?' It is little wonder that the centuries since then have only added to these notions. Wayne House takes his readers through an amazing variety of such responses—from Jesus' own time, through Jewish, pagan, and Christian references, on through the world religions, and even to the popular media today.

"Provocatively, House declares that portraits of Jesus that fail to align with the Gospels amount to an invented Jesus—a fictional character who never lived—aptly reminding us of the constant need to return to the primary sources."

GARY R. HABERMAS
Distinguished Research Professor and Chair,
Department of Philosophy and Theology, Liberty University,
and author of *The Historical Jesus: Ancient Evidence for the Life of Christ*

"Rare is the book that has the scope of this one. Rarer still that one can aim the topic at the average person. Wayne House does both as he looks at the wide variety of ways Jesus has been seen and distorted in discussions about Him that range over culture, theological history, and various religions. Alongside that comes a positive presentation of who Jesus is.

"Wayne writes so the person who knows very little about Jesus can follow the conversations His life has generated. So if you want to get oriented to Jesus, both positively as well as in terms of the theories that are off the mark, this is the book for you. Welcome to the table. Reading this book will prepare you to join in the discussion and understand the debate. Most importantly, it will help you distinguish the Jesus who lived from all those who never walked the earth."

DARRELL BOCK
Research Professor of New Testament Studies, Dallas Theological Seminary,
and author of *Jesus According to Scripture: Restoring the Portrait from the Gospels*

To Raymond M. Pruitt—
theologian, preacher, and servant of Jesus,
on his eighty-sixth birthday

Acknowledgments

Many people are due thanks for their hand in the production of this book. I must first thank those who assisted me in the writing. Dr. William Grover, colleague and friend, read through portions of the work, providing helpful ideas, and also provided research in chapter 5 on the Church Fathers. I owe special thanks to two friends and former students, soon to be Drs. Gordon Carle and Joseph Holden. Gordon assisted me in research on the resurrection of Jesus, reliability of the biblical sources, and on engaging the cults, an area in which we produced a book together. Joseph Holden helped on the chapter on Islam, an area in which he has a master's degree and which is the topic of his dissertation research. Also, I must give special thanks to Robert Drouhard, who works with me as an assistant regularly. He has checked sources and footnotes and has helped develop aspects of these chapters in a careful and dedicated manner.

Gary Taylor, a librarian at Corban College in Salem, Oregon, went far beyond the call of duty to procure books for me at the Corban Library and helped me get other books through inter-library loan. I still owe him lunch. Spring Quick at Silver Falls Library and the staff of Mt. Angel Seminary Library made books available and let me re-check them time after time. Stephen Rost reached his usual standard of professional excellence with the indexes, done under considerable time pressure.

I also wish to thank Dr. Craig Evans for writing the foreword, and Drs. Darrell Bock, Gary Habermas, and J.P. Moreland for providing endorsements.

I must also express thanks to Rod Morris, editor with Harvest House, who has labored very hard, under a tight schedule, to work through the book with me. I worked with Rod many years ago on another book with another publisher. It has been a privilege to have his careful eyes and keen insight once again coming to my aid to make a better book. Many other persons at Harvest House have been involved in the project: copy editor Paul Gossard, Katie Lane and Abby Van Wormer in marketing, Neil Isaacson in design work on the book, and especially president and publisher Bob Hawkins Jr., who liked the project from the beginning and encouraged me along the way.

CONTENTS

✠

Foreword *by Craig A. Evans*. 9
Preface. 11

Part One: The Importance of Knowing the Real Jesus
1. What's It All About? 15
2. How Jesus' Family and Disciples Viewed Him. 27
3. How the People and Leaders Viewed Jesus 41
4. What Roman and Jewish Sources Said About Jesus . . 55
5. What the Early Church Believed About Jesus. 67

Part Two: Distortions of Jesus Throughout History
6. The Prophecy of False Messiahs 79
7. The Rise of Alternate Christs 91
8. The Jesus of World Religions. 109
9. The Quest for the Historical Jesus
      Since the Enlightenment. 135
10. The Jesus of False Christianities 155
11. The Jesus of Media Scholarship. 169
12. The Jesus of Popular Religion 191

Part Three: Finding the Real Jesus
13. Who Is the Real Jesus? 223

     The Conclusion of the Matter. 253

     Appendix: A Summary of Early Heterodox
         Perspectives of Jesus 257
     Notes. 261
     Select Bibliography 301
     Index of Scriptures and Other Ancient Writings. . . . 303
     Index of Names. 309
     Index of Subjects. 313

Foreword
by Craig A. Evans

In the last 25 years or so, readers of books and viewers of television have been bombarded with one new portrait of Jesus after another, many appearing in the days and weeks leading up to Christmas or Easter, often enjoying a great deal of media attention. To be sure, Christian scholars are usually given the opportunity to respond. But that is a big part of the problem: Sane biblical scholarship and historical research are often portrayed as reactive and on the defensive. Competent scholarship, which almost always supports the traditional understanding of Jesus, rarely receives attention in the popular media. When the general public hears the cautious, conservative scholar speak, it almost sounds as if he or she is on the run. Therefore, I am not surprised that increasing numbers of people fall for the silly notion that the church has misrepresented the real Jesus or has something to hide.

It is a pity that the media create this image, for it is quite false. The major discoveries of the last half century have in fact lent strong support to the historical veracity of the New Testament Gospels and to the traditional understanding of Jesus, which the Christian church has proclaimed for two millennia. Literary finds such as the Dead Sea Scrolls and archaeological discoveries have shed important light on Jesus and His world, and in some very important instances have provided dramatic proof of the reliability of the Gospels. Yet many of the most significant discoveries are hardly referenced, if at all, in popular presentations of the historical Jesus. Indeed, many of these discoveries are not taken into account, at least not sufficiently, in some of the scholarly publications. Why is this?

A surprising number of writers, including New Testament scholars themselves, lack training in the Semitic background of the New Testament. In attending national and international conferences for more than 30 years, I am surprised how often I bump into New Testament scholars who have studied Greek and know something of the Greco-Roman world, but have only the feeblest ability (if at all) with Hebrew and Aramaic. Most know little of the Dead Sea Scrolls, the early rabbinic literature, and the Aramaic paraphrases of Scripture that developed in the synagogue. Indeed, some of these scholars have not traveled to Israel and have not visited the excavations. Knowledge of these things is vital for an accurate understanding of the proclamation and teaching of Jesus. Yet many scholars do not know it well.

This deficiency on the part of so many New Testament scholars helps explain the oddness of much of the work of the Jesus Seminar, founded by Robert Funk in 1985. Whereas many of the Seminar's fellows have been exposed to Greek literature and Greco-Roman culture and conventions, not many of them appear to have competence in the Semitic (Jewish) world of Jesus. Few seem acquainted with the land of Israel itself. Few have done any archaeological work. Few know rabbinic literature and the Aramaic paraphrases of Scripture. As a consequence of these deficiencies, it is not surprising that the Seminar has come to so many odd and implausible conclusions. The Seminar does not understand what Jesus meant by His reference to "kingdom of God." The Seminar has completely misunderstood the meaning of eschatology and holds to a skewed idea of the meaning of Jesus' favorite self-designation, "son of man." Moreover, the Seminar finds no meaningful place for Israel's Scripture in Jesus' self-understanding and teaching. The Seminar's errors are egregious and legion, as many scholars recognize.

Unfortunately, the Seminar has gained a great deal of media attention and has cultivated a series of books that advance misguided and mistaken views of Jesus and the Gospels—both those in the New Testament and those outside the New Testament. Wayne House's *The Jesus Who Never Lived* addresses just these sorts of issues.

Dr. House has written a book that skillfully and carefully navigates through the murky waters of pseudoscholarship, on the one hand, and excessively skeptical scholarship, on the other. His reader-friendly book provides the antidote needed for the poisons of suspect data and faulty reasoning. I am pleased to have this opportunity to recommend it. It is a book well worth reading.

CRAIG A. EVANS
Payzant Distinguished Professor of New Testament
Acadia Divinity College, Wolfville, Nova Scotia
Author of *Fabricating Jesus: How Modern Scholars Distort the Gospels*

PREFACE

✠

When I was contemplating the writing of this book, I naturally asked myself why I should spend the effort to enter an already glutted market with yet another book on Jesus.

Renewed interest in Jesus has arisen over the last decade, an interest not in the usual Christian market, but in circles that heretofore were largely uninterested. Even scholarly, though admittedly critical, books on Jesus have occupied the rarified air of bestseller lists. The shelves of the religion section of secular bookstores, formerly reserved for Eastern and New Age religion, with a smattering of King James Bibles and books on practical living, now boast numerous books on Jesus.

Every time a book is written that parades a new revelation about Jesus, whether *The Da Vinci Code* and variations on this theme or books from the Jesus Seminar (or arguments that orthodox Christianity was only one among myriad early Christian beliefs), defenders of the traditional view of Jesus or early Christianity have written in response.

I have benefited greatly from reading many of these books, the former to see what is being argued by those who have abandoned the historic Christian faith and the latter to gain insight into the apologetic arguments that may be used to defend the orthodox understanding of Christ and Christianity.

I do not pretend to write something that replaces or even greatly supplements the fine books that defend the historical understanding of Jesus of Nazareth, many of which are listed in the bibliography. These scholars have addressed the most important challenges to the traditional view of Jesus in great detail, at times, and the reader should consult these works should he or she desire more information on the themes they are concerned with.

So why then another book? I have endeavored in this book to provide an overview for the general reader of the ways in which Jesus has been viewed over the last 2000 years by scholars and religions throughout the world, and how the discussion of Jesus has developed in recent days. The book is not for the scholar. Nor is my task comprehensive, since that would require a book many times the size of this one.

Albert Schweitzer interacted with approximately 200 books on Jesus when he published his classic *The Quest of the Historical Jesus* in 1907. Many times this number would need to be consulted today, with many pages required simply to list the theories about who Jesus is.

> *My desire is that the... reader will receive knowledge of the real Jesus amid the current contention that there are a number of equally legitimate understandings of Jesus.*

My task is also not so adventuresome. Since many scholars have written that Jesus may be claimed by all, be they deist, Buddhist, Hindu, cultist, or critical scholar, the general reader is led to believe that Jesus really can't be known. Who He is, is in the eyes of the beholder. With this I thoroughly disagree. But to go into the scores of visions of Jesus from every angle would be to lose the everyday reader in a labyrinth from which he or she would likely not emerge. I encourage those who desire to explore this topic in greater depth to consult the bibliography for evangelical books that interact with the attacks on the traditional view of Jesus.

My task, then, is more modest. My desire is that the nonspecialist, general reader will receive knowledge of the real Jesus amid the current contention that there are a number of equally legitimate understandings of Jesus. My contention is that those who advocate a Jesus other than the one presented in the canonical Gospels and the teachings of the apostles have presented a Jesus who never existed (other than in their minds).

The Jesus who really existed in the first century AD is accurately presented by those who knew Him, and their representation of His life, works, and words provides for us the proper information on which we may build a correct understanding of the one who is the Savior of the church and the Lord of the cosmos.

Maranatha!

Part One

The Importance of Knowing the Real Jesus

Chapter One

WHAT'S IT ALL ABOUT?

I n the Broadway play and later film *Jesus Christ Superstar,* Mary Magdalene asks, "What's it all about?" as she tries to figure out who this man called Jesus really is. Certainly there are aspects about the song she sings, and suggestions made in the play, contrary to what we know from the canonical Gospels about the relationship of Mary and Jesus.[1] But she does pose some important issues. She is puzzled about how to relate to Jesus as she has with other men, and this association with Him has made major changes in her emotions, actions, and thoughts. The reason she struggles is her perception that "he's just a man."[2] If Jesus is just a man, then why does He captivate her so and cause her to evaluate herself to the depths of her soul? Such questions about Jesus and the impact of His ministry, death, and resurrection have been asked for two millennia.

Every year around Christmas and Easter the news media show an interest in Jesus. Rarely do they speak to people who believe in the Jesus who has been worshipped by the church since its earliest period until now. Rather, the fascination is with a Jesus re-imaged by people who have little interest in the historical record preserved in the New Testament.

This interest in Jesus, unconnected to the earliest tradition and history we have of Him, is not a new phenomenon. Toward the end of the first century of the Christian era, perceptions of Jesus began to arise that were different from what He said about Himself as recorded in Matthew, Mark, Luke, and John and proclaimed by the apostle Paul. Jesus has become the favorite of ancient heretics, founders of various world religions, modern novelists, Hollywood and documentary filmmakers, New Age teachers, adherents of popular religion, and over-the-edge liberal scholars. He is by far the most popular, and possibly most distorted, figure of history.

When Christianity was less than a hundred years old, we find two groups at different ends of the spectrum in their views of Jesus.[3] One Jewish group, known as the Ebionites (late first century), accepted Jesus as the Messiah from God, acknowledged His humanity, but rejected His deity. On the other side were the Gnostics (early second century[4]), who accepted Jesus as a divine figure but denied His true humanity. This rise of Gnosticism coincides with the demise, though not extinction, of Jewish Christianity, toward the end of the first century and beginning of the second century.[5] Such views of the Christ were rejected by the apostolic church, and the view supported by the New Testament was finally put in creedal form, in a number of creeds, by the end of the fifth century.

Since those early centuries various religions have been enamored of Jesus. Eastern religions see Jesus as one of the avatars, or manifestations of God,[6] and Islam considers Him a prophet (see chapter 8 for both topics). In the former, Jesus is an Eastern mystic, sometimes even viewed as having been trained in India, and in the latter as one who promoted Islam.

Muhammad was a pagan who had contact with Jews and Christians from Arabia and finally became monotheistic, in the first quarter of the seventh century after Christ[7] embracing one of the over 300 Arabian deities: Allah, the moon god. In his limited investigation into Christianity, he came to believe, as is recorded in the Qur'an, that Jesus was born of a virgin, was sinless throughout His life, performed miracles, ascended to God, and will come again in judgment.[8] He acknowledged all of these things about Jesus, considering none of these to be true of himself.[9] Nonetheless, Jesus is never considered more than one of the prophets of Islam; He is not God in the flesh. Inside the Dome of the Rock on the Temple Mount, the walls are inscribed with statements that God does not have a Son, specifically addressed against the Christian doctrines of the divinity of Jesus and the Trinity.[10] As we shall see in a later chapter, Muhammad and his followers misunderstood the Christian doctrine of God.

In the eighteenth century, with the Enlightenment came skepticism about Christianity and absolute truth in religion. Biblical scholars and philosophers began to scrutinize claims that Jesus was more than human, and for over 200 years a search, or "quest," for the historical Jesus has been pursued. We have now entered the third quest.[11] While many within the second quest remain skeptical, there is growing support among some in the third quest for the credibility of the Jesus portrayed in the New Testament.[12] In contrast to those who have little regard for biblical and extrabiblical history, scholars of both liberal and conservative persuasion now agree that within a couple of years following the death of Christ, the church preached a consistent message about His death and resurrection.[13] Christ's followers considered Him both God and man, Lord and Savior. And those who became believers in the latter part of the first century and early second century continued to accept Jesus as portrayed in the Gospels. The church's belief in Jesus' deity and humanity did not begin with the Council of Nicaea in AD 325, as encouraged by the Emperor Constantine; that belief was present from the church's very beginning.[14]

> *Christ's followers considered Him both God and man, Lord and Savior.*

THE IMPORTANCE OF JESUS

Though contemporary novelists and media sensationalists never tire of trying to find some new angle on Jesus to attract an audience, most serious historians and biblical scholars are impressed with the evidence in the Gospels for the Jesus who lived, taught, performed miracles, died, was buried, and rose again from the dead.[15] An early twentieth-century composition by a devoted believer captures the wonder of Jesus:

> He was born in an obscure village, the child of a peasant woman. He grew up in another village, where he worked in a carpenter shop until He was thirty. Then for three years He was an itinerant preacher. He never wrote a book. He never held an office. He never had a family or owned a home. He didn't go to college. He never visited a big city. He never traveled two hundred miles from the place where He was born. He did none of the things that usually accompany greatness. He had no credentials but Himself.
>
> He was only thirty-three when the tide of public opinion turned against Him. His friends ran away. One of them denied Him. He was turned over to His enemies and went through the mockery of a trial. He was nailed to a cross between two thieves.
>
> While He was dying, His executioners gambled for His garments, the only property He had on earth. When He was dead, He was laid in a borrowed grave through the pity of a friend.
>
> Nineteen centuries have come and gone, and today He is the central figure of the human race. All the armies that ever marched, all the navies that ever sailed, all the parliaments that ever sat, all the kings that ever reigned, put together, have not affected the life of man on this earth as much as that one solitary life.[16]

But believers in the divine Jesus aren't the only ones who admire Him. Marcus Borg, a member of the Jesus Seminar and distinguished professor emeritus of philosophy and religion at Oregon State University, speaks as a skeptical historian about the significance and uniqueness of Jesus:

> The historical Jesus is of interest for many reasons. Not least of these is his towering cultural significance in the nearly

two thousand years since his death. No other figure in the history of the West has ever been accorded such extraordinary status. Within a few decades of his death, stories were told about his miraculous birth. By the end of the first century, he was extolled with the most exalted titles known within the religious tradition out of which he came: Son of God, one with the Father, the Word become flesh, the bread of life, the light of the world, the one who would come again as cosmic judge and Lord. Within a few centuries he had become Lord of the empire that had crucified him.

For over a thousand years, thereafter, he dominated the culture of the West: its religion and devotion, its art, music, and architecture, its intellectual thought and ethical norms, even its politics. Our calendar affirms his life as a dividing point in world history. On historical grounds alone, with no convictions of faith shaping the verdict, Jesus is the most important figure in Western (and perhaps human) history.[17]

These words of exuberant praise from a historian who does not accept Jesus as God in the flesh further indicates the amazing manner in which a human being was able to draw devoted followers by the magnetism of His life and teachings. Jaroslav Pelikan, noted historian of Yale University, has said of Jesus,

> Regardless of what anyone may personally think or believe about him, Jesus of Nazareth has been the dominant figure in the history of Western culture for almost twenty centuries. If it were possible, with some sort of supermagnet, to pull up of that history every scrap of metal bearing at least a trace of his name, how much would be left? It is from his birth that most of the human race dates its calendars, it is by his name that millions curse and in his name that millions pray.[18]

The world would be a considerably different place, with far less progress, peace, and hope than we possess today, had He not lived.[19]

LIKING JESUS WITHOUT KNOWING HIM

Just about everyone likes Jesus. How could they not, in view of the outstanding reception He has received throughout history, right? Not really. Much of the fascination with Jesus comes from those who really don't know much about Him. Were He to confront them with His teachings and call them to a life of obedience to His will, they might be part of the recalcitrant crowd crying out, "Crucify, crucify him!" (Luke 23:21).

Today a large number of people say they are attracted to Jesus but dislike His church.[20] They see within the church people who are inconsistent in their practice of Christian ethics and fail to follow what they understand to be the teachings of Jesus. The church is viewed as judgmental, whereas Jesus said not to judge. The church speaks against sins such as homosexual relationships, whereas Jesus loved all people regardless of their sin, such as the woman caught in adultery. The church has interest in political matters, but Jesus did not involve Himself in politics and worked only to ease people's burdens. (Whether these notions are true or not will be briefly discussed in chapter 12.)

This attempt to understand Jesus is often done without any reference to what we really know about Him. We simply guess who He is and how He acted—most often, how we *think* He ought to be and act to be acceptable to the twenty-first-century mind. Apart from the appeal to divine revelation, this is the manner in which He has been viewed over the centuries, including the century in which He lived on earth.

"WHO DO PEOPLE SAY THAT I AM?"

As Jesus traveled with His disciples to Caesarea Philippi, He posed an important question: "Who do people say that I am?" (Mark 8:27). The response to this question divides light and darkness, death and life. The disciples said that some believed Him to be an important prophet, but the apostles—specifically Peter—proclaimed His deity, a truth revealed to him by the Father. It is this authentic Christ, based on credible biblical and extrabiblical sources, whom we must encounter.

Each of us is confronted with important questions and priorities in this life. Some are of minor importance, but others have lasting, even eternal significance. The most important issue we must squarely confront is our relationship with God and, consequently, our final destiny. This is true not only for people today, it was also important in the first century when Jesus the Messiah came to earth.[21] This is evident in the words of Christ that if people did not believe that He was "from above" (heaven), they would die in their sins (John 8:21-24).

> *The most important issue we must squarely confront is our relationship with God and, consequently, our final destiny.*

Jesus the Prophet of God

In general, people liked Jesus Christ, as is true even today. The Scripture says that "the common people heard him gladly" (Mark 12:37 NKJV). Saying this, however, does not mean they always understood His message (Matthew 13:10-17) or understood who He was:

> When Jesus came into the district of Caesarea Philippi, he asked his disciples, "Who do people say that the Son of Man is?" And they said, "Some say John the Baptist, others say Elijah, and others Jeremiah or one of the prophets." He said to them, "But who do you say that I am?" Simon Peter replied, "You are the Christ, the Son of the living God." And Jesus answered him, "Blessed are you, Simon Bar-Jonah! For flesh and blood has not revealed this to you, but my Father who is in heaven" (Matthew 16:13-17).

The people during that time enjoyed what so many of us greatly desire—personal communication with the Son of God—yet they failed to understand Him. Many of them were miraculously fed and healed by Him. They heard His word with their own ears and saw

Him with their own eyes. No doubt many also touched Him with their hands.[22] To have the opportunity these people enjoyed seems too wonderful to imagine.

But when Jesus asked the disciples who the people thought He was, they cited many important figures of Jewish history, from John the Baptist (apparently thought to have been raised from the dead) to Elijah, who was to be forerunner of the Messiah (Malachi 4:5), to Jeremiah, who confronted the Northern Kingdom of Israel for its sins, or to some other prophet, as seen below:

John the Baptist. John the Baptist would have been a natural choice for the identification of Jesus, particularly by those who had not encountered John personally and maybe hadn't heard the news of his death. John spent his ministry in the desert, baptizing in Bethabara beyond the Jordan, whereas the people in view here are in Galilee or maybe the Golan. Otherwise it seems unlikely they would have made such a connection, unless they believed that Jesus was the resurrected John, which is what Herod Antipas thought: "At that time Herod the tetrarch heard the report about Jesus and said to his servants, 'This is John the Baptist; he is risen from the dead, and therefore these powers are at work in him'" (Matthew 14:1-2 NKJV). In the words of D.A. Carson:

> His conclusion, that this was John the Baptist, risen from the dead (v. 2), is of great interest. It reflects an eclectic set of beliefs, one of them the Pharisaic understanding of resurrection. During his ministry John had performed no miracles (John 10:41); therefore Herod ascribes the miracles in Jesus' ministry, not to John, but to John "risen from the dead." Herod's guilty conscience apparently combined with a superstitious view of miracles to generate this theory.[23]

Though Herod's superstition may be the cause for his comments, such a view is not unheard of in literature that precedes the New Testament. Albright and Mann say, "The reappearance of dead heroes was a well-known theme in contemporary Jewish thought...[Second

Maccabees 15:12-16] speaks of Jeremiah and Onias appearing to Judas Maccabaeus, and [2 Esdras 2:18-19] refers to the coming of Isaiah and Jeremiah."[24]

Elijah. Identifying Jesus as Elijah may appear surprising, except that Jesus' ability to do miracles and the expectation of Messiah's coming might have caused the people to believe He was preparing the way for the Messiah in agreement with Malachi's prophecy:

> Behold, I will send you Elijah the prophet
>> Before the coming of the great and dreadful
>> day of the LORD.
>
> —Malachi 4:5 NKJV

The disciples had similar expectations about Elijah, whom Jesus connected to John the Baptist as His forerunner (Matthew 17:10-12).

There are indeed many similarities between Elijah and Jesus.[25] Elijah exercised control over the forces of nature, telling Ahab his land would have no precipitation for several years (1 Kings 17:1-2).

In the midst of this judgment against Israel, God sent Elijah to the Phoenician city of Zarephath of Sidon, to a widow and her son who were facing starvation. To test her faith, Elijah asked her to make him some bread from the handful of flour and the little oil she had left. After she complied with Elijah's request, the jar of flour and the jug of oil did not become empty until the famine ended (17:14-16).[26]

Later, the woman's son died, and the prophet of God brought him back to life (17:17-24). These spectacular miracles performed for a non-Israelite mother and her son reveal not only the power of God but also the love of God for all people.

Those people who saw the ministry and attitude of Jesus no doubt considered Him to be like Elijah because He also controlled the forces of nature. On the mountain near the shore of the Lake of Galilee He multiplied bread and fish (Matthew 15:29-38), and He raised a widow's son who had died (Luke 7:11-17).

Jeremiah. The last prophet to whom Jesus is likened is Jeremiah.

What in the life and character of Jeremiah served as a basis for comparison with Jesus?

Donald Hagner says there are a "number of obvious parallels between Jesus and Jeremiah, such as the preaching of judgment against the people and the temple, and especially in suffering and martyrdom."[27] The message of Jeremiah was God's judgment against an unfaithful people (Jeremiah 1:16). Jesus presented a similar kind of message when He pronounced woe against Chorazin and Bethsaida (Matthew 11:20-24).

> *The Samaritan woman at the well first viewed Jesus as a Jewish man, then a prophet, then the Messiah, and finally the Savior.*

Jesus offered healing and solace to the sick and downtrodden, but to the proud and rebellious, the words of this "prophet from Nazareth" (Matthew 21:11) were sharp and powerful. Another point of similarity may be Jesus' cleansing of the temple and His indictment of those there (Matthew 21:10-13), and Jeremiah's rebuke in his famous temple sermon (Jeremiah 7:1-15). Both texts even accuse the unfaithful of making God's house a "den of robbers."

One of the prophets. Even if there was disagreement among the people about Jesus' identity, one thing is certain: They knew He was special, for He was viewed at minimum as a prophet. Just listening and watching Jesus revealed that He was powerful and insightful. This testimony—that the people identified Jesus with the prophets—demonstrates they held diverse eschatological expectations but there was no mass acknowledgment of Him as Messiah. The occasional reference to Jesus as the Son of David, found several times before Matthew 16, does not contradict the lack of recognition of Him as Messiah.[28]

Fortunately, we also see among some non-Jews a different response. The Samaritan woman at the well first viewed Jesus as a Jewish man, then a prophet, then the Messiah, and finally the Savior (John 4:4-42).

Whether they believed He was God's Messiah or one of the great prophets of Israel, all thought He was a person of great importance with divine authority and a powerful presence and message.

Messiah, Son of God

After the disciples responded to Jesus' question about how the people viewed Him, He asked, "But who do you say that I am?" (Mark 8:29). Would the disciples have a more accurate perception of their master than the general populace? You would think that their intimate relationship with Jesus would have made His identity clear in their minds. Yet this is not what we find. Though Peter correctly says that Jesus is the Messiah (*christos,* Greek translation of Hebrew *mashiach,* "anointed one"), the Son of the living God (16:16), Jesus says that the knowledge that gave rise to this confession came from heaven rather than from human insight (Matthew 16:13-17).

Is this confession true? Or is Jesus no more than a man, as the character of Mary sings in *Jesus Christ Superstar*? The Jesus who came to earth 2000 years ago has spawned a myriad of ideas about who He was and is. No more important subject than this confronts us today. Even among those who do not embrace the bodily resurrection of the crucified Messiah and His claims to deity, there is considerable praise. As Borg said of Him, "On historical grounds alone, with no convictions of faith shaping the verdict, Jesus is the most important figure in Western (and perhaps human) history."[29]

But is He only this—or is He, as Peter confessed, the Messiah, the Son of the living God? Our crucial quest in this book is to discover the true Jesus among the various visions of Him that have been constructed since His death and resurrection.

Chapter Two

HOW JESUS' FAMILY AND DISCIPLES VIEWED HIM

Believers and skeptics have offered a plethora of perspectives of Jesus over 2000 years of history. As already noted, He has been viewed as a revolutionary, an Islamic prophet, a misguided prophetic visionary, and a mystic, among other things. In upcoming chapters, we shall see that the disparate views of Jesus' person and work depend on the particular motive and setting of the person speaking of Him. Often those who put words into the mouth of Jesus of Nazareth had no access to the canonical Gospels, or they claim these records provide inaccurate or inadequate information about Him. In contrast to some of the post-first-century literature that gives fanciful descriptions of His words and deeds, we need to listen to those who actually saw and heard Him (1 John 1:1-3).

In the next few chapters we want to examine those who embraced Him as their friend, teacher, master, and even their God, as well as those who rejected Him and His message and even contributed to His death. We shall look at the spiritual leaders and power brokers among the Jewish people, the inner circle of Jesus' new spiritual kingdom, and His family, as well as the Roman officials who affected and were affected by His life.[1] Our primary focus will be on each of these groups' perspective of Jesus' person and work, and His perspective of them.

How Jesus' Family Viewed Him

His Parents

How a mother and father see their children is inevitably somewhat different from the way other people perceive them. This is no less true for Joseph and Mary, the parents of Jesus of Nazareth. They had personal experiences surrounding His conception and birth that cannot be known by anyone else. At the very conception of Jesus, by the work of the Holy Spirit, His parents realized He was to be altogether a unique person among men. The angels who visited them gave Him titles that identified His character and work. In Matthew 1:21-23, the angel told Joseph the child was to be called *Yeshua'* (Jesus), meaning "Yahweh is salvation." He would be given this name because He would "save His people from their sins." Moreover, the prophetic text that announces this birth (Isaiah 7:14) declares that the child will be called Immanuel, "God is with us."

Mary also received an angelic visitor who told her she would be blessed to be the mother of the Son of the Highest One who would inherit David's throne (Luke 1:30-35). The magnitude of this birth was not lost on Mary who, having visited Elizabeth her cousin, "sings out" a beautiful and theologically rich poetic praise about God's work through her for the people of Israel (Luke 1:46-55).

Being visited by an angel would be an amazing occurrence for any of us, and to be told of our involvement in a miracle of God would be even more wonderful. To be told, however, that the son to be born was God coming among humanity is too much to imagine. How did Joseph and Mary react, and what would be their response to this child? Matthew and Luke tell us that their initial response was complete submission to God's will for them (Matthew 1:24-25, Luke 1:38). After Jesus was born, it seems He was treated as an ordinary child, apart from the visit of the wise men approximately a year after His birth and the hasty retreat to Egypt to save His life. He was circumcised on the eighth day and presented to Simeon the priest after the time of Mary's purification (Luke 2:22). There

Simeon made an amazing prophetic statement that was clearly Messianic in intent:

> "Lord, now you are letting your servant depart in peace, according to your word; for my eyes have seen your salvation that you have prepared in the presence of all peoples, a light for revelation to the Gentiles, and for glory to your people Israel" (Luke 2:29-32).

Luke's Gospel then speaks about the amazement of the parents, but also hints at the prediction of the cross for their son:

> His father and his mother marveled at what was said about him. And Simeon blessed them and said to Mary his mother, "Behold, this child is appointed for the fall and rising of many in Israel, and for a sign that is opposed (and a sword will pierce through your own soul also), so that thoughts from many hearts may be revealed" (Luke 2:33-35).

Years would pass before this breaking of Mary's heart along with the judgment that would come on those who rejected this "light" and "glory."

Presumably Jesus received the customary religious education and instruction in His father's craft, and Luke 2:41 indicates that His parents took Him to the Passover feast each year. The spectacular events at the initiation of His life began to fade and to be replaced by the ordinary.

Only one event is recorded in Scripture that differs from the ordinariness of Jesus' life before the inauguration of His public ministry—His visit to the temple when He was 12 years old. Seemingly, Joseph and Mary had adjusted too well to their relationship with Jesus, for when they returned to Jerusalem to search for Him and finally found Him with the teachers in the temple courts, they marveled at His understanding. Jesus, though, knew Himself and His relationship to the Father in heaven. And even though His parents failed to understand what He said to them (Luke 2:49-50), Mary "treasured up all these things in her heart" (Luke 2:51).

By the time Jesus launched His ministry, presumably when He was between 30 and 33 years of age, Mary more fully understood and embraced His role as the Messiah. At the wedding in Cana she encouraged her son to perform a miracle, even before the time He had planned, but Jesus is respectful of His mother's wishes (John 2:1-12). (The term *woman* should not be understood as a derisive one—see John 19:26.)

> *Mary knew Jesus to be the Savior of the world and the hope of Israel, the Son of God and her son.*

Mary knew Jesus to be the Savior of the world and the hope of Israel, the Son of God and her son. As His mother, she had the terrible struggle to embrace His rejection and death, and at the same time she knew He was more than her son. He stood above her and all others as God. After His death and resurrection, she joined with His disciples in worship of the risen Messiah (Acts 1:14).

His Brothers and Sisters

How did the siblings of Jesus respond to their brother? The canonical Gospels provide little evidence, and that only about the brothers. Though the brothers are mentioned by name, only two, James and Judas, appear later in the New Testament.[2]

It is said that "familiarity breeds contempt," and this may well be the case for the brothers of Jesus. They did not experience firsthand the promises and miracles that announced Jesus' conception and birth, and apart from the legendary stories found in some of the later apocryphal writings regarding Jesus as a boy,[3] there were no signs that would cause them to see their brother as different from them.

Scripture gives no evidence that the parents showed any favoritism to Jesus or that the brothers (apparently four: James, Joseph, Simon, and Judas—see Matthew 13:55) knew about the special events surrounding His birth, though you would think this would be difficult to hide. The only indication we have that this information was kept private is that Mary seemed to internalize her thoughts about Jesus (Luke 2:19,51) rather than broadcast them. At least the acquaintances of Joseph and Mary had not been told about His special nature (John 6:42).

The biblical text suggests that on at least one occasion His brothers mocked Him by urging Him to perform public works:

> Now the Jews' Feast of Booths was at hand. So his brothers said to him, "Leave here and go to Judea, that your disciples also may see the works you are doing. For no one works in secret if he seeks to be known openly. If you do these things, show yourself to the world." For not even his brothers believed in him. Jesus said to them, "My time has not yet come, but your time is always here" (John 7:2-6).

The response of Jesus to His brothers is similar to His response to His mother when she asked Him to provide wine for the guests at the wedding in Cana, that is, "My hour has not yet come" (John 2:4). However, the brothers' request appears to be laced with sarcasm, for the author John, in his commentary, says, "Not even his brothers believed in him" (John 7:5). And Jesus' response to His brothers is more terse than His response to His mother: "My time has not yet come, but your time is always here" (verse 6). He refused to go with them to the feast and "show off" for the public, but then went privately after they had left (verse 10).

Mark tells us that the unbelief in Nazareth extended to Jesus' own household: "Jesus said to them, 'A prophet is not without honor, except in his hometown and among his relatives and in his own household'" (Mark 6:4).

It is amazing that the brothers are not even at the cross with their mother when their brother is being crucified. The nature of their relationship and their lack of belief causes Jesus, as oldest son of the family, to entrust the care of His mother to John, one of the apostles, rather than to His brothers (John 19:25-27).

Fortunately, the story does not end there. After Jesus had risen from the dead, the angel instructed the women at the tomb to tell His disciples to go into Galilee (Matthew 28:7). On the way, these women were met by the risen Lord who also commands them to "tell my brothers" to go to Galilee to see Him (28:10). It's possible that "brothers" here is used of the disciples, but the term does not seem to be used this way anywhere else in the Gospels (though Peter uses *brothers* to refer to all the disciples—both men and women—listening to him in Acts 1:15-16). Though certainly we may not be dogmatic, it may be that Jesus is now seeking to reclaim His own flesh and blood. Did His brothers go to Galilee to see their half-brother as the resurrected Lord? It appears they did, because they, along with their mother, were in the upper room on the Day of Pentecost (Acts 1:14), and Paul says that the risen Messiah appeared to James (1 Corinthians 15:7). Their antagonism to Jesus (during His ministry) and their absence (at His death) has now changed. They are now disciples of the Messiah awaiting the coming of the Spirit.

His Relative, John the Baptist

John the baptizer is called a cousin in the King James Version (Luke 1:36),[4] but the Greek word simply means a relative, without further designation.[5] John was the forerunner of Jesus and was the first human to herald His coming. His appearance indicated that the prophecies of hundreds of years before were now near culmination. Jesus said that if people could accept it, John was the Elijah to come to prepare the way for the Lord (Matthew 11:14; Mark 9:13; see Luke 1:17), so that John was the greatest prophet of all (Luke 7:28; 16:16). John condemned the hypocritical Jewish leaders and ritual without substance (Matthew 3:7-10), a condemnation later made even harsher by his more famous relative, Jesus (Matthew 23).

From the text, it appears that John did not know that Jesus was the Messiah, whose way he prepared, until this was revealed to him by the sign of the Spirit coming upon Jesus in the likeness of a dove at His baptism (John 1:29-36). John's bold statement that Jesus was the

Lamb of God to take away the sin of the world, and that He fulfilled the requirement of identification as God's Messiah, seems to be undercut by a later request that John sent to Jesus when he was in Herod Antipas's prison. John asked whether Jesus truly was the Messiah. Jesus responded that He was doing the works of healing and preaching that had been prophesied about the Messiah (Matthew 11:2-6). We can hope Jesus' words provided comfort to John's heart and assurance of his doubts at his dark time of discouragement before his murder by Herod Antipas.

How Jesus' Disciples Viewed Him

Different Groupings of the Disciples

When we speak of Jesus' disciples, we must keep in mind that there were different groups. Some, such as Peter, James, and John, had very close relationships with Jesus while others did not, and some even became disillusioned and abandoned Jesus (John 6:60-66). In between these extremes were the seventy-two, who were sent on a mission to the house of Israel (Luke 10:1,17), the band of the Twelve, and other followers such as Mary of Magdala, Lazarus and his sisters, Mary and Martha, and secret followers such as Nicodemus and Joseph of Arimathea.

The Special Trio of Disciples

Whereas the 12 disciples traveled with Jesus and assisted Him in His ministry (feeding the crowds—Matthew 14:14-21; procuring a donkey—Matthew 21:1-7; preparing for the Passover—Matthew 26:17-19), He took with Him only the trio of Peter, James, and John on at least three occasions: when He was transfigured in the company of Moses and Elijah and the Father declared from heaven the Son's uniqueness (Matthew 17:1-9; 2 Peter 1:16-18); when he went to the house of a ruler of the synagogue to bring back to life his daughter (Luke 8:40-56); and when He desired their company while praying in the garden of Gethsemane before His arrest (Matthew 26:36-38).

Nathaniel, Philip, and Andrew

How did the various disciples view Jesus? It's difficult to determine except among the Twelve. Nathaniel enthusiastically accepted Jesus as the Messiah of Israel and the Son of God immediately after Jesus revealed supernatural knowledge about him:

> Jesus saw Nathanael coming toward Him, and said of him, "Behold, an Israelite indeed, in whom is no deceit!"
> Nathanael said to Him, "How do You know me?"
> Jesus answered and said to him, "Before Philip called you, when you were under the fig tree, I saw you."
> Nathanael answered and said to Him, "Rabbi, You are the Son of God! You are the King of Israel!" (John 1:47-49 NKJV).

I doubt Nathaniel understood the implications of the divine title he used at the time, and Jesus would give far greater proof of who He is in the future (John 1:50-51).

The one who brought Nathaniel to Jesus was Philip, his brother. Not much is said about him in the Gospels, but no sooner had he been called by Jesus than he went to get his brother to follow the Messiah. Philip believed Jesus to be the one "of whom Moses in the Law and also the prophets wrote, Jesus of Nazareth, the son of Joseph" (John 1:45). It is doubtful that, through this initial impression of Jesus, Philip viewed Him as the Son of God.

The Apostle Peter

Peter was the leader of the apostles. He had his hills and valleys in his relationship with Jesus and his understanding of Him. Peter's high point was correctly identifying who Jesus was after the Lord had asked the disciples about His identity. Peter's confession, "You are the Messiah, the Son of the living God" is a profound pronouncement at this juncture of his development as a disciple of "rabbi" Jesus. We learn from Jesus that this was not simply a tremendous insight on Peter's part but a revelation from God (Matthew 16:16-17). Hardly had these words come from Peter's mouth than he descends into one of his valleys. After Jesus began to explain to His disciples that He must die and come back from the dead, Peter took Jesus aside (ostensibly to not embarrass Him) and rebuked Him for this improper perspective (verses 21-22). Jesus' words to Peter are stinging: "Get behind me, Satan! You are a hindrance to me. For you are not setting your mind on the things of God, but on the things of man" (verses 21-23).

Misunderstanding Within the Apostolic Band

Jesus' person and mission were also not understood by the mother of the "sons of thunder," James and John (Matthew 20:20-28; Mark 3:17), when she asked that one of her sons be allowed to sit at Jesus' right and the other at His left in His kingdom.

As is true of all the disciples prior to Jesus' resurrection, they did not comprehend what it meant for Him to be God in the flesh. This is clear in Philip's request during their final Passover meal together that Jesus show them the Father: "Jesus said to him, 'Have I been with you so long, and you still do not know me, Philip? Whoever has seen me has seen the Father. How can you say, "Show us the Father"?'" (John 14:9). Since Jesus was the very revelation of the Father (John 1:18), to look at Jesus, God in the flesh, was to behold the Father (the invisible God).

John the Beloved

The name "John the beloved" comes from the traditional understanding that the person referred to in the Gospel of John as "the disciple whom Jesus loved" is, in fact, the writer of the Gospel (John 21:20-24).[6] John may have been a teenager when Jesus called him, and he was ostensibly the youngest of the apostles. He is depicted with soft features in at least one painting, which led some to mistakenly identify him as Mary Magdalene (see chapter 11). Several times in his Gospel, John reports Jesus claiming to be God.

The Case of "Doubting Thomas"

Thomas has been given bad press. When people think of him,

they think of unbelief. In fact, Thomas was the first to proclaim his willingness to die with Jesus (John 11:16). As for the occasion for which he receives the name "Doubting Thomas," after the death of Jesus, none of the disciples were heralding that Jesus would soon be raised. Instead they cowered behind locked doors in fear of the Jewish authorities (John 20:19).

Thomas was absent when Jesus appeared to the gathered apostles, and he refused to believe their story (John 20:19-25). Though he asked for clear proof of Jesus' resurrection, for which he has been castigated, his request is what John cites as proof of Jesus being the Word of life that came from the Father (1 John 1:1-2). "We have heard, seen, and touched Him," John says. Jesus was not unwilling to give the proof to Thomas; He simply indicated that those who believe in Him without such direct proof are especially blessed.

> *Instead of thinking ill of Thomas, we should remember his exclamation to Jesus: "My Lord and my God!"*

Recall that John's Gospel was written to provide signs that would cause people to believe that Jesus was the Messiah, the Son of God, and through believing they might have life (John 20:31). Instead of thinking ill of Thomas, we should remember his exclamation to Jesus, "My Lord and my God!" (John 20:28). This way of speaking to Jesus was sheer blasphemy if He were not God in the flesh; it was one of the many perspicuous declarations in the New Testament that Jesus was viewed as God hundreds of years before the Nicene Council.

Lazarus, Mary, and Martha

It does not appear that Lazarus, Mary, and Martha traveled with Jesus, but He did have considerable fondness for them.[7] He seemed to drop by to visit them on His trips to Jerusalem (Luke 10:38-42, John 12:1-2), since the town of Bethany was near the city.

No statements from Lazarus regarding Jesus are recorded. Such is not the case with Mary and Martha. Mary fully believes that Jesus could have kept her brother from dying (John 11:32). Her devotion to Jesus is revealed by her anointing His feet (John 12:3-8), and by her interest in listening to His teaching rather than helping her sister prepare a meal (Luke 10:39-40). The loving relationship between this family and Jesus is accented in the text, but little is known of their perspective of who Jesus was, other than Mary's confidence in His power.

Mary Magdalene

More is known about Mary Magdalene than other lesser figures among the followers of Jesus. Her name probably relates to her having come from Magdala in Galilee. Prior to the time of Jesus' passion, we hear of her only in Luke 8:2, mentioned as one of "certain women who had been healed of evil spirits and infirmities—Mary called Magdalene, out of whom had come seven demons" (NKJV).[8] She is present at the crucifixion and resurrection of Jesus, and we are able to determine that she and Jesus had a close relationship—though not in the nature of a spouse, a view advocated by Mormons and in novels such as *The Da Vinci Code*. No credible evidence exists, even in purported statements from Gnostic documents, that Jesus and Mary from Magdala were married.

According to John's Gospel, Jesus appeared alone to her near the tomb, assuring her of His intention to remain with the disciples for a while before returning to the Father (His ascension forty days later—John 20:11-18). We are not able to ascertain her perspective on who Jesus was other than when she calls Him "Rabboni," or teacher, though she must have viewed Him with awe due to His teaching and His resurrection.

Secret Disciples: Nicodemus and Joseph of Arimathea

We know that Jesus had at least two secret disciples, Nicodemus and Joseph of Arimathea. Nicodemus is most known for the encounter he had with Jesus at night,[9] as recorded in John 3. He began this private meeting with Jesus by indicating that he and possibly others of the Jewish leadership were impressed with Jesus; they were convinced He must be a teacher sent from God.

Jesus bypassed the flattery by saying a birth from above was necessary to enter God's kingdom. He then challenged this Jewish leader to be born from above, "of water and of the wind"[10] (John 3:5), figures of spiritual birth in Jewish thought equated with the work of the Spirit of God (Ezekiel 13:3; 18:31; 36:26). Jesus revealed the solution to the riddle of Agur in Proverbs 30:4, that He was the one who ascends and descends and is the Son of God (John 3:13) who has come to save those who believe in Him (John 3:14-21). The only other reports of Nicodemus are John 7:50-52, where He seeks to defend Jesus before his colleagues; and in John 19:39, where he joins in the preparation of Jesus' body for burial.

The accounts of Luke and John speak of Joseph of Arimathea. He is identified as a person who is good, righteous, and looking forward to the kingdom of God (Luke 23:50-51), but nonetheless one who was a secret believer (John 19:38). We know nothing else about him but that this member of the Sanhedrin was rich and provided the tomb in which Jesus was buried (Matthew 27:57-60).

Judas Iscariot

No discussion about Jesus' disciples would be complete without attention to Judas Iscariot. Each time the synoptic writers give a list of the Twelve, Judas's name is always last and usually with a "description which brands him with an infamous stigma"[11] (Matthew 10:4; Mark 3:19; Luke 6:16; John 18:2,5). We discover from John's Gospel that Judas was a covetous person and a thief (John 12:6) and that his disenchantment with Jesus and love of money finally led him to betray, in agreement with prophecy (Psalm 69:25; 109:8; Acts 1:16), the Lord to the Jewish leaders (Mark 14:10).

Judas never expresses faith in Jesus nor recognition of who He was, but was always "the son of destruction" (John 17:12). The highest title he ever gives to Jesus is Rabbi (Matthew 26:25)—not Lord, Messiah, or God.

There have been recent attempts to rehabilitate Judas. The so-called *Gospel of Judas*[12] argues that Judas alone understood his important part in helping Jesus achieve His destiny, and thus he is the best of the disciples. The first-century writers had far better understanding of Judas than a fourth-century Coptic document's attempt to make Judas a hero.

We have seen from a brief examination of the Gospels how family, friends, and foes understood Jesus. His family had difficulty accepting someone they were so familiar with, and even the disciples, who had differing levels of familiarity, struggled with all that Jesus had to say about who He was. Nonetheless, at least eleven of the Twelve eventually accepted Jesus as Lord, Teacher, Messiah, Son of God, and God in the flesh.

Chapter Three

HOW THE PEOPLE AND LEADERS VIEWED JESUS

We have seen that those who were closest to Jesus held Him in the highest esteem. But what of the general populace? What of the Jewish leaders and Roman officials? What did they think about Jesus? We will look into how the people in general reacted to Jesus, as well as how Jewish groups and Roman officials reacted to and were affected by Him. We will see their perspective on His person and work and additionally examine how Jesus viewed these different groups.

HOW THE JEWISH POPULACE VIEWED JESUS

His Hometown of Nazareth

The positive reception Jesus failed to receive from the people in His home community gave rise to a familiar aphorism: "A prophet is not without honor except in his hometown and in his own household" (Matthew 13:53-58). An important variation of this saying is found in Mark, where Jesus adds "and among his relatives" (Mark 6:1-6).

Both Matthew and Mark use the Greek word for one's homeland (*patris*), from which we derive *patriotic*, and then narrow the scope to one's household (*oikia*). Jesus had two kinds of opposition in Nazareth. First, those among whom He walked and worked, some for His entire life, were antagonistic toward Him. This opposition, however, may have been fresh and related only to His recent teaching. The thought seems to be, "Who does He think He is? How can this man we've known for years now come forth with these ideas and do these works?"

Their familiarity with Jesus is connected in Matthew to their knowing His father, Joseph the carpenter,[1] while Mark speaks of Jesus Himself being a carpenter. Both are true. Since sons learned the craft of their fathers ("He who does not teach his son a trade, teaches him to steal," is a Jewish saying),[2] it is natural for Jesus to have learned this skill and to have worked with His father until He entered His itinerant ministry.

Mark adds that the opposition was also among His relatives (*sungenes*), or extended family, in addition to the community and His own household.

Last of all, though He healed a few people, it was small in comparison to what He did elsewhere, because so many did not believe in Him.

The People Heard Him Gladly

Not every community was as hardened as Nazareth. Jesus walked through Galilee and even into Perea east of the Jordan River, and His teaching and miracles were widely accepted. "The large crowd enjoyed listening to Him" (Mark 12:37 NASB). Examples abound in which Jesus experienced warm association with the people. He received and blessed their children, healed the sick who came to Him, and fed those who followed Him and were amazed at His teaching (Matthew 7:28).

> *His popularity grew to such an extent that the Jewish leaders, who desired His death, were afraid to do anything.*

When Jesus healed those who were possessed by demons and could not speak, "the crowds marveled, saying, 'Never was anything like this seen in Israel'" (Matthew 9:33).

When He came into Jerusalem at the beginning of the week

before His death, the multitudes spread branches and their garments in His path, welcoming Jesus as the Son of David. The crowds acknowledged Him as the prophet from Nazareth in Galilee. His popularity grew to such an extent that the Jewish leaders, who desired His death, were afraid to do anything: "When the chief priests and the Pharisees heard his parables, they perceived that he was speaking about them. And although they were seeking to arrest him, they feared the crowds, because they held him to be a prophet" (Matthew 21:45-46).

How Groups Within First-Century Judaism Viewed Jesus

An old saying, sometimes attributed to Machiavelli, tells us that "a man is known by his enemies." This proves true in the life of Jesus. His enemies were from two camps: those who were self-seeking partisans of the Roman conquerors, and those who wanted to maintain an ethical and theological monopoly over the minds of the Jewish people. The former we see in the priestly caste of the Sadducees, primarily, and of less importance the Herodians. The latter we see in the Pharisees, who did not wield political power in the time of Jesus (though during the Maccabean period much earlier that was not the case).

Jesus was not surprised by this animosity toward Him; He anticipated it: "If the world hates you, know that it has hated me before it hated you. If you were of the world, the world would love you as its own; but because you are not of the world, but I chose you out of the world, therefore the world hates you" (John 15:18-19). There was such resistance because He was the light of the world, spreading truth and opposing falsehood: "Everyone who does wicked things hates the light and does not come to the light, lest his deeds should be exposed" (John 3:20).

The leaders of Israel could not stand being under such scrutiny, and so they acted as their forebears had earlier with the prophets. Jesus hurled this stinging indictment against these leaders after He had come to Jerusalem to fulfill His destiny:

Woe to you, scribes and Pharisees, hypocrites! For you build the tombs of the prophets and decorate the monuments of the righteous, saying, "If we had lived in the days of our fathers, we would not have taken part with them in shedding the blood of the prophets." Thus you witness against yourselves that you are sons of those who murdered the prophets. Fill up, then, the measure of your fathers. You serpents, you brood of vipers, how are you to escape being sentenced to hell? Therefore I send you prophets and wise men and scribes, some of whom you will kill and crucify, and some you will flog in your synagogues and persecute from town to town, so that on you may come all the righteous blood shed on earth, from the blood of innocent Abel to the blood of Zechariah the son of Barachiah, whom you murdered between the sanctuary and the altar. Truly, I say to you, all these things will come upon this generation (Matthew 23:9-36).

Yet, who were these foes of the Messiah? Has too broad a brush been used to paint them as more wicked than they really were? Or have we simply misunderstood the intent of the Gospel authors in describing these conflicts Jesus had with each of these groups within Judaism?

Though there were numerous factions within first century Israel, in this chapter we will set forth only the ones mentioned in the Gospels, with some of the others to be discussed in subsequent chapters.

The Pharisees

Jesus had several bouts with the Pharisees. The New Testament does not present them as having, in general, interest in the political matters within Israel,[3] but Mark shows them combining with the Herodians against Jesus (3:6), and Matthew shows a connection with the Sadducees for the same purpose (3:7; 16:1,6,11-12). The Pharisees were concerned about the interpretation of the Hebrew Scriptures, thus their regular connection with the scribes, a combination found in all four Gospels (Matthew 12:38; Mark 7:1,5; Luke 5:21; John 8:3).[4]

A major complaint that they leveled against Jesus was that he had social contact with those, such as tax collectors and prostitutes, whom the Pharisees viewed as unclean, reflecting their practice of ritual purity (Matthew 9:10-11; Mark 2:15-16). Another complaint was that He and His disciples did not follow ceremonial washing rituals (Matthew 15:1-2). Moreover, He and His disciples failed to fast as did the Pharisees (Matthew 9:14). More than once He was criticized for performing unlawful acts, such as gathering grain (Mark 2:23-24) and healing on the Sabbath (Luke 6:6-7). The Pharisees even accused Him of casting out demons by the power of Satan (Matthew 9:34; Mark 3:22-29). The miraculous acts and words that identified Him as God brought the fiercest accusations from His enemies (Matthew 9:6).

Jesus castigated the Pharisees for failing to perform the more important works of justice, mercy, and faith while they concentrated on less important matters (Matthew 23:23-24). He accused them of taking advantage of widows and faking their prayers to God (Matthew 23:14 NKJV), and many times of being hypocrites (Matthew 23:13-29).

On the other hand, Jesus did agree with the Pharisees and against the Sadducees regarding the canon of Scripture and their theology of angels, resurrection (Mark 12:24-27), and predestination (John 6:44),[5] and encouraged people to follow the teachings of the Pharisees, though not their practices (Matthew 23:3).

In spite of the general hostility against Jesus reflected in the New Testament, all Pharisees were not alike. We know from the Talmud that the Pharisees recognized different types among their own ranks,[6] and the New Testament tells us that some Pharisees were even followers of Jesus, including Nicodemus and Joseph of Arimathea.

The Sadducees

The Sadducees receive far less notice in the Gospels than is given to the Pharisees.[7] They did not have the support of the people, as did the Pharisees,[8] but because they were friends with the Romans and many were priests, they were a powerful force within Israel. The Sadducees were closely connected to the temple, and many served on the ruling council of Israel, the Sanhedrin (Acts 4:1; 5:17; 23:6). They did not believe in angels and spirits (Acts 23:8), the physical resurrection of the dead, or the doctrine of predestination held by the Pharisees,[9] as well as the Essenes. Additionally, they held only to the books of Moses as Scripture. Since they controlled the temple and had access to the governing authorities more than the Pharisees, they were probably more significant opponents of Jesus, particularly in condemning Him to death.

The Herodians

Little is known of the Herodians, but their name says much. They supported the rule of the Herodian family. They are mentioned only three times in the New Testament, once in Matthew and twice in Mark. F.F. Bruce says that their "association with the Pharisees in the question regarding the paying of tribute to Caesar suggests agreement with them in the issue at stake, that is, nationalism versus submission to a foreign yoke."[10] And this same alliance is evident also in Matthew 22:15-22, indicating that they were nationalistic rather than being friendly to Rome, as were the Sadducees. Both the Pharisees and Herodians desired to entrap Jesus to discredit Him, and as Mark 3:6 says, "to destroy Him."

The Scribes

The scribes were very important in the development of Judaism following the Babylonian exile.[11] As mentioned, they are associated several times in the Gospels with the Pharisees in opposition to Jesus (Matthew 15:1-2). He is contrasted with them in His authority: "He was teaching them as one who had authority, and not as their scribes" (Matthew 7:29).[12] This probably related to His command of the Hebrew Scriptures and argument from them, without citing rabbinic sources from oral tradition for their interpretation.

The Priests

Nearly every reference to the priests in the Gospels is in a negative light. Jesus was not their opponent per se, and He recognized the priests' legitimate function within the religion of Israel (Matthew 8:4; Mark 1:44; Luke 5:14; 17:14). However, members of the priesthood, particularly the chief priests, were in continual struggle with Jesus throughout His ministry and played a decisive role in His crucifixion.[13]

Not only did Jesus challenge their authority over the temple area with His cleansing of the peddlers (Mark 11:15-18; John 2:14-16), but the people held Him in such high regard that it fomented jealousy within them: "When the chief priests and scribes saw the wonderful things that He did, and the children crying out in the temple and saying, 'Hosanna to the Son of David!' they were indignant" (Matthew 21:15 NKJV).

It is no wonder this opposition arose, since the teachings and practice of Jesus struck at the heart of the priests' existence within Judaism. The death of a suffering Messiah would put an end to the sacrifice in the temple and the need for a priestly caste.[14] In view of all of this, we see the chief priests conspiring with the Pharisees to arrest Him and put Him to death (John 7:25-52; 11:45-57; 12:9-11). They did not see Him as a prophet, Messiah, or the Son of God. They saw Him as a "thorn in their side" that had to be removed.[15]

Jewish Leaders at the Cross

The Jewish leaders at the foot of the cross of Jesus must have felt a certain triumph as they looked up at this "thorn in their side." They believed they had conquered the one who would be their king, who claimed to be on an equal footing with God Himself, who had brought their attitudes and actions into question—they who considered themselves the rightful rulers over the people of Israel.

All three synoptic accounts of the crucifixion have these rulers of Israel gloating over their prey (Matthew 27:39-43; Mark 15:29-32; Luke 23:35). Matthew identifies them as the chief priests, the scribes, and the elders; Mark singles out the chief priests and the scribes; and Luke uses the general term "rulers." No Pharisee is mentioned in these accounts, though some probably would have been at the trial.

The Gospels reveal three levels of misunderstanding that the Jewish leaders had about Jesus. They misunderstood who Jesus was; they misunderstood what Jesus taught; and they misunderstood why Jesus came.

His identity. The ones at the cross mocked Jesus' claim that He was the Messiah, the king of Israel, and the Son of God; they failed to understand *who* He was, though these three titles were united in the same person for the first time in the history of Israel. Each king, from the time of the first king, Saul, was the "anointed one," or Messiah (1 Samuel 10:1),[16] and also was known as a son of God, though not in the exact same way that Jesus was. The future Messiah would come from the Davidic line and would occupy David's throne as the everlasting king of Israel. Israel and other lands wished for their kings to live forever (1 Kings 1:31; Nehemiah 2:3; Daniel 2:4; 3:9). The future

> *Jesus encountered difficulty because of the type of Messiah He presented Himself to be; namely, not a conquering warrior but a suffering and crucified Savior.*

Messiah would actually achieve this, according to the Hebrew Scriptures as well as the Book of Enoch, which was referenced in the New Testament and considered an important though noncanonical book by early Jews and Christians.[17]

Jesus encountered difficulty because of the type of Messiah He presented Himself to be, namely, not a conquering warrior but a suffering and crucified Savior. The response of the crowd to Jesus' declaration that He would die revealed a common perspective, one the rulers apparently shared: "We have heard from the Law that the Christ remains forever. How can you say that the Son of Man must be lifted up? Who is this Son of Man?" (John 12:34). To them it was unbelievable that Jesus could be Messiah and yet be hung on a tree to die. If He was the Messiah, the Son of God, the Jewish leaders considered His crucifixion a refutation of His Messianic claims, which He had made before even the Sanhedrin (Mark 14:60-62). Thus the taunts rang out loud that day:

If you are the Son of God, come down from the cross (Matthew 27:40).

He is the king of Israel; let Him now come down from the cross (Matthew 27:42).

[If He is the Messiah (understood),] let God deliver Him (Matthew 27:43; see Psalm 22:8).

His teaching. They also did not understand *what* He taught. The false charge that He said He would destroy the temple was miscon-strued and was never established at trial. When He had driven the money changers and peddlers from the temple, some had challenged His authority. He supported His right by saying, "Destroy this temple, and in three days I will raise it up" (John 2:19). John's commentary clarifies that Jesus meant He would rise from the dead (John 2:21-22). But before this happened, He had to fulfill the Messianic "Servant Song" of Isaiah by suffering and dying (Isaiah 52:13–53:12). As He said in Mark 10:45, "Even the Son of Man came not to be served but to serve, and to give his life as a ransom for many"—something the Jewish leaders totally failed to understand.

His purpose. The rulers did not understand *why* He came. He had told His disciples after the confession in Caesarea Philippi that it was necessary that He die (Matthew 16:21; Mark 8:31). At one juncture, the turning point in Mark's Gospel, He declared He had come to serve and to die for many (Mark 10:45; see Matthew 1:21). At another time, He said He had the power to lay down His life and the power to take it up (John 10:17-18), speaking of the coming resurrection. He told Pilate he had no control over Him except what had been given to him (John 19:10-11).

The time of Jesus' being offered up was no less planned and pre-determined than was the time of the offering of the sacrifice in the temple. The deliverance from sin and the defeat of Satan foretold thou-sands of years before (Genesis 3:15; Colossians 2:14) was near, and it was the Father's purpose and will that the Son should die vicariously for humanity (John 18:11). And the Son was willing to do so (Mark

14:36). This was not a snap decision, but something He had determined to do (Hebrews 10:5-10; Psalm 40:6-8, LXX).

Christ of St. John of the Cross, a famous painting by Salvador Dali, shows the crucifixion from the vantage point of the Father looking down on His Son. What is interesting besides this angle is that there are *no nails* in Jesus' hands and feet. It was not the nails that kept Him on the cross; it was love.

The religious leaders did not know the true significance of their mocking words, "He saved others; he cannot save himself" (Matthew 27:42). If He saved Himself, then He in fact could not save others. They jeered, "Come down"; and He could have, but only if He had surrendered the very reason He came into the world to begin with, to save sinners. They said that if He would come down they would believe. But this is putting the onus of their unbelief on Jesus, as though He had not already done enough. In fact, the fault was their evil, unbelieving hearts (Luke 16:19-31).

Moreover, the Father had not forsaken the Son, as the Jewish leaders supposed. Though Jesus appeared to be abandoned by God, the cross was not the end of the story. The writer of Hebrews later tells us He endured the cross "for the joy that was set before him." Even at this time of great stress and pain, when He cried "My God, my God, why have you forsaken me?" much was not evident to the observer on that fateful day. The psalm that Jesus quotes on the cross, Psalm 22, begins with this cry of aloneness but ends with triumph. Such is also the case with Jesus. His death was not the end; He conquered death, and in the process conquered death for all those who believe in Him as Savior.

How Roman Authorities Viewed Jesus
Jesus, the Galilean Zealot

The only record of a possible confrontation with Rome before Jesus' condemnation by the Roman governor Pilate was regarding whether the Jews should pay taxes to Caesar, a trap (a seeming dilemma) set for Him by the legal scholars and chief priests. If Jesus said that the Jews should not pay taxes, this would bring the wrath of Rome down on Him. On the other hand, for Him to agree with the payment of taxes would provoke the people. These Jewish leaders must have felt very proud of themselves for devising such a test, but "He detected their trickery" (Luke 20:23 NASB). They began by seeking to flatter Jesus and to acknowledge the accuracy and truthfulness of His teaching, a ploy of no value in dealing with the great teacher (Luke 20:21-24).[18]

Jesus' ingenious answer sidestepped this seeming conflict of loyalties and established jurisdictional authority. Give to Caesar what belongs to Caesar, but more important, give to God what belongs to God. Rome demanded only a portion of the earthly possessions the Jews had, but God demanded entire obedience. Jesus' disagreement was not as much with Rome as it was with the failure of the religious authorities to be obedient to God. As Martin Hengel rightly observes,

> Jesus' attack was directed not against the Roman rulers, but against the religious and political ruling class in Judaism itself, the Sadducaean priests and the Pharisees. It was they and not, as the Zealots believed, the Romans who stood in the way of the dawn of the kingdom of God.[19]

Jesus and Pilate

The story of Jesus and Pontius Pilate is one of the most interesting in the Gospel accounts—the governor of Rome interviewing the King of kings. Pontius Pilate is mentioned in the canonical Gospels, Philo, Josephus, and several second-century Christian books, but the first physical evidence of him was an inscription found at Caesarea Maritima in 1961.[20]

Pilate, as prefect, held absolute authority within his domain on behalf of the emperor and senate of Rome. He held the power of life and death, and the right to overturn death sentences given by the Sanhedrin. He also appointed the chief priests, controlling even the temple and temple funds.[21]

Josephus indicates that Pilate often created conflicts with the Jews.

Early in his administration he set up, inside Jerusalem, Roman standards bearing images of the emperor, an act he rescinded after six days because of the furor from the Jews. Another time he used funds from the Temple to build a water aqueduct to Jerusalem. The rebellion against this project caused Pilate to kill a number of Galileans (see Luke 13:1-2), something that caused a rift between him and Herod (Luke 23:12) and that Pilate sought to mitigate by sending Jesus, a Galilean, to him (Luke 23:6-7). The subsequent slaughtering by Pilate of some Samaritans eventually brought such discord that he was summoned to Rome for questioning by the Emperor Tiberius, in AD 36, though Tiberius had died by the time the prefect arrived in Rome.[22]

> *Pilate sought to release Him...not out of the goodness of his heart, but probably because he did not wish to yield to the demands of the Jewish rulers.*

The Alexandrian Jewish philosopher Philo, a contemporary of the apostle Paul, has nothing good to say about Pilate, viewing him as "a man of a very inflexible disposition, and very merciless as well as very obstinate."[23] Pilate was not an effective administrator and lasted only a few years (AD 26–37) as procurator of Judea.[24] The church historian Eusebius reports that, under the Emperor Gaius, Pilate "was forced to become his own murderer and executioner."[25]

Had it not been for this star-crossed moment in history where he became the man to condemn Jesus to death, Pilate's name would hardly be known by anyone. But here he is on center stage, a third-tier Roman official questioning the King of kings, unknowingly preparing the convergence of history when the seed of the woman would crush the head of the serpent (Genesis 3:15).

The favor Pilate seemed to show Jesus was probably due to his desire to irritate the Jews, but may have been colored somewhat by the persuasion of his wife based on superstitious concerns (Matthew 27:19).[26] He did recognize that many viewed Jesus as the Messiah (Matthew 27:17,22). The inscription he placed on the cross seems to be based on the charge of the Jewish leaders that Jesus put Himself forward as a king and that He decried the payment of taxes to Caesar (Luke 23:2). The former is true since the Messiah is the king of the Jews, while the latter charge was false.[27] When Pilate asked Him if He truly was a king, Jesus readily admitted it (Mark 15:2), but in John's Gospel, Jesus indicated He was not king of an earthly kingdom (John 18:33-38). Such a claim posed no threat; Jesus clearly did not portray Himself as a Zealot attempting to overthrow Rome.

Able to see through the false accusations, Pilate sought to release Him (Luke 23:13-16), not out of the goodness of his heart, but probably because he did not wish to yield to the demands of the Jewish rulers. Only when the rulers connected the release to enmity with Caesar did he relent (John 19:12).

Jesus' reception by the people of Israel, the rulers of the Jews, and the Romans is no different from what He received from His family and friends (see chapter 2). Some embraced Him as the Messiah, even God in the flesh, while others scoffed at His claims and rejected the deeds that showed Him to be the Messiah of God. The people in general enjoyed His teaching and miracles, but the opponents of Jesus, including religious sects, the rulers of the Jews, and the Romans saw Jesus as a problem to be dealt with.

Chapter Four

WHAT ROMAN AND JEWISH
SOURCES SAID ABOUT JESUS

A variety of references outside of the New Testament refer to Jesus and early Christians. Some have more credibility than others, and even those that I have chosen to include that have connection to traditions may not always be substantiated conclusively. Here I discuss only the various texts that mention Jesus in some respect.

JESUS IN ROMAN SOURCES

Authors Who Speak of Jesus

Tacitus (ca. AD 56–ca. 117). Tacitus, a Roman historian of the first century and early second century AD, was a critic of Nero. His *Annals of Imperial Rome* (ca. AD 108) have been given much attention because they appear to be an early non-Christian reference to the followers of Jesus Christ. The context is the burning of the city of Rome (AD 64). Tacitus claims that Nero tried to blame the Christians of the city for that disaster. The unpopular Christians were reported to have both scandalous worship and a disloyalty to Rome. By not giving credence to Nero's attempt to shift blame for the great fire, Tacitus is not showing support for Christians; rather he despised Nero more.

And so we find Tacitus referring to Christ in Book XV, chapter 47 of the *Annals of Imperial Rome:* "Their originator, Christus [Christ], had been executed in Tiberius' reign by the Procurator of Judaea, Pontius Pilatus."

Pliny the Younger (AD 112). Pliny was a governor in the Roman province of Bithynia in modern-day Turkey. This episode may be one of the first clear occasions when Roman officials recognized Christianity as a religion separate from Judaism. For some reason a number of Christians had been brought into Pliny's court. The initial charges are not known. What is clear is that some of those arrested would not recant their faith. Pliny was unsure whether he could execute these Christians simply for their beliefs.

To settle that question, Pliny sought an answer from his friend Trajan, the emperor.[1] Among other things, he said he gives them a chance to recant and worship the emperor before being executed, and that these Christians confess "Christ as a god." Trajan responded to his governor's inquiry by saying that indeed the Christians are to be given a chance to recant their belief.[2]

Pliny is concerned because a large number of people had become Christians in his region, causing the closing down of temples and the ceasing of festivals, though he had hope that things were going to get better. He says that by punishing the Christians, the temples are filling back up and the festivals are beginning again, and that many Christians recant and go back to worshipping the Roman gods.[3]

In the late second century the Latin father, Tertullian, shows familiarity with this correspondence between Pliny and Trajan.[4] He accurately portrays their discussion about what to do with the Christians.

Suetonius (AD 120). Suetonius was a Roman historian and a court official under Emperor Hadrian. In his *Life of Claudius* Suetonius writes, "As the Jews were making constant disturbances at the instigation of Chrestus [Latin variant of Greek *Christos*], he [Claudius] expelled them from Rome" (25:4).[5] Suetonius apparently misunderstood the police records, thinking that Chrestus was in Rome and a leader of the riots in AD 49 that brought the expulsion from Claudius.[6]

Suetonius also writes of the persecution of Christians under Nero because they professed "a new and mischievous religious belief"[7]—apparently belief in Jesus' death and resurrection, in view of what we know about early Christian proclamation.

Mara bar Serapion (second or third century). A letter written by a Syrian, Mara bar Serapion, discusses Jesus as martyred by Jews and calls Jesus their king.[8] This may be a reference to the historical Jesus, but the information is too vague for us to be certain. Some have argued that this letter is a later Christian apologetic work,[9] and many skeptics say that the Jewish person executed and called "a wise king" was either a king in the days of Babylonia or the teacher of righteousness at Qumran.[10] These suggestions are not as likely as that Mara bar Serapion was a writer in the second century and that he was referring to Jesus, but we can't be sure.[11]

Lucian (second century). I have discussed some Roman writers who mention Jesus, but I will include one Greek writer, Lucian, a second-century satirist. His comments are not intended to be complimentary; he criticized Christians for their naïveté, using the story of a man named Proteus, who duped the Christians he traveled among. Lucian displays a remarkable knowledge of Christianity.[12]

Habermas notes several salient points from the words of Lucian. Early Christians worshipped Jesus; He introduced the teachings the Christians followed. The events occurred in Palestine, He was crucified because of what He taught, His disciples followed certain teachings, all these followers of Jesus are brothers, they have a conversion, they deny the gods of Greece, they worship Jesus as a god and live according to His laws. Lucian also calls Jesus a sage, making Him like the sages of Greece. Christians view themselves as immortal, giving them no fear of death. Moreover, Christians accept Jesus' teachings by faith, which results in having little care for earthly possessions, and so they share all things in common. Additionally, the Christians held to certain sacred books, and they were easily taken advantage of due to their gullibility.[13]

In addition to the observations by Habermas, the text also indicates that Lucian is viewing Christianity in its earliest stages, not like one who had familiarity only with the Hellenized form of Christianity, since he speaks of the Jewish synagogue with its elders and rulers and the president. The mention of believers holding all things in common may reflect familiarity with information found in Acts 2:42-47, and not necessarily uniform Christian practice.

Evaluation of Roman Sources

Adolf Harnack advises that in assessing the Roman understanding of Christians, we should recognize that the Romans thought "Christians had emanated from the Jews." It is certain that the Jews were marked as a special people because of their refusal to worship images, participate in other cults, and general exclusiveness. This was viewed as "a defect in public spirit and patriotism." However, Harnack informs us that by the time of Pliny, some Romans began to make a distinction between Jews and Christians. The latter were deemed to be "enemies of the human race."[14]

Harnack also establishes for us a principal reason for the periodic persecutions of Christians in the first several centuries.[15] Rome was not upset by religions existing contentedly alongside the Imperial Cultus. The Roman Cultus was based on worshipping dead and living Caesars. The religious arms of Rome were willing to embrace other sects as long as those sects were willing to give supplication to the images of the emperors. If only Christians would compromise a bit in their homage, they probably, for the most part, would have gone unmolested. But not only did many Christians refuse to honor Caesar with divine worship, there were times and places when church leaders forbid Christians to be party even to the games or the dramas or public teaching because that would require some contact with polytheism.

The central issue in much of the Roman persecution is the refusal

> *The central issue in much of the Roman persecution is the refusal of Christians to worship the Roman deities. The worship of Christ as God precluded the worship of others.*

of Christians to worship the Roman deities. The worship of Christ as God precluded the worship of others. A stunning evidence of this is an ancient certificate attesting to what was required of Christians to avoid punishment.[16]

Conclusion

That Christians believed in the deity of Jesus was not itself an offense. Rather, the primary issue between Rome and Christians was that the latter saw God worthy of worship only in His triune nature as revealed in Christ. The refusal to recognize the emperor also as God sometimes warranted a terrible death. The broken and charred bones of the Christian martyrs in the catacombs shout of faith in the power of a resurrected Christ. On the walls of the catacombs are inscribed memorials to these saints: "Victorious in peace and in Christ."[17]

Rome's persecution of the faithful is evidence of the early Christian belief that Christ is the true and unique incarnated God, and of Rome's awareness of this Christian teaching.

JESUS IN JEWISH SOURCES

There is a maze of opinion over which Jewish sources are wholly authentic and which, if any, are instead edited or created by early Christians with apologetic motives. My purpose is not to debate these issues. Consequently, the following section will alert you to the issues and, in some cases, will provide briefly the rationale behind some of the assertions of the naysayers. But no thorough response to all issues can be attempted here.

Josephus

Josephus ben Matthias (Roman name, Titus Flavius Josephus) was born just shortly after the crucifixion of Jesus. He was educated in biblical law and history. He became an important historian and even was an advisor to, and translator and spokesman for, Titus the emperor. For these reasons it is significant if we find in Josephan literature a reference to Jesus. But the evidence for that must be carefully sifted:

Josephus allegedly wrote what has come to be called the *Testimonium Flavianum:*

"Now there was about this time Jesus, a wise man, if it be lawful to call him a man, for he was a doer of wonderful works, a teacher of such men as receive the truth with pleasure. He drew over to him many of the Jews, and many of the Gentiles. He was the Christ, and when Pilate, at the suggestion of the principal men among us, had condemned him to the cross, those that loved him from the first did not forsake him; for he had appeared to them alive again the third day; as the divine prophets had foretold and ten thousand wonderful things concerning him. And the tribe of Christians so named from him are not extinct at this day" (*Antiquities.* XVIII.33).[18]

Because well-meaning Christian apologists have made uncritical claims about its authenticity, this passage has provided fodder for those who attempt to chew up any evidences for the historicity of Christ. Josh McDowell cites the Arabic manuscript of the *Testimonium,* which includes the clause "He was perhaps the Messiah," and one might fairly infer that McDowell believes the Arabic version provides evidence for the authenticity of the earlier Greek text.

We must be careful as Christians to be accurate about our sources in determining what the truth is, whether it supports our claims or not. And we must do this in face of those who radically oppose Christianity and even the existence of Jesus Himself.

Even though I am most willing to accept the evidence for the *Testimonium* wherever it may lead, some vehemently oppose recognizing the authenticity of even a partial statement of Josephus about Jesus. The whole passage is said to be fabricated pseudepigrapha (literally, "false writings")! The motive behind such claims is to discount Christianity, and the method is to provide a rationale against any part of the *Testimonium* as authentic witness to early Christianity; these opponents truly desire that Jesus had never lived.[19]

Fine scholars who have worked on the *Testimonium,* including Steve

Mason, one of the major Josephan scholars in the world today, find support for the accuracy of much of it. Christopher Price has put together a well-organized interaction with the various views, and I have used his fine work to set forth the material in this chapter.

The Testimonium *has an authentic core of Josephan language and style.* Price, who argues strongly for the partial authenticity of the *Testimonium,* maintains that the phrase "a wise man" is not a Christian addition. It is characteristically Josephan! But the phrase "if it be lawful to call him a man" is a Christian interpolation. Also, in "a teacher of such men as receive the truth with pleasure," Price finds strong evidence for the authenticity of "receives the truth with pleasure" because it is Josephan. Even the clause "He drew over to himself both many of the Jews, and many of the Gentiles," cannot be a Christian interpolation, Price says, because it conflicts with the portrait of Jesus in the Gospels. However, "He was the Christ," Price takes to be blatantly New Testament language and so not original. While he admits that interpolations in the *Testimonium* are not Josephan, Price argues well that the language and style of some references to Jesus are authentic.

The reference to James the brother of Jesus suggests an earlier reference to Jesus. Price then moves to a second argument to establish portions of the *Testimonium* as authentic. He points out that in the reference to James's martyrdom (see *Jewish Antiquities,* 20.200), Josephus refers to Jesus as "the so-called Christ." Yet there is, Price says, a "unanimous scholarly consensus" for the authenticity of the Book 20 reference.

The Testimonium *is present in all manuscripts of* Antiquities of the Jews. Price continues his argument by saying that there are 42 extant Greek and 171 extant Latin manuscripts of Josephus's *Antiquities.* These are not older than the ninth century so, Price admits, the probative value may not be great. However, references to the *Testimonium* among Christian writers indicate it was known much earlier.

Josephus makes no connection between Jesus and John the Baptist. Then Price makes a most convincing point when he says there is a text in *Antiquities* XVIII that is "accepted as authentic by almost all scholars." John the Baptist is discussed in that text, but Josephus makes no connection of John to Jesus. Yet, had early Christian editors been active in that passage, certainly they would have made a connection.

Textual variants in the manuscript tradition suggest an authentic core. Price compares the texts of Jerome, Ambrose, the Syriac, and Arabic versions, and from these argues that while the evidence shows some Christian tampering, it also indicates that the *Testimonium* on the whole is authentic.

There is no track record of Christians making such whole-cloth inventions. And finally, Price affirms that Christian copyists were conservative and not prone to fabrication.

No less convincing are Price's thoughtful replies to objections against the *Testimonium*. For example, does the *Testimonium* really not fit the surrounding passages? It is convincing to claim that it does fit since the preceding passage is about many Jews being killed. The reference to the death of Jesus is not an interruption to that topic. Price notes too that the phrase "the tribe of Christians so named from him" is not unfitting to that time, as Tacitus and Pliny make similar statements.[20]

> "And even to this day the race of Christians, who are named from him, has not died out."
>
> —FLAVIUS JOSEPHUS

Price exemplifies how an honest researcher should go about his work. He has found, even after editing out the obvious interpolations, a convincing body of evidence in the *Testimonium* to the historicity of Jesus. And so, it does not seem inappropriate to offer the following edited version of the *Testimonium* and think that it may represent the original. The suspected interpolations are in brackets:

> About this time arose Jesus a wise man [if indeed it be right to call him a man]. For He was a doer of marvelous deeds, and a teacher of men who gladly receive the truth. He drew to himself many persons, both of the Jews and also of the Gentiles. [He was the Christ.] And when Pilate upon the indictment of the leading men among us, had

condemned him to the cross, those who loved him at the first did not cease to do so [for he appeared to them alive on the third day—the godly prophets having foretold these and ten thousand other things about him]. And even to this day the race of Christians, who are named from him, has not died out.[21]

Babylonian Talmud: Tractate Sanhedrin 43a

Rabbi Michael J. Cook, Professor of Judaeo-Christian Studies at Hebrew Union College–Jewish Institute of Religion (Cincinnati campus), has written "References to Jesus in Early Rabbinic Literature." Cook points out that statements about Jesus in the Talmud are quite rare and that some references applied to Jesus may not be about Him at all. Yet he sees the following taken from Sanhedrin 43a as a possible reference to Jesus:

> Jesus (Yeshua) was hanged on Passover Eve. Forty days previously the herald had cried, "He is being led out for stoning, because he practiced sorcery and led Israel astray and enticed them into apostasy. Whosoever has anything to say in his defense, let him come and declare it." As nothing was brought forward in his defense, he was hanged on Passover Eve...(Rabbi) Ulla said, "Would you believe that any defense would have been so zealously sought for him? He was a deceiver, and the All-merciful says: You shall not spare him. It was different with Jesus, for he was near to the kingship"...The rabbis taught: Jesus had five disciples: Matthai, Naqai, Nezer, Buni, and Todah.[22]

However, Cook maintains that the Babylonian rabbis who wrote this were not testifying to Jesus' historicity. They were merely responding to the Gospel polemic that the trial of Jesus was unfair. The rabbis merely accepted the Christian reports as true. "This is a passage about later times, not anything factual about Jesus' day hundreds of years and miles away."[23] I wonder, though. Unless these rabbis gave some credence to the historicity of Jesus, wouldn't a more efficient and simpler counter have been to say, "There was no Jesus, so there was no trial and death of Jesus"? If the rabbis accepted as true the Christian claim to the historicity of Jesus, then that acceptance is a witness, is it not? Still, there are those who say Sanhedrin 43a cannot be a reference to Jesus.

That is the motive behind Dennis McKinsey's article. He does not doubt that the rabbis were addressing a historical occasion, but McKinsey asserts this occasion was not about Jesus at all! How could it be, he argues,[24] when

1. it says Yeshua, not Jesus
2. even if the two names were identical, there were scores of people named "Jesus" (Josephus lists 28 high priests with that name)
3. Jesus is said in the Bible to have been crucified, not hanged
4. Jesus is not said in the Bible to have been stoned
5. the Bible says nothing about a herald going forth for 40 days
6. Jesus had no connection with the government
7. the Bible does not say that Jesus was accused of sorcery

But these seven arguments are not convincing even to the Jewish professor, Rabbi Cook, and they break apart against rational responses. For example,

1. The two spellings are different because one spelling is Hebrew
2. Let McKinsey provide *another* Jesus of that period who was condemned to death by the Sanhedrin
3. "Hanged" is a term for crucifixion (Acts 10:39; Galatians 3:13)
4. That does prevent a Jewish notion that He was crucified justly
5. Again, it is not the Bible but the Talmud that is under investigation
6. "Near to kingship" may simply refer to Christ's descent from David

7. Even so, some Jews of the New Testament attributed His miracles to other powers than God. The rabbis are providing their understanding, not that of the New Testament.

In the mind of these rabbis, some of the events testified to in the Gospels about the life of Christ, such as His being a teacher and His being condemned to death, are historical.

Celsus

Before moving to patristic opinions about Christ, it seems fitting to use Origen's "Against Celsus" to provide another less-than-positive evaluation of the life and person of Christ. Celsus was a typical second-century spokesman for heathenism and had only negative evaluations of Christianity. He wrote *The True Word* around AD 178,[25] but unfortunately this work is no longer available. However, we can determine some of Celsus's opinions about Christ by noting them in Origen's *Contra Celsus:*

- 1:28—Jesus invented his birth from a virgin and was actually illegitimate. He acquired magical powers in Egypt...Jesus falsely claimed to be a God,
- 4:14—Were God to come down among men, the divine nature would be altered,
- 6:78—If God desired to rescue all peoples, why would He come to just one corner of the world?

Though he rejected Jesus, Celsus clearly believed that Jesus claimed to be God incarnate.

We find within the nonbiblical Roman and Jewish writings sufficient evidence to demonstrate the historicity of Jesus; we also find substantiation of much of what is said about Him in the Gospels of the New Testament. Certainly there is not the quantity and quality of statements we would desire, but this is no surprise. Jesus was viewed in the sources as a historical person who had to be reckoned with because of the growth of Christianity, which sprang from belief in Him, but He was not considered significant in the overall view of history. The irony is, He has become considerably more significant than those Roman writers and Jewish rabbis who made mention of Him, and their own writings are known largely because of the short references they made to this crucified Jewish teacher.

Chapter Five

WHAT THE EARLY CHURCH BELIEVED ABOUT JESUS

THE CLAIMS OF THE EARLY CHURCH FATHERS

We now move into the area of what Christians in the early centuries of the church believed about Christ. Even here, there are the assertions of skeptics to answer. For example, Dan Brown has one of his characters in *The Da Vinci Code* assert that the divinity of Jesus was proposed and established at the fourth-century Council of Nicaea.[1] This assertion deserves a careful and thorough response (see chapter 11). If it is clear that Christian leaders from AD 100 to 300 affirmed the deity of Jesus Christ, then *The Da Vinci Code* is exposed as a story based on poor research despite the claim on its back cover to be "carefully layered with remarkable research." So, we begin by looking at what some of the first-century Church Fathers wrote about Jesus in various epistles and other documents.

First Century

Clement of Rome to the Corinthians (AD 30–100). This first-century Father also repeatedly refers to Jesus as Lord and as Son of God.[2]

Didache (AD 80–100). This early Syrian church manual of discipleship speaks of Trinitarian baptism on two occasions (*Didache* 7). Connecting the Son to the Father and the Holy Spirit by one name indicates that Syrian believers were taught to embrace Jesus as equal with the Father.

It cannot, therefore, be seriously and correctly maintained that ecclesiastical leaders in the first century did not subscribe to both the humanity and the deity of Jesus Christ.

Second Century

Ignatius to the Ephesians (AD 107). Ignatius writes, "There is one Physician who is possessed both of flesh and spirit; both made and not made; God existing in the flesh...even Jesus Christ our Lord."[3] In the longer version of his letter, Ignatius calls Christ "the Lord, our God, Jesus Christ." Ignatius can hardly make it more evident that he is ascribing deity to Jesus, and this is centuries before Nicaea.

Polycarp to the Philippians (AD 110–140). This Father, who writes around AD 100, calls Jesus "Lord," "Judge," and "Son of God."[4]

Mathetes to Diognetus (AD 130–200). "As a king sends his son, so sent He Him; as God."[5] This quote occurs in the context of Mathetes's discussion of the manifestation of Jesus Christ. Mathetes says He who was sent is none other than "the very Creator and Fashioner of all things." The One sent is the "immortal One" and only begotten Son of God."[6]

> *Clearly Justin, nearly 200 years before the Council of Nicaea, believed Jesus to be Christ and God.*

Justin Martyr. Justin was born about AD 114. He was martyred about AD 165. In his *First Apology* he affirms that Christians worship only God, but the Son is included in this worship of the divine because Christ is God's only Son and became Man.[7] More precisely, Justin remarks that Jesus is the first begotten Word of God and is "even God."[8]

Justin, in his *Dialogue with Trypho,* responds to arguments by Trypho about Christ not being God. Justin's remarks include "Christ is called both God and Lord of Hosts";[9] "Christ existed as God," and Christ "was God even before the creation of the world";[10] Christ is "The Word of Wisdom, who is Himself this God begotten of the Father";[11]

Jesus "is deserving to be worshipped as God and Christ."[12] Clearly Justin, nearly 200 years before the Council of Nicaea, believed Jesus to be Christ and God.

Irenaeus (late second century AD). This father is thought to have been a disciple of Polycarp. Irenaeus wrote five books against heresies. In each and every one, Christ is declared to be divine.

- Book I: Jesus Christ is "our Lord, and God, and Saviour, and King."[13]
- Book II: Christ is "the Prince of Life existing before all" and He "co-existing with the Father" is Creator.[14]
- Book III: The Son truly is Lord[15] and is properly termed "God."[16] He cites John in asserting that Christ is the Word who "was God."[17]
- Book IV: Christ is the only begotten God.[18]
- Book V: Again Irenaeus agrees with the apostle that Christ is the Word who is God.[19]

Theophilus of Antioch (AD 180). Here is yet another second-century churchman who asserts that Christ is God. Theophilus is one of the first to use the word "Trinity" of God,[20] and he says the Word, Christ, is God.[21]

Athenagoras (second century AD). Athenagoras composed *A Plea for the Christians* about 177. In it, this apologist speaks of "God the Father, God the Son."[22] He says there is "a unity of these Three, the Spirit, the Son, the Father."[23] The Father, Son, and Spirit are "united in essence."[24]

It cannot, therefore, be denied that leaders in the second-century church attributed deity to Jesus the Christ.

Third Century

Clement of Alexandria (ca. 150–211). In several works Clement attests that Jesus Christ is God in the flesh. In *Exhortation to the Heathen*, Jesus is the Word who is God,[25] and Clement's readers are urged to believe in Him who is both "Man and God."[26]

In Clement's *The Instructor,* he also asserts that Jesus is divine. Jesus is portrayed as "God the Word" and God's "beloved Son." Christ is omniscient "since He is God."[27] In Book III of this same work, Clement provides a Christian hymn he composed titled, "A Hymn to Christ the Saviour." In this Jesus is called "Christ their King," "almighty Word," and "the God of peace." Clement also writes a prayer in which the Father, the Son, and the Holy Spirit are said to be "all in One."[28]

Tertullian (ca. AD 155–220). Tertullian's Christology is preserved for us in creedal form. This statement of faith was written about AD 200—more than a century before the imagined first establishment of the deity of Jesus at Nicaea. In this Confession, Tertullian precisely states that Christ is "both Man and God,"[29] and he also makes many other assertions about the deity of Jesus.

In *On Prescription against Heretics,* Tertullian writes "this Word is called 'His Son,' and, under the name of God was seen in diverse manners by the patriarchs."[30] In the same work, Tertullian says that Jesus is both "man and God."[31]

In Books III through V of *The Five Books against Marcion,* Tertullian expands on his understanding of the Person of Christ. Christ, who was preexistent, became Man[32] when He was born of the Virgin Mary.[33] In Book IV Tertullian recounts many ministry experiences of the incarnate Christ as related in the Gospels, and thus he affirms his view of the historicity of Jesus. Tertullian argues with Marcion that Paul calling Jesus the "image of God" in Colossians does not mean that Christ is not also "truly God."[34]

Origen (AD 185-254). Origen died in his seventieth year and left a treasury of theological and biblical writings. He asserts that Jesus is divine, the Son existing in the form of God is equal to God, and the omnipotence of the Father and Son is one.[35] Origen refers to "the most excellent Trinity...Father, Son, and Holy Spirit."[36] Not less enthusiastically does Origen in his commentaries affirm the deity and humanity of Christ. For example, in his *Commentary on John,* Origen says that Christ "is God."[37] Since Christ is in the beginning with God, He is

God.[38] There are "three hypostases, The Father, the Son, and the Holy Spirit."[39]

Hippolytus (died ca. 236). Irenaeus taught this Father. Hippolytus, among other works, wrote a *Treatise on Christ and the AntiChrist*. The Word of God (Christ) who is without flesh took upon holy flesh by the Virgin.[40] The Son who was born the Word of God before all ages is the Lord of things in Heaven and on earth.[41] Hippolytus agrees with Paul in Titus that Jesus is "God and Saviour."[42]

Cyprian (died ca. 258). Cyprian, in both his epistles and his treatises, teaches the deity of Christ. Christ, who is God, from the beginning is Son of God, and in time He has become Son of Man as well.[43] Cyprian had an occasion to supervise a church council, and he records one of its members saying that baptism is to be performed "in the Trinity."[44] Another member is cited as saying, "Jesus Christ our Lord and God."[45]

Novatian (born late second century). This Father died about 50 years before the Nicene Creed of 327 when, according to some, the church gave Christ His deity. Yet in Novatian's *Treatise Concerning the Trinity,* this father clearly asserts that Christ is God. Christ is both the Son of God and truly Man.[46] Christ is shown to be God by His works and powers.[47] It is wrong to deny that "the Son of God is God."[48] In his private creed, Novatian says that Jesus is "our Lord God."[49]

No one should suppose that the church did not fine-tune its doctrine about Christ over the first few centuries of its existence. Yet this review of a number of significant Church Fathers who lived, ministered, and wrote prior to the Council of Nicaea shows that long before that Council met, belief in both the humanity and the deity of Christ had been established.

THE CREEDS OF CHRISTENDOM

A creed (from the Latin *credo,* "I believe") is an authoritative statement of belief of the Christian faith to which a follower of Christ is expected to give assent. Although there were no formal Christian creeds during the apostolic age, there was a body of distinctly Christian teachings.[50] These teachings developed over the years to become the basis for the formalized creeds of Christendom. As the fledgling church faced more and more heretical opposition, the need for more refined and definitive creeds increased accordingly.

For example, orthodox Christians found the Gnostics a formidable theological foe. Yet Christians rose to the occasion and cast out the Gnostic heresy, and in so doing refined and clarified their own orthodox convictions. The best summary of early Christian beliefs is what we call the Apostles' Creed. The Creed is built upon belief in the Trinity, yet it does not develop Trinitarian doctrine—it does not seek to explain the three-in-one doctrine of God. Its primary emphasis is upon the relationship between God and men, while also repudiating the Gnostic idea that the created world is evil or the work of an evil god. While not apostolic in authorship, it certainly is apostolic in content.

One of the earliest local creeds to become canonized was that of the Roman church, the Old Roman Creed. It is the direct ancestor of all other local Western creeds and had tremendous influence on the Eastern ones.[51] The Apostles' Creed was used in the western church as a succinct summary of the primary declarations of faith required of those who wished to be baptized, for teaching and worship. The Apostles' Creed *indirectly* refuted various heresies, such as those of the Ebionites, Marcion, the Gnostics, and the Docetists. It is still used in many churches today during worship and communion as a distillation of the Christian faith (though its primary function was not the refutation of theological heresy).

The great *battle* creeds—the Nicene Creed, the Athanasian Creed, and the Chalcedonian Creed—formed the backbone of early orthodox Christology. They were written under far different circumstances than were the Old Roman Creed or the Apostles' Creed.

The Battle Creeds

The Creed of Nicaea (AD 325) was drafted specifically to refute the claim made by Arius, a presbyter in the church in Alexandria, Egypt, that Christ was the first and greatest creation of God and thus essentially different from the Father. The Nicene Creed affirms the unity of God, that Christ was "begotten from the Father before all time," and declares that he is "of the same essence [*homoousios*] as the Father." Thus the Son is God in every way. The Creed is primarily devoted to the person of Christ, although a passing affirmation of the Father and the Holy Spirit is made. The language employed in the Nicene Creed is far more sophisticated and precise than in the Apostles' Creed, since it was designed specifically to refute a single heresy and to affirm the orthodox Christology.[52]

> *Arius was quite content to allow for a Christ who was...created by God before the rest of His universe, who was even similar to God in His nature. The Council of Nicaea was not.*

This sophisticated language was employed to refute the Arian charge that Christ was a *creature* and to affirm His co-eternality with the Father—to affirm, in other words, that Jesus Christ is God. The focal point of contention between the teaching of Arius and the orthodox position was over Christ's "essence." Two words became the hallmark of this Creed: *homoousios* ("of the same nature") and *homoiousios* ("of a similar nature"). The Nicene Creed insisted that Jesus was "of one substance with the Father," that is, of the same divine nature as the Father. The distinction, then, was the subtle difference in Greek between two words: *homo-,* meaning "same," and *homoi-,* meaning "similar."[53] Arius was quite content to allow for a Christ who was a supernatural heavenly being created by God before the rest of His universe, who was even *similar* to God in His nature. The Council of Nicaea was not.

The Athanasian Creed, which gained general acceptance by the eastern and western churches, was written by an unknown author(s) in the Augustinian tradition, the majority of scholars believe, somewhere in Southern Gaul about the mid-fifth century. It contains a clear and concise definition of the Trinity and the Incarnation of Christ, both of which must be believed in order to be saved. It is named after the great early church father, Athanasius, who virtually single-handedly defeated Arianism and saved the Christian church from "pagan intellectualism."[54]

The Creed is still in wide use in Christian churches today. It affirms that "the Father is God, the Son is God, and the Holy Spirit is God; and yet there are not three gods but one God." The articles on Christ uphold His eternal "generation" from the substance of the Father, His complete deity and complete humanity, His death for sins, resurrection, ascension, second coming, and final judgment. It behooves every Christian to study and learn this truly great Christological affirmation.

The Athanasian Creed was a milestone in opposition to theological heresy, some of which is unfortunately being recycled and proclaimed as "new revelation." The Creed's use has declined in the church today because of its length and repetitiveness, which are not to our modern taste for brevity and sound bites.

The Chalcedonian Creed. The three major heresies of the fourth century—Apollinarianism, Nestorianism, and Eutychianism (or Monophysitism)—posed the most serious threat to Christianity, specifically to the doctrines of the Trinity and of the person of Christ. The Church Fathers knew that to surrender any aspect of Jesus' divinity or humanity would sound the death knell for the Church. To put an end to the confusion, a large church council of some 500 bishops was convened in the city of Chalcedon near Constantinople (modern Istanbul) from October 8 to November 1, AD 451. The resulting statement, called the *Chalcedonian Creed* (or the Chalcedonian Definition), refuted Apollinarianism, Nestorianism, and Monophysitism.[55]

The Definition states that Jesus Christ is perfectly God and perfectly man, that He is consubstantial[56] with God regarding His divinity and with mankind regarding His humanity.[57] Moreover, humanity and deity are joined in the person who is God and man "without confusion, without change, without division, without separation."[58] This was precisely the doctrine the early church fathers fought to preserve.

The Chalcedonian Definition represents the orthodox biblical teaching (admittedly in Greek philosophical language) accepted by

Catholic, Protestant, and Orthodox branches of Christianity, as to how Jesus Christ was God and man at the same time. Rather than being an intellectually pretentious and speculative invention of Greek philosophy or ontology (a charge some cults make about this and other church creeds), the Definition's purpose was to help the church correctly understand the biblical teaching that Christ's two natures are united together in the one person. When the Definition speaks of the two natures of Christ occurring together "in one Person and one *subsistence*," the Greek word translated "subsistence" is *hypostasis*, "being." This is often referred to as the *hypostatic union*, which simply means the union of Christ's human and divine natures in one person.

Therefore, our faith rests not on an extraordinary human being who happened to be unique and the most unusual person who ever lived, but on Jesus actually being God in human flesh. "The Word became flesh and dwelt among us..." (John 1:14).

Part Two

Distortions
of
Jesus
Throughout
History

✠

Chapter Six

THE PROPHECY OF FALSE MESSIAHS

*"For false christs and false prophets will arise and
perform great signs and wonders, so as to lead astray,
if possible, even the elect."*

(MATTHEW 24:24)

Shortly before He was condemned by the court of the Jews for declaring Himself to be the Messiah, Jesus spoke to the disciples about the end of the age. The biblical text, known as the Olivet Discourse, contains far more than we can look at here. We can examine here only the meaning that Jesus intended in His statements about the coming of false christs, a coming that is a challenge even to the elect of God.

In this chapter we'll examine Jesus' teaching about false messiahs, in what sense this relates to messiah figures within Judaism since the time of Jesus until the present day, and how we should understand the future coming of false messiahs, including the Antichrist. Then we'll look at individuals after the time of Jesus until the Jewish revolt against Rome in AD 132 under Simon bar Kochba, hailed by many within the Jewish community as the Messiah. Third, we'll look at the reasons why bar Kochba was viewed as the Messiah and how this defeat by Rome had such devastating impact on the Jews and has affected the idea of the Messiah in Judaism. Last, we'll examine messiahs who have come on the scene since bar Kochba and the change in Judaism from Messiah being a deliverer from the lineage of David to messiah being merely a vague ideology about freedom and deliverance.

Jesus' Prophecy of False Messiahs

The only occurrence of Jesus speaking about persons coming after Him as pretend christs is found in the Olivet Discourse, recorded in all three synoptic Gospels (Matthew 24:1–25:46; Mark 13:1-37; Luke 21:5-36). Let us look at this portion of Scripture to discover how we may recognize those who are not truly the Messiah.

The Setting of the Prophecy

Jesus traveled with His disciples to the Mount of Olives, immediately east of the Temple Mount ("opposite the temple" in Mark 13:3) across the Kidron Valley, to a place where He sat down to teach them. Either as they were leaving the Temple Mount or were on the way to the Mount of Olives, the disciples were enamored of the beauty of the buildings. Jesus turned this fascination into a teaching session on the future destruction of Jerusalem nearly 40 years away (AD 70): "Do you see these great buildings? There will not be left here one stone upon another that will not be thrown down" (Mark 13:2).

Probably in the minds of the disciples, the destruction of the temple would be a signal of the end of the age. This association would not be unexpected, because the temple, where God's presence dwelt, had been destroyed before by the Babylonians during a time of judgment. Now with Roman control in Israel, God would come to defend His people, destroy the wicked (Psalm 36, 37), and bring in the messianic age.

> *Whereas the predictions include the soon destruction of Jerusalem, they take us in time through many centuries to the final great tribulation and the coming of the Son of Man.*

The Disciples' Question

The disciples' query of Jesus is actually two or three questions. First, they are concerned with His immediate prediction, the destruction of the temple environs: "Tell us, when will these things be?" (Matthew 24:3; Mark 13:4; Luke 21:7). But they are also concerned about the end of the age, the time of Messiah's coming in power. When Jesus answers them, He seems also to interweave these elements, something important to understand as we consider the coming of false christs and the future epitome of false christ, the Antichrist.[1]

Whereas the predictions include the soon destruction of Jerusalem, they take us in time through many centuries to the final great tribulation and the coming of the Son of Man, Jesus, in judgment. Luke more particularly connects the questioning to the destruction of Jerusalem when He mentions several verses later that Jerusalem would be surrounded by armies (21:20,24) and be dominated by the Gentiles until the times of the Gentiles would be completed (21:24), while Matthew and Mark speak of the "abomination of desolation" (Matthew 24:15, Mark 13:14), with Matthew adding "spoken by Daniel" (Daniel 9:24-27). All passages speak of certain events that give fair warning to Jesus' disciples to flee the city for the mountains.

Second, the disciples inquire about the end of the age and Jesus' coming, presumably understanding this in the sense of apocalyptic judgment (these two may be separated events in their mind).[2]

There are a number of interesting points of discussion in the Olivet Discourse relating to the timing and events. Jesus explains those things that lead up to His coming and the end of the world, such as hostility between nations, persecution of believers, general breakdown of society, and the universal spread of the gospel. He also gives warnings to His disciples on what to do when the false christs come, though Jesus recognizes one who is the ultimate false christ,[3] the "Antichrist" spoken of by Daniel (Daniel 9:25-27; see Matthew 24:15-25 on "the abomination of desolation"), by John in his letters (1 John 2:18; 2 John 7), the man of lawlessness in Paul (2 Thessalonians 2:3),[4] and the beast of Revelation (Revelation 13–14, 20).[5] This is important to understand but beyond the scope of this book. Our concern is not with the final one who seeks to take the place of (*anti*) the Christ, or Messiah, but several who emulate aspects of the final false christ.[6]

Some false christs are people like Simon bar Kochba who either were viewed by their followers, or by themselves, as being the Messiah promised in the Old Testament. Other false christs, such as Antiochus Epiphanes, Greek ruler of Syria during the intertestamental period, are those who would seek to exercise dominion over the Jewish people, or the world, in the manner that Messiah is to do when He comes in power, similar to what Jesus expresses in Mark 13 and Matthew 24. Also, John the apostle speaks of false christs who by their false teaching create distortions of the Jesus who really lived and substitute one who is but a figment of their own evil minds. Thus the term "false christs" may refer to a number of ideas in the Bible and in historical development.

The Coming of False Christs

Wrong time and place. Jesus says that false christs are coming, but they may be identified. "Then if anyone says to you, 'Look, here is the Christ!' or 'There he is!' do not believe it" (Matthew 24:23). Followers of the true Messiah should reject the claims of anyone who says he is the Messiah or those who claim to know of another Messiah. Why the warning? Because the deception of false christs, as we have seen through history, is very strong and allures many. Over 1100 persons in the last century have said that they were Christ, most of these in Africa, India, or the Orient, and many have also spread West.[7] In the West false teachers such as David Koresh of the Branch Davidians and Jim Jones of the People's Temple have made such claims.

The claims of false messiahs are themselves falsified by the wrong time of the coming and the secret nature of the coming. Such claims are judged false because when the Son of Man comes, every person on earth will know it immediately: "As the lightning comes from the east and shines as far as the west, so will be the coming of the Son of Man" (Matthew 24:27). In His appearance before the Sanhedrin, Jesus said that those who seek to judge Him will in fact be judged by Him in His coming: "Jesus said, 'I am, and you will see the Son of Man seated at the right hand of Power, and coming with the clouds of heaven'" (Mark 14:62).

Wonders and signs. Second, Jesus said that false christs' deception could be so convincing that, were it possible, even the chosen ones of God would be deceived. Homer Duncan demonstrates the gullibility of people to accept a false messiah:

> A Christian leader in India informs me, "We have a man in India who claims that when the astronauts put their foot on the moon, the Lord Jesus Christ came into him and he became Christ. He advised his disciples that he is Christ and in him alone is safety. On hearing this, many people from Germany, Europe and the USA arrived over here and they are staying with him in huts somewhere at the tip of India in Tinnevelly District. Some of them have brought in thousands of gilders and gave it all to him."[8]

What is fascinating is that all of these people, and millions like them, are deceived by mere words. Jesus said that false christs would also deceive by signs and wonders (Matthew 24:24). Signs and wonders have been used together a number of times in the Old Testament (see Exodus 7:3; Deuteronomy 4:34; Nehemiah 9:10; Jeremiah 32:20-21), generally to attest a prophet's message, but also used of the wonders of God directly (Acts 2:19).[9] Imagine when the final false christ comes and performs lying wonders and deceives the whole world, except for the elect.

FALSE MESSIAHS UNTIL THE TIME OF BAR KOCHBA
Messiahs Before Jesus

Were there self-proclaimed messiahs in the first century when Jesus gave His warning? Some scholars have argued that prior to the coming of Jesus no one had claimed the title of Messiah. This does not appear to be accurate.

The Jews, who were looking for a deliverer, considered several figures as possible Messiahs prior to Jesus, including Enoch, Melchizedek, Moses, Elijah, and Judas Maccabeus. Some were immediately prior to the birth of the Christ: Simon the Servant (4 BC—*Wars* 2.4),[10] and Judas the Galilean (30 BC–AD 6), who rebelled against Rome and was defeated by Quirinius in AD 6 (Acts 5:35-39; *Wars* 2.118).[11]

Messiahs Until the Destruction of Jerusalem

We also have evidence of messianic figures who were contemporaries of Jesus until the destruction of Jerusalem. Josephus mentions a messianic figure named Jonathan, calling him a pretender (*Wars* 7.11.1). The book of Acts mentions an Egyptian (AD 40–52) who may also be included in this category (Acts 21:37-39; *Wars* 2.261-263) and Theudas (AD 44–45) who conducted a short-lived revolt against Rome (Acts 5:35-39; *Antiq* 20:97). The last so-called messiah figure before the destruction of Jerusalem in AD 70, Menahem ben Judah, supposedly the son of Judas of Galilee (AD 66–70), led a revolt against Agrippa II before being killed by a fellow Zealot.

Geoffrey Bromiley speaks to this matter, including Judas, Theudas, and Jonathan just mentioned:

> Some commentators have, indeed, pointed out that there is no historical record of anyone expressly claiming to be the Christ prior to the destruction of Jerusalem. This, however, is probably only in appearance (see Lange, commentary on Mt. 24:3). Edersheim remarks: "Though in the multitude of impostors, who, in the troubled time between the rule of Pilate and the destruction of Jerusalem, promised messianic deliverance to Israel, few names and claims of this kind have been specially recorded, yet the hints in the New Testament, and the references, however guarded, in the Jewish historian, imply the appearance of many such seducers"(LTJM, II, 446).
>
> The revolts in this period were generally connected with religious pretentions in the leaders (Joseph BJ

ii.13.4— "deceived and deluded the people under pretence of divine inspiration"), and in fevered state of messianic expectation can hardly have lacked, in some instances, a messianic character. Judas of Galilee (Acts 5:37; Joseph Ant. xviii.1.6; BJ ii.8.1) founded a numerous sect (the Gaulonites), and according to Origen (*In Luc. Hom 25*) he was regarded by many of them as the Messiah. The Theudas of Acts 5:36, "giving himself out to be somebody," may or may not be the same as the Theudas of Josephus (Ant. xx.5.1), but the latter, at least, made prophetic claims and deluded many; e.g., he promised to divide the river Jordan by a word.

Another instance is the "Egyptian" for whom Paul was mistaken, who had stirred up a "revolt" (Acts 21:38)—one of a multitude of "imposters and deceivers," Josephus tells us, who persuaded multitudes to follow them into the wilderness, pretending that they would exhibit wonders and signs (Ant. xx.8.6). This Egyptian was to show them that at his command the walls of Jerusalem would fall down (BJ ii.13.5). Of another class was the Samaritan Dositheus, with whom Simon Magus was said to be connected. He is alleged to have been regarded as "the prophet like unto Moses," whom God was to raise up.[12]

SIMON BAR KOCHBA, THE MESSIAH DESIRED BY MANY

After Israel's bitter defeat at the hands of the Romans in AD 66–70, no messianic person arose until some 60 years later when Simon bar Kochba ("son of a star," Numbers 24:17),[13] originally Simon ben Kosiba (son of Kosiba, probably his birthplace),[14] sought to throw off the yoke of Rome. His revolt was so massive, and his early success so considerable, that Rome brought a third of its legions (approximately 50,000 soldiers), to put down the rebellion. Unlike the earlier war, where the Jewish factions fought each other as much as they fought Rome, the Jewish army under bar Kochba was unified.[15]

Apparently the rebellion occurred after Hadrian's visit to Israel in which he attempted to eliminate circumcision and make Jerusalem a non-Jewish city and rename it Aelia Capitolina, after his family. Simon led the revolt after Hadrian left the area and was supported by the famous rabbi Aqiva, who drew a connection between Simon ben Kosiba and Simon bar Kochba and declared him the Messiah.[16] Not everyone shared the enthusiasm of Aqiva. Simon bar Kochba was killed by his own people when he acted in rage against one of his followers, and then failed to manifest certain capabilities the Jewish leaders believed were essential for one claiming to be the Messiah.[17] Afterwards he was called Simon bar Koziba ("son of a lie").

> *"Bar Cochba...had the order issued against Christians that, if they did not deny and defame Jesus Christ, they would be led away to suffer the most severe punishments."*
>
> —JUSTIN MARTYR

Second-century apologist Justin Martyr, who wrote just a few years after the bar Kochba war with Rome, tells us that Simon persecuted those Jews who embraced Jesus as the Messiah: "During the recent Jewish War, Bar Cochba, the leader of the revolt of the Jews, had the order issued against Christians that, if they did not deny and defame Jesus Christ, they would be led away to suffer the most severe punishments."[18]

The way that bar Kochba treated Jewish believers should not surprise us, based on the letter he wrote to Yehonatan bar Ba'ayan and Masabala bar Shimon, the commanders at Engedi. He threatens punishment for not confiscating wheat and then tells them not to give refuge to the men at Tekoa because they had not mobilized for war: "Concerning every man of Tekoa who will be found at your place—the houses in which they dwell will be burned and you [too] will be punished."[19]

Bar Kochba probably persecuted the Jewish Christians because they would not participate in his messianic revolt. For Christians to have done so "would have meant leaving Christ. Here one Messiah was opposed to another Messiah."[20]

MESSIAHS IN THE CHURCH FATHERS

After bar Kochba, another messianic figure did not appear until AD 448—Moshe of Crete—but this does not deter many Church Fathers from identifying certain heretics as false christs.

The church father Archelaus (AD 277), who castigated Manes as an antichrist for his false teaching and his attempt to deceive believers, afterwards ridiculed him because he could not perform miracles as the true Christ:

> Yea, even although you were to work signs and wonders, although you were to raise the dead, although you were to present to us the very image of Paul himself, you would remain accursed still...You are a vessel of Antichrist...I see you perform no miracle, I hold myself entitled to entertain such sentiments concerning you....For whom have you raised from the dead? What issue of blood do you ever staunch? What eyes of the blind do you ever anoint with clay, and thus cause them to have vision? When do you ever refresh a hungering multitude with a few loaves? Where do you ever walk upon the water, or who of those who dwell in Jerusalem has ever seen you? But why should I say more on this subject?[21]

Though not mentioning any false christ or the Antichrist by name, a couple of early Church Fathers believed in the literal coming of a future Antichrist who would do miracles, even attempting to deceive the elect, but that the true Messiah would come and destroy this Antichrist.[22]

MESSIAHS SINCE BAR KOCHBA

Virtually every century over the past two millennia has seen an emergence of Jewish messianic candidates and movements. As Jews wandered from continent to continent and country to country, often circumstances occurred that affected these Jewish communities in negative ways. These tense times produced a hope for the Messiah and the arrival of potential messianic candidates and movements. Countries and kingdoms in the Arabian Peninsula, North Africa, Europe, the Americas, and Asia witnessed these phenomena. Each century was touched by messianic meltdowns that resulted in more suffering and wandering for the Jews. Raphael Patai, a former professor at the Hebrew University in Jerusalem, states,

> The number of men who, in the course of the long Diaspora history, claimed to be the Messiah is unknown and cannot even be estimated, for those who left their traces in historical records can only be a fraction of the many more who arose, created a stir, gathered a following, and then met a violent end or disappeared.[23]

Well-known candidates through the centuries, such as those already mentioned; Moshe of Crete (AD 448–470) and his abortive return to Israel through the sea, along with the exploits of Abu-Isa (AD 750), David Alroy (AD 1120–1147), David Reuveni (AD 1484–1538), Shabbatai Zevi (AD 1626–1676), and Menachem Schneerson (AD 1902–1993) usually fill books and discussions on this topic. But over 90 other Jewish messianic candidates and movements are also mentioned in history.

✠

Whatever form belief in Messiah took, it is uniformly acknowledged that the constant hope of the Jewish people for over 2000 years has been God's Messiah, as illustrated in this traditional Jewish prayer, "I believe with complete faith in the coming of the Messiah."[24]

In the biblical context the Messiah was to come from the line of David the king, and was to usher in an everlasting kingdom over which David's son would reign. The prophet Isaiah spoke of this vision of Messiah and the golden age when lamb and lion would dwell together in peace. He also foresaw the Messiah as suffering for the Jewish people. These perspectives are not in contradiction but are related to different aspects of Messiah's work. Even the Essenes at Qumran acknowledged this hope and distinction. Similarly, rabbis prior to the first century AD believed that the suffering Servant of Isaiah 52:13–53:12 was the Messiah.

Jerry Rabow concludes in his investigation of Jewish Messiahs that "the past two thousand years of Jewish Messiahs have produced a few martyrs and heroes but, it sadly appears, a far greater share of confidence men, thieves, madmen, and innocents. Past messianic movements have generally brought disillusionment and disaster to the Jewish communities involved."[25]

Jesus came as the Messiah to Israel in a period of upheaval, despair, and anticipation. But unlike the other so-called Messiahs in His time and afterward, He brought hope and spiritual salvation, and fulfilled the prophecies of the Hebrew Scriptures.

✠

Chapter Seven

THE RISE OF ALTERNATE CHRISTS

The interest in a coming Davidic Messiah was only sporadic among the Jews after the first several centuries of the Christian era, and was of little interest among Christians (Jewish and Gentile) since they considered Jesus to be the Messiah. The problem that subsequently arose in Christian and non-Christian circles was the kind of Messiah Jesus actually was. We touched on some of these issues earlier in chapter 5, but we'll take a more in-depth look here as we consider the following questions about Jesus' nature.

Was He only a human Messiah and not God, as held by the Ebionites? Was He an opposing deity to the god of the Old Testament, as found in Marcionism? Was He the teacher of wisdom rather than a physical sacrifice for sins, a nonphysical intermediary from the pure spirit, as taught in Gnosticism? Was He the total embodiment of the Godhead, with no distinction between the Father, Son, and Holy Spirit, as taught in Modalism? Was He a quasi-God, created by God, as advocated by the Arians? Was Jesus a human indwelt by God, as in Apollinarianism? Was Jesus a blending of the divine and the human into a new nature, as taught by Eutyches? Were the divine and the human aspects of Jesus separate from one another, thus resulting in two separate natures and two separate persons, as taught in Nestorianism?

As you can see, there are many visions of Jesus different from the Jesus portrayed in the canonical Gospels and taught by the eyewitnesses and apostles of the first century. Yet these alternative perspectives are contradictory among themselves. And these portrayals fall within only what is loosely called Christendom; there are Islamic, mystic, and critical views of Jesus to be dealt with in subsequent chapters.

HERESIES THAT CHALLENGED THE DEITY OF JESUS

Ebionism

The Ebionites, a Jewish sect that began in the first century, embraced Jesus as the promised Messiah but maintained an *adoptionist* perspective regarding the incarnation.[1] Under this view, Jesus is not God manifest in the flesh; rather the divine spirit entered into the human Jesus.

Though the fourth-century writer Epiphanius said that this heresy came from a man called Ebion,[2] whose ideas are supposedly interacted with in the New Testament, this does not seem to be the case. *Ebionim* ("poor ones") probably comes from a Hebrew term for the poor or downtrodden.[3]

> *The Ebionites believed Jesus was the Messiah, but He was only a human being, born of his human father, Joseph.*

We are unsure at what point in the first century Ebionism began.[4] The term, however, began to be identified with those who were poor not only in this world's wealth, but also in understanding of the Son of God. This probably began with Irenaeus, as he sought to categorize heretical views in the ancient world. But other Fathers began to pick up the broad brush without the distinctions that should have been made. Consequently, by the second century—perhaps a few years earlier—we find the Ebionites identified by ascetic practices. But Eusebius says they were also called Ebionites because of their low opinion of Jesus.[5] They are described by Epiphanius as a heretical sect, among the 80 that he lists in his *Panarion*.[6]

The Ebionites rejected much of the New Testament, but used the

Gospel of Matthew,[7] called the Gospel to the Hebrews in their writings. The Ebionites believed Jesus was the Messiah, but He was only a human being, born of his human father, Joseph.[8]

Moreover, they believed that faith in Jesus was not sufficient for salvation. Obedience to the Law of Moses was required, such as following Jewish Sabbaths, festivals, and the Day of Atonement. They considered the apostle Paul an apostate.[9]

Among their number were those who claimed they could trace their ancestry back to Jesus.[10] Their obedience to the law, according to Epiphanius, was unconventional since they were vegetarians and opposed animal sacrifice, requiring them to explain away large portions of the Jewish Scriptures.[11]

They, along with other followers of Jesus such as the Nazarenes (see below), fled to Pella on the eastern side of the Jordan around AD 68. Ernest Renan is likely correct in his assessment of the impact of this flight. It caused great tension between nonmessianic Jews and Jewish Christians.[12]

I believe Renan is wrong, however, when he says that these Christians were surprised by the destruction of the temple. Jesus had warned of it, as recorded in each Gospel, and this most likely was conveyed throughout the Jewish community by oral tradition.

It is important to distinguish the Ebionites from the *Nazarenes,* often confused in the writings of some of the late Fathers. Jewish groups were often "lumped together" once the church became largely Gentile, and they were looked down upon because of the perceived abandonment by God of the Jewish people at the destruction of Jerusalem.[13] Some Gentile Fathers became increasingly antagonistic because Jewish believers continued to follow the Law, including circumcision.[14] This is an ironic reversal of the Jerusalem Council (Acts 15). In that instance, some Jews attempted to require Gentiles to keep the Law. Now Gentiles were demanding that Jewish Christians refrain from keeping the Law. As we shall see later, the Nazarenes, though keeping the Law, also were orthodox in Christian theology, such as the Trinity, the person of the Messiah Jesus, and salvation.[15]

Arianism: Jesus the Quasi-God

Arianism arose in the fourth century AD, denying to the Son equal status with the Father. Arius, a presbyter from the church of Alexandria, Egypt, near the beginning of the fourth century AD, believed that Jesus, prior to His incarnation, was created by God, a perspective that was condemned at the Council of Nicaea in AD 325. Arius's view is contrary to how Jesus was viewed as God both in the New Testament and in scores of references by the Fathers of the second through fourth centuries. At Nicaea, however, the relation of the Father to the Son was clarified, so that the Father and Son are seen to share the exact same essence, equally God in every sense. This Nicene doctrine also corrected a variation of Arianism, called semi-Arianism, held by many at the beginning of the Nicene council, including the church historian Eusebius of Caesarea. This view posited that the Father and Son were both divine, but did not share the same essence, with the Son having an inferior nature.

Arius summarized his views in a letter to Eusebius of Nicomedia, written around 321. In it he details his conviction that Christ had a beginning:

> But what we say and think we both have taught and continue to teach; that the Son is not unbegotten, nor part of the unbegotten in any way; nor is he derived from any substance; but that by his own will and counsel he existed before times and ages fully God, only-unbegotten, unchangeable. And before he was begotten or created or appointed or established, he did not exist; for he was not unbegotten. We are persecuted because we say, "The Son has a beginning, but God is without beginning"…And this we say because he is neither part of God nor derived from any substance.[16]

More than any other theological viewpoint, Arianism threatened to become the prevailing theological definition of Christ's Person in relation to His deity for the better part of the fourth century. It was far more theologically developed and sophisticated than Ebionism. Many Christian bishops and Roman emperors adopted this view, or the diluted *semi-Arian* view, which described Christ as being *similar* in nature (*homoiousios*) as the Father, but not the *same* in nature (*homoousios*) as the Father.

The doctrine of Christ's deity is essential to Christianity. Only a person who is eternally God could redeem a lost race from sin and its eternal consequence; no finite being could bear such a burden. Only someone who was truly God and truly man could bridge the gap between God and man and reveal God most fully to us (John 14:9).

Modalism: The Jesus Who Was His Own Father

During the second through fifth centuries of the church there arose a view called Modalistic Monarchianism, or simply Modalism. Several churchmen of the second century held this view, including Praxeas, Noetus, and Sabellius. In short, Modalists said that the distinctions between Father, Son, and Holy Spirit were only superficial. God is only one person who manifests Himself in different modes to mankind. As Sabellius expresses the phenomenon, God is Father in Creation, Son in redemption, and Holy Spirit in the Church.[17] Closely related to Sabellius's view is the belief that the Father suffered as the Son on the cross.[18] The Latin Father Tertullian challenged this view:

> The devil is opposed to the truth in many ways. He has sometimes even attempted to destroy it by defending it. He declares that there is only one God, the omnipotent creator of the world, only to make a heresy out of that uniqueness. He says that the Father himself descended into the virgin, was himself born of her, himself suffered; in fact, that he himself was Jesus Christ…It was [Praxis], a restless foreigner, who first brought this kind of perversity from Asia to Rome…he put the Holy Spirit to flight and crucified the Father.[19]

The danger of this heresy was that it minimized the importance of Jesus' person and ministry by reducing him to irrelevancy, replacing his redemptive act with that of the one God, the Father. However, it was not the Father who was incarnated, who suffered and died and rose again, but the eternal Son of God, distinct and yet one with the Father in essence. Since the church taught that Jesus was the only name under heaven by which sinful man could be saved, this heresy posed a profound challenge to the unique work of Jesus the Christ.

HERESIES THAT CHALLENGED THE HUMANITY OF JESUS

Gnosticism: Jesus the Phantom Human

There is considerable debate today about the origin and nature of Gnosticism. Was it prior to Christianity? Did it develop from Christianity or was it an alternate expression of the Christian faith from its very beginning? Were the Gnostics possibly Jewish or an evolution from Judaism, borrowing certain aspects of Christian imagery or theology, mixed with Jewish history and theology and Zoroastrianism from Persia, and heavily dipping into neo-Platonic thought? Debate is fierce in scholarly circles, and it has spilled over into the general public through media-driven views about Jesus and early Christianity through members of the Jesus Seminar, the novel *The Da Vinci Code,* and now the *Lost Christianities* of Bart Ehrman. We will deal with each of these in later chapters. Let us confine ourselves now to the early Gnostics and what they thought about Jesus.

The Gnostics were followers of a variety of religious movements that believed that the way of salvation was provided by the learning of and implementation of secret knowledge, or *gnosis.* Until 1945, we had only the Church Fathers' writings about the Gnostics. Then, in Upper Egypt near Nag Hammadi, a peasant found a cache of 11 Coptic codices and fragments, now referred to as the Nag Hammadi Library.[20] Contained in this collection are Gnostic, non-Christian Gnostic, and Christian-Gnostic writings, the most famous of which, the *Gospel of Thomas,* possibly exemplifies the latter.[21] In this book are the purported sayings of Jesus. An apocryphal gospel, its composition has generally been dated around AD 140 in Syria, though some scholars have attempted to date it to around AD 50, before the canonical Gospels were written.

Gnosticism was a sect, distinct from apostolic or Palestinian Jewish Christianity, but since it was syncretistic it incorporated elements from both Judaism and Christianity. The teachings of the Gnostic groups were bizarre and bewildering, having no systematic theology per se.

The early Church Father Irenaeus, in the latter half of the second century, wrote a list of a variety of Christological heresies that were due to Gnostic influence. Of particular interest is his reference to the *docetic* view (central to most Gnostic thinking) that Jesus Christ was a human being in appearance only:

> Among these, Saturninus came from Antioch...like Menander, he taught that there is one Father (*unum patrem incognitum*), who made angels, archangels, virtues, powers; and that the world, and everything in it, was made by seven angels. Humanity was also created by these angels...He also declared that the Saviour was unborn, incorporeal and without form, asserting that he was seen as a human being in appearance only. The God of the Jews, he declares, was one of the angels; and because the Father wished to destroy all the rulers (Principes), Christ came to destroy the God of the Jews.[22]

Another important witness to the docetic heresy was Ignatius of Antioch. Writing several years prior to his martyrdom about AD 107, he notes that early docetism taught that Christ did not actually suffer in reality, but only suffered in appearance, and was thus not truly human.[23] Probably the apostle John alludes to this heresy when he says that anyone not acknowledging that Jesus came, and remains (perfect tense in Greek), in the flesh has not come from God (1 John 4:2-3).

Central to Gnosticism was the notion of *dualism,* the world of matter and spirit in conflict with each other. The Gnostic needed to free himself from the material, inferior, physical world, and this was achieved by attaining a certain *gnosis* or knowledge that was accessible to only an elite group. Within the bodies of the more spiritual individuals in the world are sparks of divinity that await salvation through secret knowledge given by the redeemer docetic Christ. Thus awak-ened, the Gnostics fly from their prison bodies at death and bypass hostile demons along their way to be reunited with God.

Most Gnostic groups believed that Jesus was the one who came into the world to convey this knowledge to this elite group. Gnostics also believed, similar to Plato, that the human soul was trapped in a material "cage," and the goal of life was to be released from this body. They also held in general that the material universe was created by an imperfect *emanation,* called the *demiurge,* who emanated from the perfect divine spirit.

The demiurge was often identified with the God of the Old Testa-ment and seen as the counterpart to the God of the New Testament, represented through Jesus. The God of Jesus was pure spirit and there-fore good, whereas the God of the Old Testament created the universe of matter and, therefore, was evil.

Cerinthianism. Cerinthianism, even like Marcionism discussed below, does not reflect many of the Gnostic ideas found at Nag Hammadi and in the Church Fathers, but it is often grouped with Gnosticism. Its founder, Cerinthus, lived around AD 100 in Ephe-sus—the same city, according to persuasive tradition, that the apostle John resided in at that time. An early tradition developed that John and Cerinthus encountered each other in a bathhouse in Ephesus, and that John is reported to have said, "Let us fly, lest even the bath-house fall down, because Cerinthus, the enemy of the truth, is within."[24]

The heresy of Cerinthus is one that the reader of the New Testament may easily discern. The apostle John's emphasis on the Word becom-ing flesh in John 1:14 may have been addressed against the teaching of Cerinthus, and there is little question that the following statement from John's first epistle speaks of the teaching of Cerinthus:

> This is the one who came by water and blood, Jesus Christ;
> not with the water only, but with the water and with the
> blood. It is the Spirit who testifies, because the Spirit is
> the truth. For there are three that testify: the Spirit and

the water and the blood; and the three are in agreement. If we receive the testimony of men, the testimony of God is greater; for the testimony of God is this, that He has testified concerning His Son (1 John 5:6-9, NASB).

One may easily see that John counters the Cerinthian view that Jesus was no more than a righteous man upon whom the Christ descended at baptism and left before the death of Jesus on the cross.

Though he is often included in discussions of Jewish believers, there is little evidence to suggest that Cerinthus was a Jew. He did, however, embrace certain ideas, such as millennialism,[25] common to early Jewish Christian theology and the second-century Fathers influenced by this thinking.

Around the middle of the second century an apocryphal document called the *Epistle of the Apostles* speaks about Cerinthus alongside Simon Magus (Simon the Magician of Acts 8). This document considers them both to share the same heretical Gnostic views, though Simon is said to be the father of this heresy.[26] The *Epistle* strongly argues for the true humanity of Jesus against docetic views, aligning Cerinthus with this docetic perspective.[27] However, what we know of the teaching of Cerinthus from other sources indicates that even though he held aberrant views about Jesus, he does not appear to be docetic, and maybe not even a Gnostic, particularly due to his beliefs of a future earthly millennium. He shares ideas with Ebionism—for example, its adoptionist theology that the *logos* merely inhabited a special human being, rather than the orthodox view of the union of God and man in Jesus.[28] The late second-century theologian Irenaeus describes Cerinthus's erroneous concept of Christ:

> He suggested that Jesus was not born of a virgin (because that seemed to him impossible), but that he was the son of Joseph and Mary in the same way as all other men but he was more versed in righteousness, prudence and wisdom than other men. And after his baptism, Christ descended upon him in the form of a dove from that Principality

that is above all. Then he proclaimed the unknown Father and performed miracles. At the end, however, Christ flew away again from Jesus. Jesus suffered and rose again, while Christ remained impassible, being a spiritual being.[29]

Valentinianism. This heresy is named after its founder, Valentinus, and is probably the most sophisticated of the various Gnostic perspectives, receiving more attention from the Church Fathers than any Gnostic group other than Marcionism. Valentinus lived around AD 100 to 160 and founded a school of theology in Rome. He had hoped, some have said, to become the bishop of Rome, but after this fell to another, he developed his Gnostic doctrine and, according to Tertullian, "applied himself with all his might to exterminate the truth; and finding the clue of a certain old opinion, he marked out a path for himself with the subtlety of a serpent."[30] His teachings are probably expressed in what today is known as the *Coptic Gospel of Truth,* referred to by Irenaeus.[31] Speaking of the same "gospel," Tertullian says of Valentinus, "A Gospel of his own he likewise has, beside these of ours."[32]

This complicated system consists of a number of emanations from the Supreme Father, who in turn branch into other emanations, or aeons, constituting the *pleroma.* The Father also created a pair of aeons, Christ and the Holy Spirit. Jesus the Messiah was in a bodily form, but since he was the image of the demiurge, he was actually of ethereal material from outside the world. The purpose of the Savior was to bring enlightenment to those who were spiritual and could enjoy in nonphysical form the presence of the demiurge.[33]

Marcionism. Marcion (ca. AD 144) bears the dubious distinction of being one of the most well-known heretics in the early centuries of the church. He was the son of a wealthy shipowner and used that wealth to spread his vision of Jesus. His ideas continued in the West for at least 300 years, and in the East were picked up and became part of Mandaeanism. Both were characterized by belief in a demiurge, a common component of various forms of Gnosticism.

A defining perspective of Marcion is his anti-Semitism. He taught that Christianity and Judaism were totally different, and that the God of the Old Testament was different from the God of the New Testament. He rejected the Hebrew Bible altogether and accepted only Luke's Gospel[34] and the letters of Paul (except the pastoral epistles and the letter to the Hebrews, viewed by many as from Paul). He argued that Jesus' teachings are incongruent with the wrathful God of the Old Testament, and that Paul's contrasts of law and grace, works and faith, flesh and spirit were the essence of true religion.

> *Marcion...denied the resurrection of the body and the second coming of Jesus to judge the dead, because the good god of the New Testament does not punish those who reject him.*

For Marcion, "Christ Himself is not the Messiah; He did not fulfil the predictions of the Old Testament, but came to save us from the God of wrath, in whose clutches we presently languish."[35] Jesus was not the Son of the God of the Old Testament, Yahweh, who in Marcion's thinking was an intermediary deity called the demiurge, a being between the absolutely pure spirit and the evil material world. The Christ was sent by the pure supreme spirit to give humans knowledge leading to salvation. Marcion also denied the resurrection of the body and the second coming of Jesus to judge the dead, because the good God of the New Testament does not punish those who reject Him but merely leaves them to the demiurge, who will cast them into hell.

Though Marcion is often regarded as a Gnostic, in many ways his perspectives, like that of Cerinthus above, were not in accord with the philosophical speculations of most of Gnosticism, which included a plethora of aeons, emanations, or the like. For Marcion, "Christ was God Manifest not God Incarnate."[36] The Gnostics relied on secret wisdom; Marcion relied on the New Testament—but only after he had purged all passages that differed with his theology.

Mandaeanism. The Mandaean religion is a Gnostic sect that came to ancient Babylonia and Persia from Syro-Palestina in the first or second centuries AD. It imbibed from various religions, including Judaism and Christianity, but particularly from Gnosticism. The term derives from the Aramaic word *manda,* meaning "knowledge."[37]

The primary doctrine of Mandaeanism is that the human soul is captive inside a body and material world, and may be saved only through knowledge, as well as an ascetic lifestyle. Moreover, salvation comes through a redeemer who dwelt on the earth, triumphed over evil forces, and can now assist others to ascend to final reunion with the Supreme God. The Mandaean idea of redeemer may have come initially from the Christian view of Jesus, but Mandaeans considered Jesus a false Messiah, with John the Baptist becoming the focus of the religion.[38]

Manichaeism. The Manichaean Gnostic religion comes from Mani (ca. AD 216 to 276), a man born of a wealthy Persian family, who probably was influenced by Mandaeanism. He is said to have received a vision that told him that he was the prophet of a new and final religion. He traveled to India, where Buddhism influenced him. When he arrived back in Persia, he spread his beliefs and sent his followers to the Roman Empire.

Mani considered himself the last prophet in the line of Zoroaster, Buddha, and Jesus, all of whose teachings were incorporated into his new religion. Mani's teaching also shows considerable influence from Gnosticism, in which there are two spheres, light and darkness, with the former ruled by God and the latter by Satan. At one time these spheres were separate, but with the invasion of the kingdom of darkness on the kingdom of light, a mixture occurred. Similar to Gnostic thought, the body was evil, and the human soul was spiritual, a part of the kingdom of light. Salvation comes through knowledge of the kingdom of light, which had been imparted by various teachers, ending in Mani.[39]

The great Church Father Augustine had been Manichaean before converting to Christianity, after which he wrote polemical works against the false teaching.[40]

Apollinarianism: The *Logos* (Word) Dwelt in a Man

Apollinarianism, advocated by Apollinaris of Laodicea (ca. 310 to ca. 390), argued that Jesus did not possess a human soul and spirit but that the divine Logos indwelt the man Jesus beginning with the baptism by John.

Apollinaris was for many years a pillar of orthodoxy, as well as friend of the irrepressible Athanasius. Most of his works, now lost, are staunch defenses of orthodox Christianity. His heretical views about the Person of Christ notwithstanding, he has been regarded as a man of distinguished intellect and style. He was the mentor of Jerome and a writer of volumes of otherwise orthodox literature.[41]

Apollinaris and his followers believed that the orthodox view of Jesus was too vulgar. Their solution was to claim that Jesus possessed a human body and a divine soul, a composite of one part humanity (a body) and one part deity (a soul).[42]

In a letter he wrote to the bishops of Diocaesarea, Apollinaris describes his thesis with the assertion that the Word did not assume a "changeable" human mind in the incarnation, which would have led, in his view, to the Word *being trapped in human sin*.[43] This was his great concern and undoubtedly the motivation that propelled him in formulating this heretical view. For Apollinaris, the Word, rather, assumed "an immutable and heavenly divine mind." Here lies the rub: Christ cannot be said, then, to be *totally human*, since Christ now had a human body and a divine mind; the mind and spirit of Christ were from the divine nature of the Son of God.[44]

HERESIES THAT CHALLENGED THE INTEGRITY OF THE NATURES OF JESUS

The Hypostatic Union

The early church struggled to understand biblical texts that attested both to Christ's deity and humanity. How could two natures unite in one person without a confusion or diminishing of the two? How could Jesus be omnipotent and yet weak? How could He be in the world and yet be present everywhere? How could He learn things and yet be omniscient? The Chalcedonian Definition was the solution to the problem of two distinct natures in Christ that retain their own properties yet remain together in one person. Far from being the product of Greek philosophical or speculative thought, the Chalcedonian Definition is a theological definition that the Bible itself demands.

Everything that is true of the Son's human and divine natures is integral to His Person. Thus, when Jesus said, "Before Abraham was, I am" (John 8:58), He did not say, "Before Abraham was, my divine nature existed." He is free to talk about anything that either His divine or human nature does as something that *He* did. Very simply, whatever can be said of one nature or the other can be said of the *Person* of Christ; He does not possess a separate person in tandem with each nature. Also, when Paul says in 1 Corinthians 2:8 that if the rulers of this world had understood the wisdom of God, "they would not have crucified the *Lord of glory*." "Lord of glory" refers to Jesus' divine nature, yet Paul speaks of the "Lord of glory" being crucified. Although Jesus' divine nature was not crucified, it was true of Jesus as a *person*.[45]

In this way, we can now understand Mark 13:32, where Jesus says that no one knows the hour of His return, not even the angels in heaven, *nor the Son,* but only the Father. While Jesus *remained* what He was, fully divine, He also *became* what He previously had not been, fully human. In the incarnation, Jesus did not give up any of His attributes of deity; He did, however, take on new attributes—a humanity that was not His before.

The Communication of Attributes

Once we conclude that Jesus was fully man and fully God, and that His divine nature remained *fully* divine, and that His human nature remained *fully* human, we can now ask whether there were qualities, or *attributes,* that were *communicated* from one nature to another. We maintain with the historic Christian church that there were.

From the divine nature to the human nature. Even though Jesus' human nature did not experience change in its essence, since it was united with the divine nature in the one person of Christ, Jesus' human nature gained 1) a worthiness to be worshipped and 2) an ability to resist all temptations, both facets of His nature that did not belong to the human community before.

From the human nature to the divine nature. Jesus' human nature gave Him 1) the capacity to experience physical discomforts, pain, and death; 2) an ability to appreciate and understand *by experience* what we experience; and 3) an ability to be our substitute sacrifice, which the Son as God alone could not have done. The unfathomable nature of the incarnation causes all the miracles of the Bible to pale in comparison. In some way, the transcendent, infinite deity joined Himself permanently to humanity; the Creator took upon Himself creatureliness, without ceasing to be God.

The early church creeds are extremely important in coming to appreciate the doctrine of the Person of Christ. Their importance lies in the fact that they were formulated in direct response to heretical doctrines about God, the Trinity, and Christ, which, if not refuted, would have emptied Christianity of its unique saving message for mankind. Only the Jesus of Holy Writ can expiate human sin. Heretical movements attempt either to rewrite the history of the early church creeds or to deny their relevancy altogether.

> *Only the real Jesus of history...could offer salvation. No counterfeit Jesus could save. The early church knew this all too well, something the contemporary church has sometimes forgotten.*

Some Christians proclaim, naively, that neither they nor their faith community have any use for the ancient creeds. They boast of their relationship with a "living Lord" who is not boxed into some ancient category of thought or expression. Their tune alters dramatically, however, when they are pressed to *describe* the Jesus they share this relationship with. The moment they attempt to describe "their" Jesus, they fall back upon a creedal statement of faith.

The Jesus of false religions is a fictitious person radically different from the Jesus of the creeds and classic Christian orthodoxy. Only the real Jesus of history, as foretold in the Old Testament and declared in the New, could offer salvation. No counterfeit Jesus could save. The early church knew this all too well, something the contemporary church has sometimes forgotten.

How the divine and human natures related became the subject of two heresies of the late fourth and early fifth centuries. The first heresy was known as Nestorianism, after Nestorius the Patriarch of Constantinople. His conception of the divine and human natures of Jesus was declared heretical at the councils of Ephesus and Chalcedon, though it is uncertain he truly believed what was condemned. The heresy of Nestorianism claimed that the human and divine natures of Jesus were entirely separate from each other, resulting in two persons with two natures. The human nature was tempted, suffered, and died. Mary was the mother of the human Jesus only, not the mother of the Son of God. Thus the Council of Ephesus (AD 431) declared Mary the "mother of God" (*theotokos*), not to exalt Mary, but to clarify that the one person who was Jesus was also God.

In contrast with Nestorianism, Eutyches argued that Jesus did not have two distinct natures in one person. Instead, the divine and human natures blended into another third nature, with the divine absorbing the human. Consequently, the divine nature was tempted, suffered, and died.

WHY THE RISE OF A NEW JESUS?

Even such a brief introduction to the various ways that the concept of Jesus the Messiah developed within Christian communities in the three centuries following His sojourn on earth reveals a kaleidoscope of perspectives. None of these nonapostolic views of Jesus are true representations of the Jesus who was born of the Virgin Mary in Bethlehem during the reign of Caesar Augustus. The person who was

God and man, without mixture or separation of the two natures, was distorted, sometimes beyond recognition, by people who introduced ideas foreign to the Messiah.

The Messiah's deity was not an invention of the New Testament authors or the church, but was spoken about in the Old Testament (Isaiah 9:6f; Daniel 7:13-14). As well, His true humanity is clear from 1) numerous passages in the New Testament, 2) the expectation of being of the seed of the woman (Genesis 3:15), and 3) is ultimately demonstrated in His suffering, His death, and His physical resurrection.

Those heterodox doctrines of ancient times or modern speculation all fall short, or go beyond, the only credible account—found in the canonical Gospels—of who and what Jesus was.

Chapter Eight

✠

THE JESUS OF
WORLD RELIGIONS

In our post-Christian Western world, a confusion of religion and philosophy is occurring so that the line between religions is no longer clear. For example, near the end of his book *Living Buddha, Living Christ,* Buddhist monk Thich Nhat Hanh says, "When you are a truly happy Christian, you are also a Buddhist. And vice versa."[1]

Examples of this kind of thinking within Christian ranks are displayed by the St. Francis Chapel at Santa Clara University, which hosts a weekly practice of "mindfulness and Zen meditation," and the exhortation of Jesuit Father Robert E. Kennedy to his students: "I ask students to trust themselves and to develop their own self-reliance through the practice of Zen."[2] Marcus Borg, controversial Jesus scholar and professor of philosophy and religion at Oregon State University, says that both "Jesus and Buddha were teachers of wisdom,"[3] and he tells his students "that if Jesus and the Buddha were ever to meet, neither would try to convert the other—not because they would regard the task as hopeless, but because they would recognize each other."[4]

JESUS AMONG THE GODS

Is Jesus merely another god among the many gods of world religions? Is He only a holy man or prophet who espoused religious philosophies and morals similar to what were in vogue prior to His time, and maybe even borrowed from other religious teachers before Him?

Teachers of world religions have argued both of these perspectives. Only Christianity asserts that He was not only a man, but was also the one God over the universe. Such an exclusivist perspective has caused some scholars to consider Christianity dangerous. In a symposium on Buddhism and Christ, Professor Borg asserted that the most prevalent forms of Christianity through the centuries have been "dangerous, destructive, and degraded."[5]

The various religions of the world acknowledge that Jesus is an important figure, and oftentimes embrace Him as one of their gods, prophets, or "enlightened" holy men. Is this enough? The best information we have about Jesus is recorded by people in the first century of the Christian era who had either firsthand information about Him or talked to those who were eyewitnesses. These sources are far superior to later sources about Jesus, whether they be Gnostic, Islamic, Hindu, or Buddhist.

In view of the religious and historical context into which Jesus the Messiah came, is He truly identifiable as one who borrowed from other religious traditions outside Judaism? Are His life, nature, and teachings truly compatible with the other world religions? Is the idea of all religions leading to the same conclusion even possible, other than in symposia where professors seek to find common ground for sake of collegiality and openness to a liberal worldview? We hope to discover the answers to the above questions in the following analysis.

IS A JEWISH MESSIAH COMPATIBLE WITH NONBIBLICAL RELIGIONS?

Few would dispute that Jesus was a historical person born approximately between 7 and 4 BC in Israel, and even that He died on the cross and possibly rose from the dead (except for adherents of Islam and some secularists). But the reasons for these events bring a parting of the ways in religious traditions. When one examines the Jesus of whom many religions speak, He loses the historical setting of ancient Israel. The Jesus who walked the roads and hills of the land of Israel in the first century was Jewish in His heritage physically and religiously. He saw Himself—as did His disciples, especially after the resurrection—as the Son of God and Messiah to Israel promised in the Hebrew Scriptures.

Unlike the mystic teachings of Buddhism and Hinduism and other Eastern religions, the prophecies and fulfillment of prophecy in the life of Jesus are concrete. He truly was born of a virgin; He truly did live a sinless life; He truly did die on the cross as the suffering Messiah to vicariously redeem His people; He truly did rise from the tomb in the flesh,[6] as prophesied by the Law, the Prophets, and the Writings; He truly did ascend to the position of power in the heavens; and He truly will descend again to gather His church and judge the peoples of the earth who have rejected His offer of salvation.

> *Only by the most ingenious method of reading the Old and New Testaments could a person create compatibility between these teachings about, and by, Jesus the Messiah and those of the other religions of the world.*

Only by the most ingenious method of reading the Old and New Testaments could a person create compatibility between these teachings about, and by, Jesus the Messiah and those of the other religions of the world. Yet in the writings of many who profess other religions, we discover beliefs about Jesus that are far afield from the Jesus presented in the canonical Gospels. We will examine only the largest of non-Christian religions—Hinduism, Buddhism, and Islam—to demonstrate their views of Jesus and how they have misunderstood, distorted, and created a Jesus who never really lived.

TRADITIONS OF JESUS' TRAVELS IN THE EAST

Early Life of Jesus

Some have argued that during his childhood Jesus went to India and to the Himalayas and the Ganges valley. It is said that in the Himalayas He received "spiritual initiation" from holy men and then returned to Jerusalem a short time after His thirtieth birthday. He then did miracles and spoke powerful words, but escaped before He could be put to death and traveled back to India, where He lived in Kashmir, His grave allegedly being there even today.[7]

But neither Jesus nor His disciples ever mention such a visit in the writings of the New Testament, nor is this found in the writings of the Fathers of the church. The teachings that Jesus purportedly received in India are absent in the Gospels, except by exaggerated imagination. There is a tradition that the apostle Thomas went to southern India, but there is no historical evidence that Jesus was ever there.

Post-crucifixion Travels

Some also say that Jesus visited the East after the resurrection, but this has no more historical support than that He visited North America, as in Mormon doctrine.[8] Let us examine these arguments.

According to Hinduism. A tradition persists in Hindu literature that Jesus visited India during the reign of King Shalivahan.[9] Reportedly Jesus said that He was Yuz Asaf, and that He "had become known as Isa Masih," or Jesus the Messiah. This is found in writings that allegedly date to AD 115 or after.[10]

But attestation for this view is scattered, inconsistent, and written, at the earliest, nearly 100 years after the resurrection. Also, the preaching of Thomas in India may have caused a joining of the stories about Jesus with the legends of India.

According to Buddhism. Buddhism has some of the same deficiencies regarding the presence of Jesus after the crucifixion. We must remember that Buddhism and Hinduism have been in close association, and that Siddhartha Gautama, the founder of Buddhism, received his philosophical and religious training in India. Buddhism's alleged associations with Jesus, as in Hinduism, are at least 100 years after the time of Jesus on earth.

Attempts to identify Jesus with Buddha are superficial at best and again come into being at least a hundred years after Jesus' crucifixion. The similarity is explained by Mirza Ghulam Ahmad:

The events of the life of Jesus thus became known to the Buddhists, and at this point in history the story of the life of Gautama Buddha had not yet been recorded. Ahmad further speculates that when the life of Gautama Buddha was being recorded the events were confused and mixed up with the events of the life of Jesus Christ. This is his explanation for the similarity between the life stories of the two. Here are some similarities:

1. Both fasted for 40 days
2. Both tempted by the devil
3. Both refer to themselves as "the light"
4. Both teach forgiveness and to "love thy enemy"[11]

Pagan religions, Christian heretical groups, and Eastern religions borrowed the powerful story of Jesus. The accounts of His life, miracles, death, and resurrection were added piecemeal and often carelessly from the Gospel story being preached throughout the Roman Empire and as far as India within decades of Jesus' ascension. These fragments of information on Jesus are wrongly taken as indications of Jesus' personal contact with these cultures; whereas, in reality, Jesus traveled less than 100 miles from His home. His efforts were given to training 12 apostles to carry His message throughout the world, rather than attempting to do so Himself. He came to provide salvation through His death and resurrection. After His ascension, He sent the Spirit to be with those who spread His word throughout the world in a way that He could not in His human body (John 14:26; 16:5-16; Acts 1:8).

According to Islam. Muslim doctrine disavows that Jesus died on the cross and rose from the dead. Rather, Muslims believe He ascended back into heaven in anticipation of returning to the earth again at a future date to convert people to the worship of Allah.

It is not uncommon to hear Muslims talk about Jesus traveling among them. Some legends say that after the death of Judas on the cross, Jesus went to Damascus for a period of two years around the time that Paul encountered Jesus near the city.[12] He is said to have preached to the king of Nisibis in southeastern Turkey.[13] Another view is that Jesus traveled to Afghanistan where He performed miracles,[14] while other legends have Him with His mother in Pakistan relying on Sura 23:50 in the Qur'an for a hint of this travel: "And We made the son of Marium [Mary] and his mother a sign, and We gave them a shelter on a lofty ground having meadows and springs." Supposedly Israel has no such kind of place, so eastern Pakistan is chosen, since there is a tradition about Jesus and Mary living there, and Mary being buried in a tomb on a hilltop there. A few isolated and ambiguous sayings of Jesus are said to be on inscriptions near Kashmir, India, and it has been speculated that these may be the "sayings," or *logia*, mentioned in the second century by Papias, a disciple of John.

All of these comments about Jesus in Damascus, Afghanistan, Pakistan, and India are based on isolated sources that are scanty at best, with no historical framework. Additionally, that the *logia* of Papias would have come from India, rather than Asia Minor where he worked under the apostle John, is incredible.

THE JESUS OF HINDUISM

The Alleged Reliance of the Life of Jesus on the Story of Krishna

A common myth one hears is that the story of Jesus is in reality a retelling of the story of Krishna. Part of this relies on the belief that even some of the Church Fathers did not consider the religion taught by Jesus as being new or unique. The first historian of the church, Eusebius of Caesarea (ca. AD 283–371), allegedly wrote, "The religion of Jesus Christ is neither new nor strange," and St. Augustine of Hippo (AD 354–430), supposedly wrote, "This, in our day, is the Christian religion, not as having been unknown in former times, but as having recently received that name."[15]

This alleged support among the Fathers of the church for Christianity being based on other religions is highly questionable, based on meager or improper documentation and a misunderstanding of the context.[16] Both these references are from a dubious source of the nineteenth century, Kersey Graves, who provides little evidence for what he says, but is quoted freely by specious books and websites about Jesus.[17]

Similarities of Jesus to Krishna

Comparison of the life of Jesus to Krishna. According to Hinduism, sometime between 1200 and 900 BC,[18] Krishna, the eighth avatar or manifestation of the god Vishnu, was born.[19] Some within Hinduism argue that there are considerable similarities between Jesus and Krishna that indicate, to them, that Jesus is a further manifestation.[20] Including Jesus as a manifestation of an Eastern deity is not unusual in Hinduism, Buddhism, and Baha'ism, but some attempt to closely connect Krishna and Jesus. One writer says there are more than 100 points of comparison between them.[21]

Let's look at a few examples of supposed similarities between Jesus and Krishna found in the Bhagavad-Gita and the New Testament:

1. The Bhagavad-Gita speaks of Arjuna being "the beginning, middle and end of all beings."[22] In the Book of Revelation, Jesus says, "I am the Alpha and the Omega, the first and the last, the beginning and the end."

   In expressing the idea of eternity, which is present not only in Hinduism but in many world religions, the mention of being the first and last should not be considered that unusual. But there is a difference between these two similarly worded ideas. The Hindu speaks of Krishna being the beginning, middle, and end of *all beings,* while the text of Revelation stresses the eternal nature of the *Lord's being.*

2. Supposedly the story of Asita in the Bhagavad-Gita[23] is similar to the story of Simeon with the baby Jesus in Luke 2:25-35. Stephen Van Eck, in an article titled, "Hare Jesus: Christianity's Hindu Heritage," makes the following claim: "His advent was heralded by a pious old man named Asita, who could die happy knowing of his arrival, a story paralleling that of Simeon

in Luke 2:25."[24] But the Bhagavad-Gita has not one word that parallels Luke's account.[25]

3. The Bhagavad-Gita speaks of the kingdom of God and talks about a stumbling block similar to words found in the New Testament: "If one is thus situated even at the hour of death, one can enter into the kingdom of God."[26] But the sense of the phrase is different from the New Testament usage. The Hindu term for "kingdom of God" here is *Baikuntha* and refers to the "abode of God."[27] The Hindu "kingdom of God" is achieved after a person has rid himself of all impurities in the soul, through right karma,[28] and requires that the person leave "bodily human form" to enter the kingdom[29] from which there is no return.[30] Adherence to Hinduism is not necessary: "Having gained enlightenment and finally salvation…these man gods reached the kingdom of God in their lifetime. All paths…all religions and spirituality lead one towards the one and only final goal… the abode of God, aka Baikuntha in Hinduism."[31]

> *If we were to eliminate as invalid the events in Jesus' life that appear to come from Krishna, then most of the key Christian beliefs about Jesus would have to be abandoned.*

So "kingdom of God" is not an equivalent to *Baikuntha*. The Greek phrase *basiliea tou theou* ("kingdom of God") is found approximately 70 times in the New Testament and is a major theme in the Old and New Testaments. It refers to God's rule over His world and specifically over believers—and not, as in Hinduism, to an after-body abode of God.

Dismissing these supposed similarities is not difficult since they are ambiguous and easy to explain. But what about comparisons between Jesus and Krishna that aren't so easy to explain? Krishna supposedly was born of a virgin; his family had to travel to pay a tax; his father was a carpenter; his birth was attended by angels, wise men, and shepherds;

he was pursued by a tyrant who killed infants in pursuing him; his father was warned to flee; he was baptized; he came to save humanity; he did miracles and told parables; he was crucified and rose again; among a number of other alleged similarities.[32]

At first glance it appears that Christianity is in dire straits, being just one more religion based on traces of other ancient religions. Some would conclude that it has little to offer once the supposed dependence on Krishna is removed.

If we were to delete from the Gospels the events in Jesus' life that appear similar to Krishna's story, we would end up with:

- A very human, itinerant, Jewish rabbi-healer.
- A teacher who largely followed the teachings of Hillel (a liberal Jewish rabbi from the first century BCE).
- An observant Jew who had a special relationship with God—a kinship so close that Jesus referred to God by the familiar term *Abba*.

This is very close to the image of Jesus portrayed by many liberal theologians in their quest for the historical Jesus.

If we were to eliminate as invalid the events in Jesus' life that appear to come from Krishna, then most of the key Christian beliefs about Jesus would have to be abandoned: His virgin birth, incarnation, sinless life, crucifixion, descent into hell, resurrection, ascension to heaven. We would also have to reject the Bible's criteria for salvation, belief in the Trinity, the inerrancy and inspiration of the Scriptures, and so on.

But these apparent similarities between Jesus and Krishna may be explained a number of ways. People often have similar experiences in similar situations, and some of the similarities between the two can be explained in this manner. Others may be the result of stories from the life of Jesus working their way into Hindu stories about Krishna. Numerous websites reference these identical events in the life of Krishna and Jesus. The likely source for all this is, again, the highly unreliable nineteenth-century book by Kersey Graves.[33]

Graves conveniently provides no sources or citations, which is one of many reasons his book has been long discredited by scholars working in the field of comparative religion. But that doesn't keep this popular idea from appearing on numerous websites—none providing sources or citations (and rarely mentioning Graves' book). There's good reason for this absence of evidence. The *Bhagavad-Gita* (first century AD) doesn't mention Krishna's childhood, and the stories of Krishna's childhood recorded in the *Harivamsa Purana* (c. 300 AD) and the *Bhagavata Purana* (c. 800-900 AD) don't mention the gifts at all. Even if they did, those works were written well after the birth of Christ, making such a claim absurd.[34]

The Teachings of Jesus Compared to Krishna. Various passages from the Bhagavad-Gita have some wording that may be found in the New Testament.[35] Common ideas of life and death, obedience and judgment, as well as statements that speak of deity are present in all religions.[36] One does find minor connections between some words of Krishna and of Jesus the Jewish Messiah. Let's look at a few examples.

The Bhagavad-Gita (2:11) says that a wise person does not lament for the living nor for the dead, and Jesus says in Matthew 8:22 that disciples are not to delay following Jesus while they wait for the death of their relatives. Jesus uses dead here in two different senses: spiritually dead and physically dead. The words are similar but the meaning is different.

Another example is the theme of God's impartiality or that He does not show favoritism (Bhagavad-Gita 9:29; see Romans 2:11; Matthew 5:44-45). However, the text of Bhagavad-Gita bears little resemblance in meaning to Matthew 5:44-45. The Hindu text says that those persons who are balanced, free from contamination, and have several positive attributes are dear to the god Krishna. This is not the meaning of Matthew's text. It only says that believers in God are to love people who do not do positive acts or have proper attitudes. And the sense of Romans is that God is open to provide evidence of Himself to all people by doing good to them.

Although Hinduism is older than the Christian faith, certain shared terms and teaching are not surprising. There is an important contrast, however, between the religion of Krishna and the Bible. The former has a pantheistic (all is God) emphasis, while the latter sees a distinction between God and the world. Additionally, Krishna's personhood and God's nature in Hinduism are similar to the ancient Modalistic error in contrast to the orthodox doctrine of the Trinity (discussed in chapter 7). Though Hinduism, and worship of Krishna in particular, are older than Christianity, the oldest *existing* writings of Hinduism date hundreds of years after the writing of the New Testament documents, and the author of these Hindu texts may have borrowed from Christian and other sources.

Why Jesus Is Not Krishna nor Christianity Compatible with Hinduism

Belief that Jesus and Krishna are one and the same requires acceptance of the Hindu belief in reincarnation. Jesus was born possibly as much as several thousand years after Krishna lived (provided that Krishna really lived). But unlike Krishna, Jesus came in fulfillment of Old Testament prophecies, revealed Himself as both the great God of the universe and as man, died for the sins of humanity, and rose physically from the dead. Moreover, since these events are based on the Hebrew Scriptures, written long before Eastern ideology came into the Near East, and represent a culture largely antagonistic to foreign religious viewpoints, there is little likelihood that Jesus reflects a Far Eastern view of the world. Furthermore, though there are some superficial comparisons between Jesus and Krishna, the differences between the Jewish Jesus and the Hindu Krishna are most compelling. Jesus and Krishna are not the same.

Christianity and Hinduism are incompatible religions, being at the extremes from each other at many different levels—their views of God, the nature and work of the Messiah, sin and salvation, among other matters. Hinduism's perspective of religion lies within the subjects of philosophy and ethics, not in history. Mahatma Gandhi reveals this view when he says, "I may say that I have never been interested in a historical Jesus. I should not care if...Jesus never lived."[37]

Gandhi clearly does not understand the essence of Christianity. If Krishna did not live, it would be unimportant; the same is not true of Jesus. The historicity of Jesus is essential to the eternal salvation promised to the Christian. If He did not die and rise again, then we are still in our sins (1 Corinthians 15:12-19).

THE JESUS OF BUDDHISM
Similarities of Jesus to Buddha

Comparison of the life of Jesus to Buddha. There is little evidence proving the existence of Buddha. Everything we know about his life comes from Buddhist writings produced many years after the supposed events. Legend says that Buddha, born as Siddhartha Gautama, was the son of royalty in what is now southern Nepal. He was married at age 19 and had one son. Sometime around age 30 Siddhartha ventured out of his cloistered palace and supposedly saw for the first time an old man, a sick man, a dead man, and an ascetic. He was so moved by these images that he left his life of leisure, as well as his family, and became a wandering monk.

He wandered for six years looking for inner peace through asceticism, finally arriving in a northeastern Indian town. He sat under a giant fig tree (bodhi tree) and determined to stay there until he received enlightenment. After 49 days he was "illuminated" and became the Buddha, meaning "Enlightened One." He began to preach his message through the countryside, converting his fellow ascetic monks, then his family, and even a king. He lived to the age of 80. After his death he was cremated, and his ashes were distributed to several cities around India. His alleged remains are venerated at several shrines around Asia.

There are a few similarities between Jesus and Buddha. Like Buddha, Jesus began His public ministry around the age of 30. It could be said that a sign initiated both their ministries—Buddha's enlightenment under the tree and the descent of the Holy Spirit at Jesus' baptism (Luke 3:21-22)—but there are also significant differences. They both fasted for long periods before their ministries began, though for Jesus it was a time of testing, not self-contemplation as in Buddha's case. Jesus also lived a simple life similar to Buddha.

Teachings of Jesus compared to Buddha. Some have argued that Buddha and Jesus taught virtually the same message, and there are some similarities. Both taught that suffering is real and has a cause. Both taught that a person should be compassionate to those around them. They both emphasized a change in thinking from the prevalent religious teaching of their day, but in most other areas they have little similarity.

Why Jesus Is Not the Buddha

Some propose that Jesus was a reincarnation of Buddha because their teachings seem to be so similar. Buddhists believe that when a person dies he is reborn. Depending on how well he followed the teachings of Buddha, he may be reborn as an animal, a person, or even a nonphysical being. Eventually, if one becomes enlightened through perfect adherence to the tenants of Buddhism, he will attain a cessation of desire and self and enter into the state of nirvana. Buddha was not very concerned about the idea of deity. This has led to a wide variance of opinion over the role of deity in Buddhism. It ranges from no deities to Buddha himself being the highest deity among many.[38]

For Jesus, there is only one life upon earth. Jesus taught that eternal life with the Father or eternal punishment apart from the Father is the final state of mankind, not a recurring cycle of death and rebirth. Man can do nothing of himself to attain this life. Jesus taught that it is the opposite of looking inward that one finds peace. It is only through looking to Jesus in faith that we may attain eternal life with the Father. All this shows that Jesus had a vastly different idea about deity than did Buddha.

Buddhism is so far from what Jesus actually taught, let alone the thinking that Jesus was simply a reincarnation of Buddha himself, that one wonders why the comparison is even made.

Why Christianity Is Not Compatible with Buddhism

Beyond the superficial similarities, there are far more differences between the teachings of Jesus and Buddha. They range from the prescribed activities all the way to the philosophical foundation of Buddhism. These differences are significant and prove that Jesus was not a Buddhist. We will examine the Buddhist core teachings: the Four Noble Truths and the Eightfold Path.

The Four Noble Truths are 1) Suffering exists, 2) suffering has a cause, 3) suffering can be eliminated, and 4) there are ways of eliminating suffering.

In Buddhism, suffering is caused by craving, desire, and attachment. However, Jesus taught that suffering is caused by sin.

For Buddhism, pain, distress, anxiety, and dissatisfaction exist within each of us, having been created by our own desires.[39] This is the first truth. This teaching reflects the belief in Buddhism that matter is transitory—it exists only in perception. So any suffering is the result of internal faultiness. Jesus taught that suffering does exist, but that it is a reality of living. It is far more than some internal perception.

The second truth relates to the cause of suffering. In Buddhism, suffering is caused by craving, desire, and attachment. However, Jesus taught that suffering is caused by sin, whether from the fallen world we live in or by the actions of others and ourselves. In Mark 5:26, a woman had suffered many years from a medical condition. The text gives no indication that her suffering was the result of craving, desire, or attachment. Also, in Luke 13:1 Jesus is asked about the suffering of a certain group of Galileans. Jesus said, "Do you think that these Galileans were worse sinners than all the other Galileans, because they suffered in this way? No, I tell you; but unless you repent, you will all likewise perish" (verses 2-3). These victims suffered because of Pontius Pilate's sin, not theirs. When Jesus and the disciples begin the Passover meal Jesus tells them, "I have earnestly desired to eat this Passover with you before I suffer."

For Jesus, the suffering He speaks of wasn't a result of desire; far from it.

The third truth of Buddhism's Four Noble Truths is that suffering can be eliminated. Jesus taught not only that we will suffer, but also that it is necessary:

> "Blessed are those who are persecuted for righteousness' sake, for theirs is the kingdom of heaven. Blessed are you when others revile you and persecute you and utter all kinds of evil against you falsely on my account. Rejoice and be glad, for your reward is great in heaven, for so they persecuted the prophets who were before you" (Matthew 5:10-12).

Further, Jesus taught that it was necessary for Him to suffer. Mark 8:31-32 says, "He began to teach them that the Son of Man must suffer many things and be rejected by the elders and the chief priests and the scribes and be killed, and after three days rise again." After Jesus was resurrected, He taught the disciples, showing them why the events surrounding his crucifixion and resurrection had to happen.

> He said to them, "These are my words that I spoke to you while I was still with you, that everything written about me in the Law of Moses and the Prophets and the Psalms must be fulfilled." Then he opened their minds to understand the Scriptures, and said to them, "Thus it is written, that the Christ should suffer and on the third day rise from the dead, and that repentance and forgiveness of sins should be proclaimed in his name to all nations, beginning from Jerusalem" (Luke 24:44-47).

The fourth truth describes the path a person must take to achieve the cessation of suffering and the achievement of peace, what is known as the Eightfold Path.

The Eightfold Path is right view, right intention, right speech, right action, right livelihood, right effort, right mindfulness, and right concentration.

The first point of the Eightfold Path is "right view." But it isn't just any view. A person must have a proper view of all of Buddha's teachings to have "right view." Only by study of the Buddha's teachings can one fulfill this requirement.[40] However, Jesus taught that it is only when we believe Him that we can have eternal life. We must know who Jesus is by studying His words, not those of the Buddha.

The second point is "right intention," or "right thought." The Buddha said this involves three areas: the intention of renunciation, the intention of good will, and the intention of harmlessness.[41] While Jesus did talk of leaving everything, it was leaving everything to follow Him exclusively (Matthew 16:24). Jesus taught His followers to pray for their enemies, but He taught that intention of good will is not enough. When Jesus saw a need, His compassion spurred Him to action. Jesus also never taught that we should be harmless at all times. He even instructed His followers on one occasion to arm themselves (Luke 22:36).

The third, fourth, and fifth points of the Eightfold Path are sometimes grouped together. They are right speech, right action, and right life. "Right speech" involves not lying, not slandering, not using harsh language, and not engaging in idle chatter. These points seem to have resonance with Jesus' words, but they are general moral instructions that are found in most of the world's great religions. "Right action" for a Buddhist involves refraining from any action that is "unwholesome"[42] (this means no taking of life, human or otherwise), not stealing, and not engaging in illicit sexual intercourse. Although Jesus never prohibited killing (in fact, He said, "I have not come to bring peace, but a sword"—Matthew 10:34), the other precepts are also universal in nature. No major religions promote stealing or illicit intercourse.

The Buddhist teaching of "right living" deals with how one earns their living. It is to be earned legally, peacefully, honestly, and without harming or causing others to suffer. The Buddha himself is said to have prohibited five specific occupations that violate these tenets: dealing in weapons, any job that involves trading in living beings (raising animals for the purpose of slaughter, slave trading, and prostitution being examples), meat production or butchering, and creating or dealing in poisons and intoxicants (alcohol or other drugs).[43] There is no indication that Jesus ever prohibited people from any occupation, and He did not disapprove of temple sacrifices of animals. He, in fact, ate the Passover lamb. He interacted with several soldiers, not at any time urging them to give up their profession. Rather, He taught that whatever we do, we are to do it to glorify the Father (Matthew 5:16).

"Right effort" is the sixth point of the Eightfold Path. Buddha taught that effort was required because "each person has to work out his or her own deliverance."[44] This is, of course, antithetical to what Jesus taught. It is only through the work of Christ that we are delivered. He said, in John 6:44, "No one can come to me unless the Father who sent me draws him. And I will raise him up on the last day."

For Buddha, the ultimate truth of all things is visible by looking into one's self. This is the foundation of the seventh postulate of the path, "right mindfulness." Mindfulness is "presence of mind, attentiveness, or awareness." In order to be "right" one must "remain in the present, open, quiet, and alert, contemplating the present event."[45] Jesus did not teach this. We are to meditate on His words and think of how to apply the teaching to ourselves. We are always to think about Jesus. This is because it is in God we find truth, nowhere else.

The last teaching of the path is "right concentration." This is "an intensification of a mental factor present in every state of consciousness...a deliberate attempt to raise the mind to a higher, more purified level or awareness."[46] Again, Jesus never taught this kind of self-meditation. Rather, we are to concentrate on following His teachings and how to apply them to our lives. Then we are to go out and tell others of His teaching. It was not Jesus' goal that we strive to attain some supraconscious state, but that we may know and follow Him.

THE JESUS OF ISLAM
The Claims

Islam is the faith from which Judaism and Christianity sprang. One often hears that Judaism, Christianity, and Islam share a common origin, each being able to trace back to their common father, Abraham.

Consequently, they are said to worship the same God. Beyond this popular misconception, it is understood within these groups that this is not so.

Islam, for example, though it follows the formation of Christianity by 600 years and the Jewish faith by 2000 years (not even counting the patriarch Abraham), considers itself the founder of both: "Islam regards itself, not as a subsequent faith to Judaism and Christianity, but as the primordial religion, the faith from which Judaism and Christianity are subsequent developments."[47] This becomes obvious in two texts from the Qur'an:[48]

> Abraham was not a Jew nor a Christian, but he was (an) upright (man), a Muslim; and he was not one of the poly-theists. (*Al 'Imran:* The Family of Amran, 3:66).

> And they say: Be Jews or Christians, you will be on the right course. Say: Nay, (we follow) the religion of Abraham, the upright one, and he was not one of the polytheists (*Al Baqarah:* The Cow, 2:135).

From these two passages we discover that the Qur'an does not consider Abraham either a Jew or a Christian, but a Muslim. Conse-quently, it is Muslims who truly represent the faith of Abraham. Not only Abraham but also various prophets and leaders, such as Noah, Joseph, Moses, David, and Solomon, are considered Muslims. In the New Testament John the Baptist and Jesus (*'Isa*) are included (*Al An'am,* 6:85-87).

The fact that Muslims believe in only one God does not in any way prove that they worship the God of Abraham. The God of the Bible was worshipped thousands of years before Muhammad was born. When he chose the moon god of the pagan pantheon, Allah, as the god of Islam, he was not reaching back to the true God of the Hebrews, Yahweh, and the one that Jesus called Father. Allah is a pagan deity embraced by Muhammad and his followers in moving Arabia to monotheism, but he is not the true God.[49]

Another difficulty with Islam's claims about Jesus is that the Qur'an was written centuries after the Hebrew and Greek Scriptures. No historical source would support the claim that any writings of Islam predate either the Hebrew Scriptures or the Christian Scriptures. Moreover, the Islamic faith is considerably different from the faith of the biblical text, coming into existence in the seventh century, with its teachings being an adaptation of the Jewish and Christian Scriptures that preceded it. And though Islam believes that the Scriptures are corrupt, and the Qur'an a corrective, we have in our possession the only texts of Scripture Muhammad would have been aware of,[50] and they are substantially different from the teachings and supposed historical facts of Islam.[51]

> *No historical source would support the claim that any writings of Islam predate either the Hebrew Scriptures or the Christian Scriptures.*

Jesus was the greatest prophet until Muhammad. The Qur'an recognizes Jesus as the Messiah (*Al Baqarah* 2:87, *Al Ma'idah* 5:110), the "Word of Allah" (*An Nisa'*, 4:171), and the son of Mary (Mariam), a virgin, and says He was born under a date palm tree (*Maryam* 19:22). As a child Jesus did many miracles, including speaking from His cradle (*Al 'Imran* 3:46; *Al Ma'idah* 5:110; *Maryam* 19:30) and giving life to clay birds (*Al 'Imran* 3:49). He also foretold the coming of Muhammad (*As Saff* 61:6).

In Islam Jesus is known as 'Isa and is a prophet of Islam—in fact, the greatest next to Muhammad. Supposedly He was a loyal Muslim ("one who surrendered"), and teacher of Islam ("surrender") (*Al 'Imran* 3:84). However, the message (*Injil,* or gospel, *Al Ma'idah,* 5:46) of Jesus was eventually lost and then corrupted by later Christians, so that the Qur'an is the only reliable guide to the true teachings of Jesus: "Surely the (true) religion with Allah is Islam. And those who were given the Book differed only after knowledge had come to them, out of envy among themselves" (*Al 'Imran:* the Family of Amran, 3:18).

In contrast, Jesus is never called 'Isa[52] outside of Islam, not even close as a variant between Hebrew, Aramaic, or Arabic. The name for Jesus in Hebrew is *Yeshua'*, meaning "Yahweh is salvation." This comes into Greek as *Iesou-s*. Furthermore, the Qur'an has many factual errors as it uses largely hearsay knowledge of Christian teaching.[53]

Also especially significant is that Jesus is portrayed in the Qur'an as superior to Muhammad in every respect, posing the question as to why His teaching would not be accepted above the teaching of Muhammad, making Him the greatest prophet of Islam, even if He is not viewed as the Son of God.

Differences Between the Jesus of Islam and the Real Jesus

He was born of a virgin. According to the Qur'an, Jesus was born of the virgin Mary, who is the only woman named in the Qur'an (Sura 3:42; see 21:91; 66:12; 23:50), something often reiterated in the Qur'an by the use of "son of Mary" in referring to Jesus (*'Isa*). Jesus was created by the word of God (Sura 3:47) and was spared the "touch" of Satan: "When any human being is born, Satan touches him at both sides of the body with his two fingers, except Jesus, the son of Mary, whom Satan tried to touch but failed, for he touched the placenta-cover instead" (Sahih Bukhari, vol. 4, Hadith 506).[54] None of the above is declared to be true of Muhammad.

He is the Messiah of God. Jesus is also not only called 'Isa in the Qur'an but also *Al-Masih* (the Messiah), similar to *ha-mashiach* in Hebrew, sometimes in combination with 'Isa and at other times by itself. The Hebrew word means the "anointed one," referring to the king of Israel, particularly of the Davidic line.[55] Many Muslim interpreters, however, seek to relate *Al-Masih* to the Arabic word *sah*, that is, "to wander, to survey, to go on pilgrimage."[56]

The understanding of "wander" for the Hebrew *mashiach*, however, is untenable. The term speaks of one who has been anointed by Yahweh, sometimes a priest or other anointed leader, but most importantly the redeemer of Israel (Daniel 9:25), and in the New Testament the one who came to give Himself for His people (Matthew 20:28; Mark 10:45; John 1:1-18). It is also understood to be synonymous with the Son of

God (Matthew 16:16; 26:63; Mark 1:1; Luke 4:41; John 11:27; 20:31). No such parallel may be found between Jesus and Muhammad.

He is the prophet of God. To Muslims, Jesus is a great prophet, second only to Muhammad. He is said to have received the *Injil,* or gospel, to give to the Jewish people (Sura 19:31; 4:169; 3:48; 4:46), something in agreement with the New Testament (Luke 4:18; 10:21). But even though many considered Jesus a prophet, He did not consider Himself to be only a prophet; He was greater than all of the prophets, including Abraham (Matthew 22:45; Luke 11:31-32; John 8:54-55).

He performed miracles. Jesus was a worker of miracles, according to the Qur'an, including, it seems, the feeding of the 5000 recorded in Mark 6:30-44 (Sura 5:112-114). Also, the Qur'an speaks of Jesus giving life to people—without specific details, but possibly referring to Jairus's daughter (Mark 5:35-43), the widow's son at Nain (Luke 7:11-17), and Lazarus (John 11:38-44). It is possible that Qur'anic materials rely on stories told to Muslims by Christians.

At other times the miracles given by the Qur'an are similar to apocryphal legends, such as Jesus bringing clay birds to life,[57] and may partially be explained by the fact that Jesus' miracles in the Qur'an are recorded without explanation, but the Gospel accounts demonstrate that the miracles ("signs" in John) are done to prove that He was the Messiah, the Son of God (John 20:30-31), including the greatest miracle of all, His resurrection from the dead.

Jesus' prediction of Muhammad. One of the more unusual claims of Islam is that Jesus prophesied about the coming of Muhammad: "And when Jesus, son of Mary, said: O Children of Israel, surely I am the messenger of Allah to you, verifying that which is before me of the Torah and giving the good news of a Messenger who will come after me, his name being Ahmad" (*Al-Saff,* Sura 61:6).

This passage is thought to refer to Muhammad, but the problem relates to the name Ahmad. Maulana Muhammad Ali seeks to correct this confusion: "We are here told that Jesus had given the good news of the advent of a Prophet whose name was Ahmad coming after him.

That our Prophet was known by two names, Muhammad and Ahmad, is a well-known fact of history."[58]

In reality, the use of *Ahmad* for Muhammad began to occur approximately a century after the writing of the Qur'an and is a corruption in the Qur'anic text. Second, this alleged prophecy of Jesus is unknown until the Qur'an, 600 years after His earthly ministry, so it is without historical credibility.

Last of all is the supposed prediction of Muhammad in John 14:26-27, the promise of the Holy Spirit. The word for helper in the Greek text is *parakletos,* meaning "one who comes to the aid of another, an advocate, or counselor."[59] Muslims have argued that the text was corrupted and should be *periklutos.*[60]

This argument is without merit:

1. No extant manuscript of the gospel of John has *periklutos* as a variant reading. As stated earlier, the manuscripts that have *parakletos* were the manuscripts in circulation at the time of Muhammad and so would not be a corruption of some earlier time. This is the only New Testament Muhammad could have referred to. It is common for Muslims to claim that the New Testament is corrupted when it differs with the Qur'an, but this violates the Qur'an itself, which considers the New Testament inspired by Allah because none can change the Words of God (Sura 6:34; 10:64).

2. The term *parakletos* is used to refer to the Holy Spirit by name, not Muhammad (John 15:26). For the verse to refer to Muhammad, it would require not simply a corruption of the word but a total rewriting of the passage.

3. The word *periklutos,* the alleged correct reading, is a Greek word of the classical period and does not occur in New Testament, Byzantine, or Patristic lexica, so it is doubtful it was used during the time the Greek New Testament was written. It means "famous" or "renowned."[61] This would hardly fit the context of what the *parakletos* is to do, to aid the believer, not to promote Himself.

4. The *parakletos* does not speak of Himself but of Jesus, which would require Muhammad to lead people to Jesus, not to Himself or to a new religion.

5. Jesus would send the Holy Spirit to make Himself known, so if Muhammad were the Paraclete, one would have to conclude that the Qur'an came from Jesus.

6. The fulfillment was to be with the disciples; 600 years later would be too late.

7. Last, the Paraclete would live forever with the disciples, while Muhammad lived only 63 years.[62]

Why Jesus came. According to Islamic teaching, Jesus came to call Israel to obedience to Allah, but calling the Jewish people to return to the proper practice of Islam (wrongly viewed as preceding Judaism) is hardly the reason why Jesus came to the earth. The biblical text tells us He was the lamb of God to take away the sin of the world (John 1:29), to save His people from their sins (Matthew 1:21), to give His life as a ransom for many (Mark 10:45).

> *Jesus...will kill an imposter Messiah, marry and have children, live a total of 40 years, and be buried beside the grave of Muhammad.*

The second coming of Jesus. Our last consideration, how Jesus is viewed as the coming judge, is based on two verses in the Qur'an. Sura 4:159 says, "And there is none of the People of the Book but will believe in this before his death; and on the day of Resurrection he will be a witness against them." This verse, according to Muslim interpretation, indicates that Jews and Christians ("People of the Book") believe in the death of Jesus on the cross, and Jesus will use this against them on the day of Resurrection. Another verse, Sura 43:61, says, "And this [revelation] is surely knowledge of the Hour, so have no doubt about it and follow me. This is the right path." This passage occurs in a chapter concerning Jesus as a prophet, and this verse indicates that Jesus asks people to follow Him in the right path of Allah (Sura 43:64).

Muslims believe that eventually all Jews and Christians will believe Jesus when He comes again to occupy a subordinate role under a Muslim leader and demonstrate complete adherence to Islam. Supposedly He will kill an imposter Messiah, marry and have children, live a total of 40 years, and be buried beside the grave of Muhammad.

Obviously the coming of the Christ in Christian thought is totally contrary to what we discover in the Qur'an. Jesus comes to take His church to Himself in the resurrection, and in my understanding of the Scripture, when He comes after the tribulation period He will establish the kingdom promised to David and to Israel. In the former portion of His second coming He rescues His bride (1 Thessalonians 1:10; 4:15-17; 1 Corinthians 15:50-54); in the latter portion He comes as a judge and king over the earth (Revelation 19:11–20:6; 22:7-13).

WHY ALL RELIGIONS *CANNOT* BE TRUE

Often it is argued that all religions will lead a person to God. Supposedly each religion possesses an aspect of the total truth, and eventually everyone will arrive at the same place through one's own chosen path. The following illustration is often used to explain how differing viewpoints can all be an important part of the total truth.

Six blind men come upon an elephant and begin to debate what is before them. One man touches the side of the elephant and says it is a wall. Another blind man takes hold of the trunk and says it is a snake. Another touches a leg and calls it a tree, while another calls a tusk a spear. The fifth blind man holds the tail and thinks it is a rope, and the last blind man thinks the ear is a fan. None of the blind men had all of the truth; each had a portion of the truth.

The same, it is argued, is true with world religions. Each religion seeks to explain the truth about God, with each one having a portion of the truth. Only by putting all of the information together can we arrive at the whole truth.

What is implicit in this argument is that there is no absolute access to truth. All of us are searching for the truth, but we are like the blind men in this story who have incomplete understanding of God. What is not acknowledged in this illustration is that none of the blind men came to any truth. They were wrong about what they were examining and never got the overall perspective that let them know they really were touching an elephant. The men needed to be cured of their blindness so they could see the folly of their analysis and recognize the elephant in front of them.

As this analogy plays out, all the religions of the world never really come to a knowledge of God because people are blind and incapable of knowing the truth. Scripture says that the god of this world has blinded the minds of those who are perishing (2 Corinthians 4:4); the revelation of God is necessary to bring people to truth (Matthew 16:17; John 6:65).

Since the various world religions have contradictory positions about the nature of God, sin, salvation, and other beliefs, all of them cannot be correct about what is true. A basic law of logic is called the law of noncontradiction. Two propositions that are opposite of each other cannot both be true in the same way at the same time. My students cannot both be physically in my classroom during my lecture and at the same time not be in my classroom. This would be a violation of the law of noncontradiction. But they can be physically in my classroom and not be there mentally (wandering minds), which is called a paradox.

Truth is both objective in nature and discovered, not invented. It is what corresponds to reality. For example, the earth is round, not square. If one is true the other is not true. I cannot make something true that is not already true; I can discover that it is true and accept it or reject it. Some would say that truth is not absolute, or that it is relative. Such views are self-defeating. To say there is no absolute is to state an absolute. To say there is no objective truth is to recognize one. To say that all truth is relative is to make an absolute statement.

Truth by necessity is also always narrow. If I were to say that every religion is true, I would by necessity exclude any other viewpoint about the truthfulness of religions. What is really true about the world excludes all other possibilities about the statement of truth that we make. Two plus two is four, and no matter what a person might say it can never be six, ten, five hundred, or some other number. All other statements of truth are like this.

When we place various religions or cults side by side, we will discover a plethora of viewpoints that contradict each other and contradict the Bible.[63] They cannot all be true, and those contrary to the Bible are simply false.

Jesus did not say that the Holy Spirit was the Spirit of diversity but of truth and that He would lead the apostles into the truth (John 16:12-15). Jesus also said that He was the truth, the way, and the life (John 14:6), not a truth, a way, and a life. No one can come to the Father except through Him. This is narrow and exclusive.

✣

Christianity, as traditionally believed for 2000 years, is "dangerous, destructive, and degraded" in the eyes of the members of a symposium on Jesus and Buddha, as we saw at the beginning of this chapter. To believe that Jesus is the unique Savior of the world, that He is God in the flesh, and that belief in Him is necessary to have eternal life is supposedly a harmful viewpoint. The issue not addressed in this statement is whether Christianity, as historically understood, is true.

The attempt to make Christianity merely one among other religions is the approach that would have been approved by Rome, which held to inclusivism. It was the claim of Christians that Jesus was the only Savior, God, and Lord that brought them to a collision with Roman authorities.

Christianity, however, did not succeed in the ancient Roman world by demoting the Christ to one religious leader among many. And neither will this approach succeed in the present era. The Jesus of the world's religions is a Jesus who never lived. The true Jesus of the canonical Scriptures had unique purpose in coming to earth, and His teachings contradict those of the other religions of the world.

✠

Chapter Nine

THE QUEST FOR THE HISTORICAL JESUS SINCE THE ENLIGHTENMENT

Toward the end of the eighteenth century, the Enlightenment had gained the high ground in Western Europe in all areas of human endeavor. The influence of the Roman Catholic Church had waned. The Reformation, which had removed the blinders from the eyes of the general public and the chains from the intelligentsia, allowed scholars to think and teach apart from the authority of the Roman Church. Rationalism ruled, so that no subject, including the nature and work of Jesus, was safe from fresh investigation and possible rejection in favor of either agnostic or deistic notions.

To the average Christian reading the New Testament, there is no distinction between the Jesus presented by the authors of the Gospels and epistles and the Jesus the orthodox church has believed in from the beginning. To many scholars, though, a plain reading of the Jesus in the Bible is unacceptable. These men and women have been affected by the naturalism coming from the Enlightenment, and the miracles and other supernatural events recorded in the Gospels are discounted as incongruent with modern knowledge.

This trend away from the historic view of Jesus as God who entered human history has been expressed in three quests for the historical Jesus.[1]

Jesus scholar Darrell Bock provides a helpful summary of these three quests: "an 'antidogmatic' first quest; a second, 'new' quest grounded in historical and tradition criticism as well as in Greco-Roman background; and a third quest rooted in the study of Jesus in his Jewish context."[2]

One needs to understand that these quests overlap, with persons pursuing older quests while other quests are in progress. Today many scholars adhere to the methodology and assumptions of the second quest, which began in the early 1950s, including the later radical positions reflected in the Jesus Seminar, while more constructive work on Jesus and the Gospels, including the work of many evangelicals, is occurring within the third quest, which began in the late 1960s or early 1970s.

THE FIRST QUEST

The Beginning of the Quest

What is known as the first quest for the historical Jesus may be traced to 1778 when Gotthold Lessing published the work of Hermann Samuel Reimarus (1694–1768) titled *Fragments*[3]—published posthumously because Reimarus feared recriminations due to the contents of the work. In this book he argues that there was incongruity between the Jesus who really lived and the way in which the writers of the Gospels presented Him. Jesus had no intention of beginning a new religion, Reimarus claims, and was very much a follower of first-century Judaism. Jesus did, however, see Himself as a political Messiah. After the disciples stole His body from the tomb and then proclaimed His resurrection, the more spectacular picture of Jesus arose to foster a Jesus movement.

> *Reimarus's denial of the supernatural Jesus of the Gospel accounts, the risen Lord and God, bore bitter fruit in the rationalism of the early nineteenth century.*

The Fruits of Reimarus's Efforts

Reimarus's denial of the supernatural Jesus of the Gospel accounts, the risen Lord and God, bore bitter fruit in the rationalism of the early nineteenth century. Several scholars began to explain away the supernatural elements in the life and teaching of Jesus. C.F. Bahrdt (1741–1792)[4] and K.H. Venturini (late eighteenth century),[5] for example, wrote of Jesus and His disciples as conspirators who faked His death on the cross. Albert Schweitzer said of these scholars that they "first attempted to apply, with logical consistency, a non-supernatural interpretation to the miracle stories of the Gospel."[6] Their literary attempt to connect Jesus to the Essene community earns from Schweitzer the title "The Earliest Fictitious Lives of Jesus."[7]

The Giant of the First Quest

Perhaps the most notable scholar of this post-Reimarus period was David Friedrich Strauss (1808–1874),[8] who denied the historical reliability of the Gospel records, particularly the supernatural events.[9] This was in contrast to an earlier first-quest scholar, Heinrich Paulus (1761–1851), who had given some historical credence to the New Testament. But, except for the virgin birth, Paulus had discounted all miracles even though they appeared to be miraculous "since that which is produced by the laws of nature is really produced by God, the Biblical miracles consist merely in the fact that eyewitnesses report events of which they did not know the secondary causes."[10]

Strauss, however, believed the Gospels contained a considerable mythic number of elements rather than historical information about Jesus. He believed these myths should be understood as creations of the Gospel writers, who had Messianic expectations. From Strauss's perspective, however, these myths, such as the virgin birth, are legends that seek to honor Jesus in the same way that legends are told in the Greek world about its key historical figures. In spite of this, Strauss believed that Jesus would receive more honor if there were no "legend" of the virgin birth and Joseph had been recognized as His real father.[11]

The Beginning of Source Criticism

Concurrent with this new criticism of the life of Jesus arose investigation of what is known as the synoptic problem, a critique of the first three Gospels. *Synoptic* comes from two Greek words meaning "to see together," and is applied since Matthew, Mark, and Luke share many of the same sayings and events in the life of Jesus. Prior to the rise of source criticism in the mid-nineteenth century, the majority of scholars held that Matthew was the first Gospel written. H.J. Holtzmann (1832–1910), in 1863, substituted Mark for Matthew as the first Gospel. He argued that Matthew and Luke, in fact, depended on Mark's Gospel and on an undiscovered hypothetical source of the sayings of Jesus to construct their Gospels. Holtzmann's unnamed source document was given the title *Q* (from German *Quelle,* "source") by Johannes Weiss (1863–1914) in 1890. There is no written source document representing Q, but the majority of critical scholars believe that either a document or oral tradition of the sayings of Jesus was used by Matthew and Luke, along with Mark, to write their Gospels. Today other sources, sometimes named *M* and *L,* have also been postulated in addition to Q, but discussion of this is beyond the scope of this book.

Conservative Resistance

Not all scholars followed the move away from the historical Jesus to the Jesus of legend. While an onslaught of scholars were deconstructing the Gospel accounts, conservative scholars such as Adolf Schlatter (1852–1938)[12] and Alfred Edersheim (1825–1889),[13] a Jewish convert to Christianity and professor at Oxford, held firm. In *The Life and Times of Jesus the Messiah,* Edersheim argued that these various scholars' conclusions were greatly colored by their worldview. In a word, the Jesus they discovered at the end of their studies was already determined by the only Jesus they would allow at the beginning of their research. Rather than being influenced by a careful study of the Gospels, they were bound to an antisupernaturalistic view of reality, which circumscribed their understanding of Jesus and the Gospels.

The Jesus of the First Quest

Critical scholars of the eighteenth and nineteenth centuries agreed that the Jesus portrayed in the Gospels was largely created by the faithful in the first and second centuries of the Christian era, but they were not unified about the portrayal itself. Two primary pictures of Jesus emerged. The dominant perspective was Jesus the moral reformer, who emphasized the brotherhood of man and the fatherhood of God. His teaching centered on how to live one's life in service of God and man. For the classical liberalism of the nineteenth century, this example of Jesus was the essence of the Christian religion.

Johannes Weiss articulated the minority view. He said that Jesus was an eschatological prophet who expected the end of the world in His time. This emphasis by Jesus caused many to be unreceptive to His teaching. Sharing this view also was Albert Schweitzer, who argued that the ethical emphasis of many of the first-quest scholars were simply reflections of the liberalism of those who were writing about Jesus. They brought their worldview values to the Jesus quest. Schweitzer forcefully argued that there was insufficient information in the Gospels to do a life of Jesus; the proper view of Jesus was that He was an apocalyptic prophet who attempted to bring in the kingdom of God, but failed in His attempt. Schweitzer's book sounded the death knell for the first quest.

The Period of No Quest

End of the First Quest

Three major scholars spell the end of the first quest of the historical Jesus: William Wrede (1859–1906); Albert Schweitzer (1875–1965), as mentioned above; and Martin Kähler (1835–1912). Kähler gave the first major critique of the first quest,[14] but he received little attention until recent days.

At the heart of Kähler's perspective is the belief that the Gospels are not objective reports of Jesus but confessions of early believers in Jesus.[15] Thus the Jesus being pursued by the first quest was little like the Christ of faith.[16]

The adopted wisdom of scholars prior to Wrede was that Mark represented the best information about the historical Jesus, with Matthew and Luke being merely supplemental and John inconsequential. Wrede challenged even the historical credibility of Mark. He said that the identification of Jesus as Messiah was a theological addition by the church after the resurrection. This enabled Mark to explain why Jesus did not set Himself forth as Messiah in Mark's Gospel; Mark invented the Messianic secret, whereby he is able to acknowledge Jesus as Messiah and yet hide the secret until the resurrection.[17]

In contrast to Wrede, Schweitzer considered Mark's portrayal as basically historical, in agreement with earlier scholars in the Jesus quest.[18] Nonetheless Schweitzer dismantled the position of the first quest because he, as well others, believed it was impossible to separate the Jesus of the Gospels from the historical Jesus. But he then erected a Jesus of his own who was eschatological in nature.

Schweitzer says the rationale behind much of the quest for the historical Jesus was to do away with the orthodox dogma of Jesus taught in the church for nearly two millennia, which made critical studies of Jesus impossible. He points out that the scholars of the first quest decried the methodology of orthodoxy but at the same time gave little attention to their own portraits of Jesus, which reflected their idealist, rationalist, socialist, or romanticist views. If the mistake of orthodoxy had been not to ask questions about the Jesus of history, the failure of the historical quest had been to form Jesus into a nineteenth-century figure matching the ideology of the biographer.[19]

Schweitzer sought to remove Jesus from the milieu of the nineteenth and twentieth centuries, in which He fit the image of a modern ethical teacher or idealist, and place Him in the first century AD. He believed, with Wrede, that Mark had a strong Messianic element, but the difficulty was deciding the nature of the Messiah. Schweitzer believed that Jesus, along with many of His day, strongly held to an imminent coming of God, and came to believe that He was the Messiah. Before Jesus was able to bring about this coming kingdom of God, however, He was arrested and put to death.[20]

How does this eschatological Jesus who died in the first century relate to the current day, according to Schweitzer? For him, the significance of Jesus is not in His history but in His spirit. Hugh Anderson summarizes the importance of Schweitzer's work:

> Whereas the Liberals, in their search for the truly human lineaments of Jesus, lost the Christ-character or the kerygma-character of his history, Schweitzer, himself no less resolved on scientific objectivity, all but submerged the historical Jesus in the dogmatic "concept of the Christ."[21]

A Time of Optimism

German theologian and writer David Strauss had represented an optimistic classical liberalism that had considerable appeal in the nineteenth century. He was unconcerned with the Gospels' portrayal of Jesus and more interested in Jesus as the great example for how we should live. In view of this, supernatural elements of the Gospels were unimportant to him, including a belief in the deity of Jesus.[22]

The optimism of this period was brought to a screeching halt with the horror of World War I; the idea of evolutionary progress was largely crushed. Man's sinfulness was hard to deny, but the idea of goodness of man was difficult for the liberal mindset to abandon. Nonetheless it was weakened.

The Division of Faith and History

The first quest ended in pessimism that the historical Jesus could be discovered.[23] Those who abandoned the first quest held that they were too optimistic regarding the tools of criticism with which they sought to uncover the Jesus beneath the myth, and that there was little possibility through the power of historical investigation to untangle the faith of the Church from the Jesus who had actually lived.[24]

An additional feature that gave rise to the abandonment of the quest was the embracing of existentialism in religious studies. The attempt to discover the historical Jesus was considered irrelevant and illegitimate because the Christian faith is built on belief in Christ rather than having certain knowledge of the historical Jesus. Consequently, it was unimportant who the historical Jesus really was.

With World War I, liberalism lost its footing, allowing for the prominence of the writings of a brilliant theologian by the name of Karl Barth. His commentary *Epistle to the Romans* in 1918 shook the liberal theological world with his emphasis on the sovereignty of God and the sinfulness of man. Though Barth did not bring theology back to an affirmation of earlier classic theology, his neo-orthodoxy gained the upper hand on liberal theology. Unfortunately, Barth and his followers had no interest in the historical Jesus. His existential, or encounter, theology was interested only in a personal encounter with God in a Word of God that was beyond, or above, the text of the Bible.

> *Barth and his followers had no interest in the historical Jesus... only in a personal encounter with God in a Word of God that was beyond, or above, the text of the Bible.*

Rudolf Bultmann Controls the "No Quest" Approach

Stepping onto the stage of the "no quest" attitude and the existential philosophical milieu was form critic Rudolf Bultmann, a giant in New Testament studies. A Lutheran scholar lauded as a great preacher, Bultmann considered it an expression of unbelief to need facts and history to underpin the Christian Gospel. His concern was to communicate the good news of Jesus as the Savior of mankind without the myths surrounding the story of Jesus in the Gospels (hence the term *demythologization*). These myths were no longer acceptable to "scientific humans," who had grown beyond belief in miracles and a "three-story universe" in which angels and demons resided. Since faith eschews need for proof, the desire to build Christianity on knowledge of the historical Jesus was unneeded and even counterproductive to Christian belief.

Additionally, Bultmann contended that not only does current belief in Jesus not require knowing the Jesus of history, but that the first Christians also had little interest in such information. Bultmann said,

"I do indeed think that we can know almost nothing concerning the life and personality of Jesus, since the early Christian sources show no interest in either, are moreover fragmentary and often legendary; and other sources about Jesus do not exist."[25]

For Bultmann, the faith of the early Church was expressed in a Christ of faith, not in a Jesus of history. He sought to uncover the faith of the early church by uncovering the written sources and oral traditions that developed around Jesus. The proclamation (*kerygma*) about the Christ of faith, not the historical Jesus, was his concern. Though Barth and Bultmann disagreed on many things, they did agree that the quest for the historical Jesus was unneeded, if not impossible.

The Second Quest (The New Quest)

New Critical Methodology

After World War I many scholars began to move from *literary* or *source criticism* to what is known as *form criticism*. In *literary criticism* scholars attempt to determine the sources behind the final form of a text, such as the New Testament, giving consideration to the temporal proximity of the event to the recording of the event. *Form criticism,* on the other hand, concerns itself with different patterns or forms that can be discerned within the text (genres such as psalms, parables, hymns), usually developed from oral tradition, and how they fit into the historical context.

After World War II biblical critics added another type of analysis, *redaction criticism.* Those who use redaction criticism are interested in an author's theological ideas and how those ideas have shaped the author's material. In discovering an author's molding of a passage, a critic looks to vocabulary, style, comparison of similar accounts, and repetition of themes.

The Beginning of the New Quest

The second quest of the historical Jesus began with Ernst Käsemann (1906–1998), a student of Rudolf Bultmann, with his publication of the essay "The Problem of the Historical Jesus"[26] in 1954. He believed that one could avoid the errors of a past in the new quest, a quest that was both historically and theologically necessary.[27] Käsemann offered two methodologies to approach the new quest. The first was his theory that is sometimes called the "criterion of dissimilarity." Supposedly we may arrive at the historical Jesus by including only material that "is not derived either from primitive Christian teachings or from Judaism. When Gospel material originates from neither of these sources, one can be reasonably sure that the material is historical."[28]

The second criterion to determine an authentic story or saying of Jesus is to find multiple attestations of the words in independent traditions, and stories that simultaneously are in agreement with material already determined to be reliable.

Differences in the New Quest from the First Quest

This new quest is different not only in methodology from the old quest, but also its focus on Jesus and history is different. The first quest sought to find evidence within the Gospels that could substantiate knowledge of the historical Jesus; the second, which accepted the inseparable distance between faith and history, was uninterested in substantiating the historical Jesus and instead focused on the *kerygmatic* Christ, the Christ preached by the church. Charles Anderson explained that this was so because "the significance of Jesus for faith was the great overriding factor in the life of the early church. [Käsemann] feels that this was so much the case that it almost completely replaced his earthly history."[29]

Käsemann questioned whether the phrase "historical Jesus" is valid because of his concern that some might believe a life of Jesus can be written. Having said this, he did believe that the Christ of faith had an earthly existence. Not to do so would be to neglect the important primitive Christian recognition of the identity between the exalted Christ and the earthly Jesus. Second, he was concerned that such de-emphasis of the earthly Jesus might give rise to a docetic view of Jesus (that Jesus only *seemed* to have a physical body). Last of all, he acknowledged that within the Gospel tradition there is compelling evidence for some things in Jesus' life being historical.[30]

Even more important than Käsemann's analysis is the work of Günther Bornkamm. He also denied the possibility of constructing a biographical or psychological life of Jesus. He accepted form criticism, in which the events of the life of Jesus are given in *pericopes* (sections or portions) that cannot be connected in a sequential account. Consequently, the Gospels are given not to provide history but to proclaim Jesus. On the other hand, to abandon interest in history altogether is to lose the earthly Jesus. Bornkamm believed that a balance could be maintained through the use of historical criticism. He also believed that Jesus did not believe Himself to be a Messiah, but Bornkamm did think that Jesus' ethical teaching was authentic.[31] For Bornkamm, Jesus was a "transcendent personality who called people to repent."[32]

Evaluation of the Second Quest

Norman Geisler says that the contrast between the first and second quests is that "the old quest sought discontinuity between the Christ of Faith and the Jesus of history amid assumed continuity. The new quest was concerned with the person of Christ as the preached word of God and his relation to history."[33]

As stated earlier, advocates of the second quest believe they can discover the distinction between the Jesus of history and the Christ preached by the church by the use of two methodologies. They are concerned with far less information than the first quest because their criterion of dissimilarity does not allow Jesus to share either Jewish or Christian beliefs.

This, of course, is an indefensible position because it removes Jesus from the very milieu in which He lived. Even critical scholar Morna Hooker recognizes the inadequacy of the criterion of dissimilarity. She says that some of Jesus' perspectives *must* have overlapped those of the Jewish leaders and some His followers, yet the criterion disallows this consideration. To exclude such details is to cause as much distortion, she says, as including too many details.[34]

THE THIRD QUEST

Why a Third Quest?

The second quest has produced few results, so we have now moved on to the third quest. The genesis of this quest is usually dated to 1970. Unlike the previous two quests, which had a narrow focus and were largely philosophical, not historical, in their approach, the third quest is an interdisciplinary approach, gaining information from archaeology, history, and texts. These are then judged against the disciplines of anthropology and sociology to seek to understand Jesus. They are much broader in possible perspectives of Jesus, too numerous and complex to develop in this chapter (but discussed in various websites and books).[35]

A More Positive Approach, but Still Not Correct

The third quest has more support across liberal and conservative circles and, on the whole, has been far more constructive in understanding the Jesus who actually lived. A number of scholars, such as E.P. Sanders, Ben Meyer, Géza Vermes, Bruce Chilton, and James Charlesworth, have rightly been seeking to reconnect Jesus to His Jewish heritage, viewing Him as a Jewish teacher in the first century who embraced Judaism and Jewish thinking.[36]

A few examples of these more positive studies will suffice. Jewish scholar Vermes considers Jesus a rabbi and Galilean holy man. Meyer sees Jesus as a preacher to God's chosen people, Israel, offering community. Sanders focuses on Jesus' cleansing of the temple as the event that offended His Jewish audience and eventually brought His death.[37]

Moreover, conservative scholars such as I. Howard Marshall and N.T. Wright, who give much more credibility to the Gospel materials and eyewitness testimony, also are involved in the new quest.

The Jesus Seminar

On the very heels of the second quest comes the Jesus Seminar. It has the negative approach to Jesus like the second quest, but is sometimes listed with the third quest, due to its occurrence during the same period. This group has developed some destructive approaches in its intent to minimize the credibility of the canonical Gospels and give unusual credence to Gnostic texts from the second century (these they have tried to date far earlier than is generally accepted). Moreover, many within the Jesus Seminar see the New Testament creating a Jesus from pagan myths and Hellenistic influence.

> *A number of Jesus Seminar members believe there were numerous variations of Christianity from the very beginning.*

A number of Jesus Seminar members believe there were numerous variations of Christianity from the very beginning, with orthodox and heretical existing side by side as alternate and legitimate views of Jesus and Christianity. Supporting this perspective is the belief that both canonical and noncanonical scriptures have equal value in arriving at a proper understanding of Jesus. Several documents (the Nag Hammadi texts—see page 96) used by Gnostic Christianity were formerly assigned to the second and third centuries, but now, some within the third quest consider these works to have been written in the first century and to be in competition with the canonical Gospels of Matthew, Mark, Luke, and John. Especially significant has been the *Gospel of Thomas,* made prominent by the Jesus Seminar and even included in the book *The Five Gospels.*

AN EVALUATION OF THE QUESTS FOR THE HISTORICAL JESUS

Criticisms of the historical quests for Jesus may be brought on three levels: presuppositions that underlie the study, the methodology used in dealing with the Gospels, and misunderstanding of the value and authenticity of noncanonical works.

Presuppositions of the Quests for Jesus

The first criticism of the quests for Jesus relates to the presuppositions of the quests. With the exception of the conservative resurgence, all the quests have been built on premises that are simply assumed to be true:[38]

1. There is the rejection of the supernatural acts of God as recorded in the Gospels. Such out-of-hand repudiation limits the researcher in determining what genuinely happened in the historical situation recorded by the Gospel writer.

2. The Gospels are then dismissed as nonhistorical documents in spite of the repeated attestations of historical persons, places, and events. Since all historical works share a worldview milieu, both of the writer and era being written about, the theological orientation of the Gospel writers no more invalidates the historicity of their texts than does any other ideology. Each text must be investigated in its own right.

3. It is invalid to separate a fact from its value. For example, the spiritual significance of the virgin birth is meaningless apart from the biological fact of it. As well, one cannot separate the death of Christ from its value.

4. It is creating a false dichotomy to separate the Jesus who lived in history from the Jesus who is proclaimed by the church. This presumes that the Gospels do not set forth the authentic Jesus who existed and that the church set forth an idealized, nonhistorical Christ.

5. The form-critical assumptions—that the various layers of the Gospel tradition can be peeled away—must be rejected, for the composition of the Gospels is much tighter and more integrated than form-critical arguments would aver.

6. The view that the Gospels contain myth is a misunderstanding of what myth really is in literature.

As Norman Geisler says,

> Simply because an event is more than empirical does not mean it is less than historical. The miracle of the resurrection, for example, is more than a resuscitation of Jesus' body—but it is not less than that. As C.S. Lewis noted,

those who equate the New Testament with mythology have not studied too much New Testament; they have not studied enough myths.[39]

Myths attempt to explain the nature of things, how they came to be. They in general do not teach requirements for belief and behavior, as the Gospels in general do.

7. The quests fail to make the starting point where the evidence is the best, namely, Jesus' own background and era, how He addressed Israel, and how that led to His crucifixion.

Methodologies of the Quests for Jesus

The first quest, steeped in the empiricism popular at the time, tried to apply empirical rules to studying the Gospels. In the end, scholars gave up the quest, as described above. For them, there was simply no way to verify the historicity of the Gospels using standard empirical methods.

The second quest sought to strip the Gospels of all of the later information that, in their estimation, strengthened the church's position. They also wanted to extract Jesus from His Jewish setting, thinking Jewish elements were also additions made to establish Jesus as the promised Messiah. To this end they chose as authentic only those things in the Gospels that were not in direct support of church doctrine and not too Jewish. This practice, of course, left those of the second quest with very little actual information. As described below, they also gave extrabiblical writings much more credence than is warranted. This has led to some rather outlandish claims. Martin Hengel, reviewing Barbara Thiering's comparison of the Qumran sect with Jesus, says,

What is new is the distorted, idiosyncratic, polemical approach to Christian origins based on an eisegesis [the interpretation of a text by reading into it one's own ideas] of the Dead Sea Scrolls, especially the Pesharim, by B. Thiering. She claims to be able to discover—from reading the New Testament in light of her interpretation of the Dead Sea Scrolls—that Jesus was married, divorced, and remarried. Her precision is astounding: Jesus was betrothed to Mary Magdalene at Ain Feshka [= Cana] at 6:00 P.M. on Tuesday, June 6, 30 C.E. Mary Magdalene decided to divorce Jesus in March 44, after "the birth of Jesus' third child." This reconstruction is imaginative eisegesis. Readers of this Festschrift need no demonstrations that Thiering has offended the science of historiography, which at best can approximate probabilities.[40]

The third quest's methodology has greatly improved over those of the previous two. Now, using modern research techniques involving a broad cross-section of disciplines, scholars are seeking to reattach Jesus to His historical setting. However, the new quest continues to suffer from previous false presuppositions and an unjustifiable use of extrabiblical sources. To further complicate the issue, some scholars have fallen prey to "media scholarship" (which I will discuss in chapter 11). This has led to questionable conclusions based not so much on the evidence, but on what will sell.

Incorrect Understanding about Extrabiblical Documents

As noted above, extrabiblical material has become popular in the quest for the historical Jesus, and certainly may be helpful. But such sources, particularly with no manuscript evidence, are highly suspect. Geisler says,

> In the most recent radical quest there is a misdirected effort to date the New Testament late and to place extra-biblical documents of Q and The Gospel of Thomas [early]. But it is well-established that there are New Testament records before 70, while contemporaries and eyewitnesses were still alive. Further, there is no proof that Q ever existed as a written document. There are no manuscripts or citations. The Gospel of Thomas is a mid-second-century work too late to have figured in the writing of the Gospels.[41]

Though considered by many scholars as historically credible as the Gospels that we possess, the fact is that Q does not exist, but is merely a hypothetical document thought to be the source for some of the Gospels' material. *The Gospel of Thomas* (among others such as *The Gospel of Judas* and *The Gospel of Philip*) is part of the Nag Hammadi Library found in Egypt. It is considered a work supporting Gnosticism, if not of Gnostic origins itself, an issue still being debated. Neither Q nor *Thomas* deserve equal footing with the canonical Gospels. The *Gospel of Thomas* is much later than the synoptic Gospels, and one entire copy and a fragment are all that exist of this work, hardly enough to characterize it as a reliable source for the historical Jesus. "Q" cannot even be studied because it does not exist except in reconstructions among scholars, who are often at odds with each other over the issue.

Consequently, there is no compelling reason for these two works to be used when attempting to find the historical Jesus.

Conclusions

Though the different quests all set out to distinguish the Jesus of history from the Jesus of the New Testament, they have all failed because of their erroneous presuppositions and bad methodology. Yet this has not stopped the newest quest from coming up with different versions of the Jesus of history. However, this does not mean there is nothing of value to be gained from the third quest. On the contrary, with the renewed interest in Jesus there are opportunities for further historical exploration.

Fertile Areas for Research Stemming from the Third Quest

N.T. Wright offers several avenues of investigation he believes are important questions, many of which have been only partially covered, that must be addressed by current scholars: [42]

    1. How did Jesus relate to the Judaism of His day? In what ways were Jesus' aspirations the same as that of His contemporaries

and how did they react to Him? What did He say or do that related to their hopes for the immediate future?

2. What really were the aims of Jesus? Though Jesus is portrayed as coming only to save the world through His death, were there other things that motivated Him daily, and what did He desire people to do to respond to Him properly?

3. Why did Jesus need to die? On one extreme is the view that He died as a revolutionary against Rome, while on the other side is the perspective that He was a "bland Jesus, the mild Jesus, the Jesus who was so thoroughly like any other ordinary Jewish holy man that it is hard to see why anyone would have wanted to oppose him, let alone crucify him."[43] Wright poses the question as to whether Jesus believed He was called to a violent death.

4. What was the cause of the early church's origin? Directly related to this issue is the meaning of Easter, a point that has had little serious historical research.

5. Wright poses the clear distinction between the issue of what the Gospels are and whether they are in fact true. Whether they were written by Christians is irrelevant to whether they are true. Moreover, in what genre are they written, and does this tell us anything about the authors of the Gospels?

In conclusion, Wright says,

These, I suggest, are the questions that ought now to be addressed in serious historical study of Jesus. They are also the starting-point for serious *theological* study of Jesus. It will not do, as we have seen many writers try to do, to separate the historical from the theological. "Jesus" is either the flesh-and-blood individual who walked and talked, and lived and died, in first century Palestine, or he is merely a creature of our own imagination, able to be manipulated this way and that.[44]

In order not to fall into the trap of many of the questers, we need to recognize that trying to determine what "historical" is proves counterproductive to knowledge. Our concern should be to find out what really happened, *not* what we will allow to have happened based on a naturalistic worldview. This is not to say that history does not require interpretation, but we do need to understand that history is not merely subjective. There is objective fact that can be known.

How Jesus Is Presented in the Gospels: Some Scholarly Insight

Most critical scholars believe it is not possible to gain a true understanding of Jesus from the Gospels, because they are not historical documents; instead they are but statements of the church's faith, interwoven with mere fragments of historical fact. Wright speaks to this. He acknowledges that the Gospels are products of theological reflection, but this does not invalidate them as historical. He admits they are written from a particular point of view, but that is true of all history. Moreover, though the Gospels are not strict biographies, they are "theologically reflective biographies."[45]

Second, the Jewish mind was fully inclined toward history. This is true in the Jews' look to Abraham and the fathers, to the Exodus, the connection to David, and the anticipation of Messiah's coming to earth to usher in His kingdom. Wright says that the Jewish person would not have considered that God had redeemed His people yet, since Rome ruled over them, there was disobedience to the law, and the world was still sinful:

> *The complaint about the Gospels' lack of chronological order as an indication of their nonhistorical nature is without merit... since this is what real history looks like.*

> Something had to happen in the real world...A "spiritual" redemption that left historical reality unaffected was a contradiction in terms. If the gospels, seen in terms of the pagan culture to which the church went in mission, are

inescapably *biographies,* then, seen in terms of the Jewish culture which gave them their theological depth, they are inescapably *theological history.*[46]

The complaint about the Gospels' lack of chronological order as an indication of their nonhistorical nature is without merit. Wright calls those who make such arguments naïve, since this is what real history looks like.[47]

The Future

The third quest may yet blossom into something very useful for scholars and laity alike. By putting to use modern methods of research, we may be able to gain a better insight into these "theological histories" and the Jesus portrayed in them. While we may hesitate to say that this research proves the New Testament true, it certainly gives us evidence against the claim that it is *not* true. Moreover, because of the widespread interest in Jesus generated by these quests, we have been given an opportunity to present Jesus' message of salvation, and we should take advantage of it.

Chapter Ten

✠

THE JESUS OF FALSE CHRISTIANITIES

Heretical Views of Jesus in Contemporary Cults and Unorthodox Religions

That there is nothing new under the sun receives no greater evidence than in comparing the heresies following the first century with modern "false Christianities." The first four centuries of Christianity saw the rise of six basic heresies about the person of Christ: heresies that either denied the actuality (Ebionism) or the fullness (Arianism) of Jesus' deity, that denied the actuality (Docetism) or the fullness (Apollinarianism) of His humanity, that divided His person (Nestorianism), or that confused His natures (Eutychianism). All distortions of the orthodox Christian doctrine of the person of Christ are merely variations of one of these six heresies.[1]

Most of the earlier heresies have found their way to the modern world. Unlike the world religions (discussed in a previous chapter), which do not consider themselves part of the Christian religion but have adopted Jesus in some respects into their religious "hall of heroes," most of the advocates of recent adaptations of early Christian heresies do view themselves as Christian.

Even though they present themselves as being Christian, or at least related to Christianity in some important aspects, they deny the essential doctrines of the Christian faith. Often, researchers of religions and religious traditions have classified theses groups as cults, or occasionally religious movements. Since the term *cults* has at times been used to identify groups that are viewed as strange or extreme, such as the Branch Davidians or the followers of Jim Jones, I need to clarify that I am using the term only in the sense of a false "Christian" religion that holds to beliefs or practices incongruent with the historic Christian church. Thus I am distinguishing a cult of Christianity from orthodox or historic Christianity in terms of its false religious beliefs or practices, not in sociological or psychological terms.

THE FOCUS ON JESUS

The cults of Christianity differ from the orthodox faith at many points, but the major consideration for this book is how they view Jesus the Christ. In other religions of the world, the moral teachings of the religion provide the essence of the religion. Buddhism would continue if Buddha had never lived. Islam could still have a vital belief in Allah even if Muhammad were not his prophet.

This is not true of Christianity. Christianity would not have survived the persecutions of the early centuries or blossomed to its magnitude today apart from belief in the special nature and work of Jesus. Jesus is not merely appreciated for His teachings or respected for His high morals. He is worshipped, adored, and obeyed as the sovereign God and creator of the universe, the Savior of His people.

The Jesus of the cults, however, is no more the real Jesus than the Jesus of the ancient heresies or of the world religions. For this chapter, then, we shall first consider the orthodox view of Jesus as portrayed in Scripture and defined in the church creeds.

The church has consistently taught that Jesus is both God and man. Scriptural texts, particularly from the New Testament, abound with references to His Person. The Gospel of John, for example, is the christological tour de force for the proclamation of Christ's divinity:

"In the beginning was the Word, and the Word was with God, and the Word was God" (John 1:1). This is the stunning proclamation borne on the lips of those who had lived with Jesus for over three years and affirmed by the infant church. It is this proclamation that the church has sought to preserve.

We recognize that this uniqueness of God's Son presents difficulty as we seek to proclaim this truth. How could Jesus be both God and man? Was He part God and man, more God than man, or the other way around? Does it really matter what we believe about this incarnation of the Logos of God as it affects our eternal salvation? Rather than maintaining the biblical balance that the church has historically held, false Christianities distort the meaning of Scripture to arrive at their doctrines of Jesus.

UNORTHODOX RELIGIONS ON THE DEITY AND HUMANITY OF JESUS

Numerous groups espouse belief in Jesus in some way, and it is beyond my intentions to deal with these in any depth.[2] But we will look at a few representatives of these heretical views.

The Church of Jesus Christ of Latter-day Saints

Mormon teaching on Jesus' natures. Mormons believe that Jesus is "a god" or a godlike being. Perhaps no other group using the name Christian represents the paganization of Christian doctrine more than Mormonism, otherwise known as the Church of Jesus Christ of Latter-day Saints.

The Mormon church does not have a systematic presentation of beliefs and even takes pride that there is disparity in their doctrinal views.[3] Their theology can change according to the whims of whatever president happens to be in office at the time. For example, the founder of Mormonism, Joseph Smith, had considerably different perspectives from his successor, Brigham Young, and yet Mormons see no difficulty with this. The Mormon church merely acknowledges that the Mormon president speaks for a different generation of Mormons. The current view is what must be believed for salvation, and not former viewpoints that have been abandoned or discredited.[4]

Common to all Christian cults is the employing of Christian terminology devoid of historic Christian meaning. Thus a cult will look Christian in its use of Christian terminology, but redefining the terms renders them heterodox. Mormons use this tactic. A member of the Latter-day Saints would say that he is a Christian since he follows Jesus, but when investigated one finds that this Jesus is but one god (Yahweh) among millions.[5] For Mormons, Jesus is not the second person of the eternal, indivisible God.[6]

> *In Mormon theology Jesus once existed as the eldest of many spirit-children of God the Father through sexual intercourse with a number of goddess wives.*

The humanity of Jesus is also distorted. In Mormon theology Jesus once existed as the eldest of many spirit-children of God the Father through sexual intercourse with a number of goddess wives. "He [Jesus] was the most intelligent, the most faithful, and the most Godlike of all the sons and daughters of our Heavenly Father in the spirit world."[7] And, "Among the spirit children of Elohim [the Father] the firstborn was and is Jehovah or Jesus Christ."[8] According to the Mormon belief system, Jesus is not the eternal Son of God as understood in Christian orthodoxy but the spirit-brother of Lucifer, and he was chosen over Lucifer to redeem humanity. One of Mormonism's authoritative writings gives this account:

> The Holy Scriptures give an account of a great council which was held in the spirit world before man was placed on the earth. This meeting...was presided over by God our eternal Father; and those in attendance were His Sons and daughters...Eternal Father explained to the assembled throng...the great "Gospel plan of salvation."... The appointment of Jesus to be the Savior of the world was contested by one of the other sons of God. He was

called Lucifer…this spirit-brother of Jesus desperately tried to become The Savior.[9]

Rather than being the eternal Son of God, Jesus had a beginning and is no different in nature from His "brother," Lucifer (now Satan). He is not a single person with two natures, but a single spirit-being who was conceived and became a man of flesh and blood through sexual intercourse between His Father, Elohim, and the Virgin Mary. This belief is clearly affirmed by several leaders within the Mormon church.

> I was naturally begotten; so was my father, and also my Savior Jesus Christ. According to the Scriptures, he is the first begotten of his father in flesh, and there was nothing unnatural about it (Apostle Heber Kimball).[10]

> Christ was begotten by an Immortal Father in the same way that mortal men are begotten by mortal fathers (Apostle Bruce McConkie).[11]

> CHRIST NOT BEGOTTEN OF HOLY GHOST… Christ was begotten of God. He was not born without the aid of Man and *that Man was God* (Joseph Fielding Smith, former president).[12]

Response to Mormon teaching on Jesus' natures. As we saw above, Jesus in the Mormon pantheon is the Yahweh (Jehovah) of the Old Testament, with Elohim as his Father, one of millions of gods and goddesses that inhabit the Mormon universe. This is a purely contrived notion that cannot be supported by the Old Testament Scriptures. The names Yahweh (Jehovah) and Elohim are used together in dozens of passages to refer to the same being (Exodus 3:15; Deuteronomy 6:4; Psalm 95:3-7; 99:6-8; 100:3; Jeremiah 7:28; 10:10), who we discover in the New Testament is three Persons in one, not two separate persons.

In Mormonism, Jesus' humanity undergoes a most amazing transformation. First, He was born a spirit-being through the sexual activities of His Father, Elohim, and one of His spirit-wives. Second, He becomes a human through the Virgin Mary. The Scriptures declare, however, that Jesus has existed for all eternity as the Son, one of the three Persons, along with the Father and Holy Spirit, of the one God. He did not come into existence after the Father (Micah 5:2; Psalm 90:2; John 1:1; Colossians 1:17). Neither is He the spirit-brother of Lucifer, since, as God the Son, He is Lucifer's creator. The belief that Jesus was conceived through the sexual union of Elohim and the Virgin Mary is a patently flagrant violation of the biblical teaching that He was miraculously begotten by the Holy Spirit, and Mary remained a virgin until after Jesus was born (Matthew 1:18-20; Luke 1:26-38).

Centuries after the Messiah Jesus walked the earth, Arius and his followers declared Him a creature, merely "like" God (*homoiousios,* similar essence). Athanasius and his supporters opposed this view with their entire intellectual might, affirming at the Council of Nicaea that the Son is eternal and one essence (*homoousios,* same essence) with the Father. Sixteen centuries have passed and Mormons, and well as other false Christianities, perpetuate the same false teaching. Mormonism is Greek mythology decked out in Christian language, advocating the ancient Greek view of the eternal nature of the material universe. Far from possessing a Christology, Mormonism has transformed the majestic, eternal Son of God into a semidivine, quasi-Greek god.

Jehovah's Witnesses

Jehovah's Witnesses' teaching on Jesus' natures. The ancient Arian heresy that vexed the church of the fourth century has seen its resurgence in the Jehovah's Witnesses also. Although not a mirror image of Arius's theology, the Jehovah's Witnesses believe that Jesus is a created being, an inferior to Jehovah God: "Christ was the first of God's creations [Col. 1:15; Rev. 3:14],"[13] and "he [the Word] was created before all the other spirit sons of God, and that he is the only one who was directly created by God."[14] According to the Watchtower, Jesus never claimed to be Almighty God,[15] but He is "a god," that is, the Word was a powerful godlike one.

Jesus' humanity does not fare any better: "[W]hen God sent Jesus to earth as the ransom, he made Jesus to be what would satisfy justice, not an incarnation, not a god-man, but a perfect man,"[16] "equal of the perfect man Adam."[17]

But what was the role of Jesus prior to becoming this perfect man? Jehovah's Witnesses believe that He was Michael, the archangel, who was the first and the greatest of God's creation: "[T]he Son of God was known as Michael before he came to earth,"[18] and "before being born on earth as a man Jesus had been in heaven as a mighty spirit person...he served in heaven as the one who spoke for God."[19] After the resurrection of Jesus as a spirit-creature, apparently He resumed His former position as Michael: "War broke out in heaven: Michael [who is the resurrected Jesus Christ] and his angels battled with the dragon."[20]

In common with many ancient heresies, Jehovah's Witnesses believe that Jesus did not become the Messiah until His baptism: "Jesus came to John to be baptized! On that occasion he was anointed with the holy spirit and became the Messiah, or Christ,"[21] and He was awarded the gift of immortality at His resurrection.[22]

This is only a sampling of the Jehovah's Witnesses' distorted theology about the deity and humanity of Christ. It is unfortunate that many orthodox Christians are not as concerned about Christ's true identity as are the Jehovah's Witnesses. An Arian cult, in their zeal for this one issue, has put us to shame.

Response to the Jehovah's Witnesses' teaching on Jesus' natures. The Scriptures teach and the Chalcedonian Definition affirms that the Son of God had two natures, one divine and one human, and that these natures are united, without mixture, in one person. No mere mortal could satisfy the judgment of God against sinful humanity. God put on human nature to become that satisfaction on the cross and to rise from the dead, bringing a new order to humanity. Rather than being Michael the archangel, Jesus is the creator of all creatures and things:

> He is the image of the invisible God, the firstborn over *all creation*. For by Him *all things* were created that are in heaven and that are on earth, visible and invisible, whether

thrones or dominions or principalities or powers. *All things were created through Him and for Him. And He is *before all things,* and in Him *all things* consist (Colossians 1:15-17 NKJV, emphasis added).

The Greek text of this passage indicates that Jesus is prior to all of creation, creator of all things, and for whom all things were created. The text uses "firstborn" (*prototokos*) with an active force ("first-bearer"), rather than the passive idea of "first cre-ated" (*protoktistos*). This distinction is supported by the conjunction that begins verse 16, "for" or "because," stating a *cause* for the preceding statement, namely, that *all things* (repeated four times for empha-sis) were created by Jesus, of whatever sort they are (heaven-earth, visible-invisible,

> Jehovah's Witnesses place Jesus under the category of "a god," not the Almighty God.

thrones-powers-rulers-authorities). This is similar to John 1:3, where the apostle says, "All things were made through Him, and without Him nothing was made that was made" (John 1:3 NKJV).

So how do Jehovah's Witnesses answer this clear passage in Colos-sians? They simply add words in their New World translation that are not found in the Greek text. Their translation adds the word "other" to each statement speaking of creation, such as, "all *other* things were created." There is no warrant in the Greek text for including these words in the translation; they are arbitrary and self-serving.

What about the use of *firstborn?* Doesn't this indicate that Jesus was created? No, because the word *prototokos* also may mean "preeminent." Several times in Scripture the term is used to indicate one who is pre-eminent, even if not the first male child born to parents. An example is found in Jeremiah 31:9, where Ephraim is declared God's "first-born," even though we discover in Genesis 41:51-52 that Manasseh, not Ephraim, was the literal firstborn. What does this mean? Only that *firstborn* does not always refer to a chronological order of rank. One can have the honor of firstborn bestowed upon him.

Additionally, in contrast to the false teaching of Jehovah's Witnesses, nowhere in the Bible is Jesus referred to as a creation of God. He is, in fact, described as the creator of all that exists (John 1:3; Colossians 1:16), the one who is the same "yesterday and today and forever" (Hebrews 13:8).

As we learned above, Jehovah's Witnesses place Jesus under the category of "a god," not the Almighty God. But such an idea is incongruent with passages in John's Gospel. For example, in John 10:34-36 Jesus declared Himself to be the Son of God, the equivalent of deity in the Jewish culture, and in John 5:17-18 He reveals Himself as the one who sustains the universe with the Father (see Colossians 1:17). In John 8:58 He identifies Himself as the I AM, and in John 10:30 as being one with the Father, both statements causing the Jews to take up stones to kill Him "because You, being a Man, make Yourself God" (10:33 NKJV).

In John 1:1, the Jehovah's Witnesses translate the phrase "the Word was God," as "the Word was a god,"[23] indicating once again their propensity to translate the Greek text to suit their theological bent. The Greek text of John 1:1, as reflected in most English translations, teaches the personal relationship of the Father with the Son from all eternity ("In the beginning was the Word, and the Word was facing [Greek, *pros*] God"; see 1 John 1:2, "facing the Father"), but then also that this Word was God as to His nature. The latter use of *God,* according to Greek grammar, states the quality of the being: whatever it is to be God is what the Word was.

But this person is not only fully God, He is fully man. When Jesus said, "Concerning that day or that hour, no one knows, not even the angels in heaven, nor the Son, but only the Father" (Mark 13:32), He voluntarily functioned in His humanity, which was not privy to the knowledge present in the divine nature. God the Father's position to Jesus is "greater" (*meizon*), not "better" (*kreitton*), as the Greek words indicate. Greater speaks of rank; better speaks of nature. Hence, Jesus as both God and man could experience the attributes of His divine nature as well as the limitations of His human nature. Submission, such as we see in Jesus' prayer in the Garden of Gethsemane (Luke

22:42), does not make the one in submission inferior in nature to the one in authority (see Ephesians 5:22f).

Finally, the claim that Jesus did not become the Messiah until His baptism is contradicted by Luke 2:25-35, where Simeon, who had been searching for the Messiah, declares that the child Jesus is the Messiah. Also, the angel announcing Jesus' birth declared, "For unto you is born this day in the city of David a Savior, who is Christ [Messiah] the Lord" (Luke 2:11).

Mind Sciences

Mind Sciences' teaching on Jesus' natures. Mind Science groups are those that have adopted a largely Eastern or Gnostic view of the world, and also of Jesus Christ. They are represented by a plethora of religious groups and movements, such as the Theosophical Society, Christian Science, Unity, A Course in Miracles, and various New Age groups. The Theosophical Society[24] reveals Eastern influence when it defines Jesus as divine, but also declares that all people are innately divine, "so that in time all men become Christs."[25] One Theosophical writer, in summing up his group's view of Jesus, said that most would agree that the Christ did come 2000 years ago to establish a religion, but also claimed we cannot avoid the view that He had many predecessors—christs and saviors who have come numerous times throughout human history.[26]

The Christ, apparently, had descended on several persons like Jesus. In Christian Science, Jesus and Christ are not the same person. Jesus is the man; Christ is the spiritual idea or element of God: "Jesus is the human man, and Christ is the divine idea, hence the duality of Jesus the Christ."[27] From the writings of Religious Science, the fastest-growing wing of the mind sciences, we read, "JESUS—the name of a man. Distinguished from the Christ. The man Jesus became the embodiment of the Christ, as the human gave way to the Divine idea of Sonship."[28] And, "Christ is not limited to any person, nor does he appear in only one age. He is as eternal as God. He is God's idea of Himself, His own Selfknowingness."[29] We too can become a christ, according to this thinking, as we follow after the Christ spoken of in the Bible.

Response to Mind Sciences' teaching on Jesus' natures. Jesus' humanity as understood in the Mind Science cults is considerably different from orthodoxy. For Mind Science, He was an example to us of a man who also became a christ. As Mary Baker Eddy says, "Jesus demonstrated Christ; he proved that Christ is the divine idea of God the Holy Ghost, or Comforter, revealing the divine Principle, Love, and leading into all truth."[30] From the writings of Religious Science we learn, "To think of Jesus as being different from other men is to misunderstand His mission and purpose in life. He was a way-shower and proved His way to be a correct one."[31] And from the Unity School of Christianity we learn, "The difference between Jesus and us is not one of inherent spiritual capacity, but in difference of demonstration of it. Jesus was potentially perfect, we have not yet expressed it."[32]

According to Mind Science groups, Jesus is the temporal man, while the Christ is the eternal aspect of God that indwelt Him. Consequently, it was not the corporeal Jesus who was one with the Father, but the spiritual idea, the Christ, who dwells forever in the "bosom of the Father." But in 1 John 2:22-23 we read,

> Who is the liar but he who denies that Jesus is the Christ? This is the antichrist, he who denies the Father and the Son. No one who denies the Son has the Father. Whoever confesses the Son has the Father also.

Jesus never claimed that the Christ dwelt in Him, nor did the apostles write such, but that He in fact was the Christ (Matthew 26:63-65; Mark 14:61-64; 15:2; Luke 4:21; John 4:21-26).[33] Recognition of who Jesus is enables us to enjoy the salvation that He offers, and to miss this understanding is to miss Jesus the Messiah altogether. Following the death of Lazarus, Jesus and Martha, Lazarus's sister, spoke about this:

> Jesus said to her, "I am the resurrection and the life. Whoever believes in me, though he die, yet shall he live, and

everyone who lives and believes in me shall never die. Do you believe this?" She said to him, "Yes, Lord; I believe that you are the Christ, the Son of God, who is coming into the world" (John 11:25-27).

At another time Jesus said,

"I told you that you would die in your sins, for unless you believe that I am he you will die in your sins...When you have lifted up the Son of Man, then you will know that I am he, and that I do nothing on my own authority, but speak just as the Father taught me" (John 8:24,28; see Deuteronomy 32:39; Isaiah 43:10,13; 48:12).

Mind Science groups do not understand that Jesus is the name of the Son of God in the flesh (Matthew 1:21), while the Christ, or Messiah, is not a name, it is His title or office (Matthew 16:16).

Jesus was never a trailblazer showing us the way to being a christ; He is God of very God, while being also man of very man, two natures in one person (Colossians 2:9; Philippians 2:6-11).

United Pentecostal Church

The United Pentecostal Church's teaching on Jesus' natures. Early in the third century, a person named Sabellius (see chapter 7) developed a doctrine known as *Modalism* in its most sophisticated form.[34] Often referred to as Sabellianism, this school of thought taught that the Godhead is composed of one person who may be designated at times by Father, Son, or Spirit. There is no ontological distinction within the Godhead, only designatory significance among them based on their operation within creation. Father, Son, and Holy Spirit are identical and successive revelations of the same God or person.[35] Jesus was not the co-eternal Son of God, but God who operated as the Son of God on earth. (A similar idea *patripassianism*, expresses the belief that the Father suffered in Christ since he was identical and actually present in the Son.[36])

The modern equivalent to the modalistic idea of the Trinity and the person of Christ may be found in the United Pentecostal Church.

On the positive side, the UPC holds a strong view of the Deity of the Christ:

- "One cannot over-emphasize the supreme deity of Christ."[37]
- "Jesus Christ is the incarnation of the one God."[38]
- "Jesus is God with us, the eternally blessed God, the image of the invisible God, God manifested in the flesh, our God and Savior, and the express image of God's substance."[39]
- "Jesus is both God and man at the same time."[40]

At the same time, however, they reject the distinction of the Son from the Father:

- "If there is one God and that God is the Father (Malachi 2:10), and if Jesus is God, then it logically follows that Jesus is the Father."[41]
- "Jesus is the Father incarnate. 'His name shall be called…The Mighty God, The Everlasting Father' (Isaiah 9:6)…'I and my Father are one' (John 10:30)…'He that hath seen me hath seen the Father' (John 14:9)."[42]

Response to the United Pentecostal Church's teaching on Jesus' nature. Ancient and contemporary modalists use select verses to argue that Jesus and the Father are one "person," yet they completely disregard other portions of Scripture that differentiate between the persons of the Godhead. Furthermore, *natures* do not converse with one another; *persons* do. In attempting to appeal to logic, modalists violate the rules of logic by maintaining that the Father and the Son are one person, confusing essence with person. They teach that, in a sense, God the Father was actually in Jesus. "God the Father dwelt in the man Christ…The divine nature of Jesus Christ is the Holy Spirit…which is the Spirit of the Father."[43] And, "the deity of Jesus is none other than the Father Himself."[44]

In order to hold to this position, one must make a farce out of the prayers of Jesus to His Father, including His prayers in Gethsemane, as well as the words God the Father spoke about the Son at His baptism and transfiguration. Persons talk to persons, so Jesus' prayers to the Father require two persons. The view advocated by the UPC denies the incarnation and is little more than Dynamic Monarchianism (see appendix), a view Unitarians hold today.

When modalists affirm that "Jesus is not just a part of God, but *all* of God is resident in Him,"[45] they unwittingly agree with the orthodox creeds of the church that say Jesus is "Light of Light, true God of true God" (Nicene Creed), and "We...teach men to confess one and the same Son, our Lord Jesus Christ, the same perfect in Godhead

> *Modalists...*
> *misunderstand how*
> *the person of the Son*
> *in His humanity*
> *could communicate*
> *with God the Father.*

and also perfect in manhood; truly God and truly man" (Chalcedonian Definition). The orthodox faith believes that the Son is not part of God, but God Himself. But the creeds, and biblical faith, also recognize a distinction between the Persons who are that one God.

Modalists not only misunderstand the distinctions of the persons within the one essence of God, but they also misunderstand how the person of the Son in His humanity could communicate with God the Father. For them, natures communicate with each other: Jesus' human nature converses with His divine nature. As we have responded above, conscious *persons* communicate with one another; *natures* do not.

In John 1:1-5 the Word is said to be "with God" and indeed "was God." The language allows for no other conclusion than that the person spoken of is someone who is in some way alongside of or "with" (Greek *pros,* literally "toward") the person of God while being God at the same time. Only the orthodox doctrine of the Trinity provides a solution to this conundrum.

✠

Chapter Eleven

THE JESUS OF
MEDIA SCHOLARSHIP

Jesus has always been a popular figure. Jesus sells, and the media lose little time in using Jesus as a topic to sell papers and books. Anytime Jesus is discussed, it brings an audience, especially if the discussion is controversial. This has not been lost on the scholarly world either. Recent efforts by some in academia seem driven more by the desire for the spotlight than sound scholarly work.[1]

Although there have been many efforts to find the "real" Jesus and what this Jesus supposedly said, we will focus on three of these efforts: The Jesus Seminar, *The Da Vinci Code,* and recent work by Bart Ehrman.

THE JESUS OF THE JESUS SEMINAR
What Exactly Is the Jesus Seminar?

According to the official website of the Westar Institute, "The Jesus Seminar was organized under the auspices of the Westar Institute to renew the quest of the historical Jesus and to report the results of its research to more than a handful of gospel specialists."[2] It began in 1985 and continues as of 2006 on a new phase, the Jesus Seminar on Christian Origins, which is a "new history of early Christianities and Christian writings."

The original Jesus Seminar was composed of approximately 70 scholars from North America, though the people involved varied from time to time and fluctuated in number. Few, if any, could be considered evangelical or sympathetic to evangelical perspectives. Most are radical critics of the Bible, and only a few are well-known scholars in the field of New Testament studies. New Testament scholar Ben Witherington III says that the Jesus Seminar is not sponsored by either the Society of Biblical Literature (SBL) or the Society for the Study of the New Testament (SSNT), the major scholarly organizations in biblical studies.[3] Several members of the group, however, such as Robert Funk, John Dominic Crossan, and Marcus Borg, have achieved some degree of celebrity.

What Are the Presuppositions and Prejudices of the Jesus Seminar?

The Seminar works under several presuppositions and prejudices. First is the rejection of the supernatural. As Robert Funk wrote,

> The Christ of creed and dogma...can no longer command the assent of those who have seen the heavens through Galileo's telescope. The old deities and demons were swept from the skies by that remarkable glass. Copernicus, Kepler, and Galileo have dismantled the mythological abodes of the gods and Satan, and bequeathed us secular heavens.[4]

Anything supposedly done by Jesus that included supernatural elements is immediately suspect. Even sayings of Jesus that seem supernaturally derived are suspect. Funk wrote, "Whenever scholars detect detailed knowledge of post-mortem events in sayings and parables attributed to Jesus, they are inclined to the view that the formulation of such sayings took place after the fact."[5] Since the Seminar considers the Jesus of the church to be different from the historical Jesus, the only connection with the "sage from Nazareth is limited to his suffering and death under Pontius Pilate."[6]

For the Seminar, the Gospels are actually seen in opposition to the creeds, and are "understood as corrections of this creedal imbalance."[7]

Additionally, there is severe skepticism that the writers of the Gospels could remember all that Jesus said since it was passed along orally. Instead, they are said to have made Jesus sound "Christian" by making up some of His sayings. Furthermore, the Gospel writers couldn't even remember how Jesus talked, so these insertions don't sound like Jesus and are borrowed extensively from the "fund of common lore or the Greek scriptures."[8]

The Gospel writers, in an attempt to make Jesus into the messiah, "began to search the sacred writings or scriptures...for proof that Jesus was truly the messiah." This led them to "make the event fit the prophecies lifted (and occasionally edited) from the Old Testament."[9]

Without providing any evidence, the members of the Jesus Seminar also contend that Jesus and his disciples were "technically illiterate."[10] They also reject the New Testament canon, the accepted works of orthodoxy, saying, "Canonical boundaries are irrelevant in critical assessments of the various sources of information about Jesus."[11] Apparently for the Seminar, those who assembled the canon were not as qualified as they to evaluate the texts. It is more likely they believe the councils who assembled the canon were hopelessly biased, as are the many, many scholars who have upheld the canon through the centuries. Only the Jesus Seminar is objective enough to find the actual words of Jesus, they suppose, even if those words differ from what has been considered authentic for almost 2000 years.

All in all, the Jesus Seminar comes to its work with an elitist view of themselves in regard to scholarship and history.

The Methodology of the Jesus Seminar

The Seminar continues the approach to Jesus research begun in the nineteenth century, called higher criticism, which believes that contemporary biblical scholars are able to distinguish the Jesus of history from the Christ of faith, the Jesus who was only a human from the mythical figure from the heavens.[12] Any miracle is considered a myth, added later to reflect later beliefs. Thus there can be no virgin birth, walking on water, or resurrection. Before they even began their work, the Jesus Seminar decided that anything in the Gospels that supports Jesus being more than just a human cannot possibly be true.

The Jesus Seminar decided popular majority was the best way to ascertain Jesus' actual words. "Voting was adopted, after extended debate, as the most efficient way of ascertaining whether a scholarly consensus existed on a given point."[13] This decision to vote was apparently voted on. About this method, Ben Witherington III says, "Only in a thoroughly democratic society where the assumption that the majority view is likely to be right and to reflect a true critical opinion on the 'truth' could the idea of voting on the sayings of Jesus have arisen."[14]

The Criteria Used by the Jesus Seminar

The Jesus Seminar uses "seven pillars of scholarly wisdom" to guide its decision making. Most of these pillars are directly attributable to eighteenth- and nineteenth-century German scholars and their assumptions. So while claiming to be a fresh look at Jesus scholarship, the Jesus Seminar is really a rehashing of old (and largely outdated) liberal thinking. Moreover, the Jesus Seminar doesn't give any rationale for the adoption of these criteria, most of which are circular in reasoning. Instead of pillars, these points are blocks in an arch, all mutually dependent on each other for support. If one block is knocked out, the whole arch falls.

The first pillar is *the assumed distinction between the historical Jesus and the Christ of faith.* These two portrayals cannot be the same person, because there is a difference between the "Christ of faith encapsulated in the creeds" and the "historical Jesus...uncovered by historical excavation."[15] To the contrary, one cannot separate faith from history, because faith must have an object. If it isn't the real Jesus as He is seen in the Gospels, then there is no reason for the existence of Christianity. Genuine faith is not an unreasonable faith (1 Corinthians 15), but is based on evidence that explains the facts. The overwhelming evidence supports Jesus as He is seen in the canonical Gospels.

The second pillar, again an assumption, says that *the synoptic Gospels, along with the* Gospel of Thomas, *are much closer to the original sayings and deeds of Jesus than the Gospel of John.* The Gospel of John is the "spiritual" Jesus.[16] This makes sense, considering that the "Christ of faith" from the creeds looks similar to the Jesus found in John's account, and that the Seminar has already assumed the church created the "Christ of faith." Further, the Seminar refuses to even consider the arguments about dating John's Gospel, or that the "spiritual" element could be John seeing Jesus from a different angle.[17]

The third and fourth pillars are similar to each other. The third pillar is *the assumption that Mark was written before Matthew and Luke, becoming the basis for both.* As a result, anything found in Matthew and Luke in common with Mark is likely a copy of Mark, not necessarily an original saying of Jesus. While their first point may have merit, and is even accepted by many evangelical scholars, it has not been demonstrated that Mark has inauthentic sayings of Jesus.

The fourth pillar is *the assumption of an independent source for material common to Luke and Matthew, but independent of Mark, called the "Q" document* (Q standing for *Quelle,* meaning "source"). This is a completely hypothetical document, because no such manuscript has been found. Certainly it can be surmised that Luke and Matthew used *something* as a source to write their Gospels, but it could be an oral tradition known to both of them and not a document. To the Seminar, however, anything found in Matthew and Luke that is common to each but not found in Mark is likely to be from Q and not an original saying of Jesus.

The third and fourth pillars show the Seminar's fallacious use of discontinuity—the discipline of looking for authentic evidence of an event by finding things common among each account. What one does with this information is important. In a normal legal case, one looks for lack of discontinuity to corroborate a story. Three witnesses with the same story are better than two. The more witnesses, the more likely their story is true. The Jesus Seminar has argued the exact opposite. Stories that are similar among the Gospel writers are said to be *inauthentic* because they have so much corroboration. The only way for this to be true is if all the writers had the agenda to make up Christianity by copying each other (except John, who apparently didn't go along with the conspiracy).

The fifth pillar is *the assumption that Jesus never said anything about the coming of the end of the world.* According to the Jesus Seminar, it was John the Baptist who preached this message of impending judgment and cataclysm. Jesus is said to have "rejected that mentality in its crass form, quit the ascetic desert, and returned to urban Galilee." The disciples misunderstood everything Jesus taught them, so when He died, they reverted to the things John the Baptist had taught them. This, coupled with the disciples' emerging view of Jesus as a cultic figure akin to the "Hellenistic mystery religions," led them to overlay their own "memories" of Jesus on top of His actual sayings and parables. For the Seminar, this means the "Jesus of the gospels is an imaginative theological construct." The Seminar sees this fifth pillar as "liberation" for Jesus from the prevailing view. For them, modern scholarship is a "search for the forgotten Jesus."[18]

> *According to the Jesus Seminar...the disciples misunderstood everything Jesus taught them, so when He died, they reverted to the things John the Baptist had taught them.*

This argument assumes that the apostles learned a great deal from John the Baptist at an undisclosed time before Jesus began His ministry, and then learned nothing from Jesus, whom they followed for three years. It also assumes they were heavily influenced by Greek paganism, rather than being thoroughly Jewish. It completely disregards the possibility that Jesus spoke about the coming kingdom because He actually knew about the kingdom. Again, this also assumes the Gospel writers were all together in some conspiracy to change what Jesus actually said to fit their own theological system.

The sixth pillar is *the assumption that an oral culture is incapable of preserving the original words of Jesus,* unlike our writing-based culture today. Therefore only those sayings that are short, provocative, memorable, and oft-repeated are considered original. For the Jesus

Seminar, people are simply not able to remember long dialogues, let alone whole stories. This pillar betrays the underlying elitism of the Jesus Seminar. It is as if they are completely ignorant of oral cultures.

It also further exemplifies their dismissal of the supernatural. Jesus Himself said, "The Helper, the Holy Spirit, whom the Father will send in my name, He will teach you all things, and bring to your remembrance all things that I said to you" (John 14:26 NKJV).[19] Even if we were to grant, contrary to what this verse says, that the writers of the Gospels were not supernaturally assisted in their recounting of Jesus' words and deeds, the Jesus Seminar completely fails to acknowledge the human capacity for memorization.[20]

The seventh pillar is *the assumption that there has been a reversal of the burden of proof.* The Jesus Seminar says that in previous times it was assumed that the Gospel narratives were true, and the burden of proof was on proving the sayings and events that are recorded there false. For the Jesus Seminar this is no longer the case. They assume that scholarship has done such a good job proving the Gospel accounts false that it is now up to academia to find what bits are true (or at least close to true), and they are the defenders of the Gospel accounts.[21]

Again, as has been discussed at length, this is an assumption that is far from decided. Many scholars would deny this point. With so much evidence for the orthodox view of Jesus, and more being discovered as time goes on, it is all but impossible to disprove the Gospels, let alone assume it has already been done.

An Evaluation of the Jesus Seminar

Using the faulty criteria above, the Jesus Seminar has voted that 82 percent of the content of the Gospels is not the actual words and deeds of Jesus. According to the Jesus Seminar, the only verses from the canonical Gospels that are virtually certain to have come from Jesus, and are therefore the sum total of His teaching, are the following:

- paying taxes (Matthew 22:21c, Mark 12:17, Luke 20:25b)

- not resisting when attacked, or sued, going an extra mile (Matthew 5:39-42a, part of Luke 6:29)

- loving enemies (Matthew 5:44a, fragment of Luke 6:27b)

- praying "Our Father" (only that fragment of Matthew 6:9)

- expecting the unexpected (Matthew 20:1-15)

- statement that "God's domain belongs to the poor," the hungry will be fed, and those who weep will laugh (Luke 6:20-21)

- giving to everyone who begs (Luke 6:30a)

- showing compassion (Luke 10:30-35)[22]

- the statement that "God's imperial rule" is like leaven hidden in dough (Luke 13:20b-21)

- the statement that shrewdness is commendable (Luke 16:1-8a)

Only 18 percent of the Gospels—including the noncanonical Thomas—are even considered the *possible* words of Jesus, with even less of that percentage "most likely" the words of Jesus, leaving us a disjointed sage separated from His context. Witherington argues that the Jesus of the Jesus Seminar was not controversial, was passive until questioned or criticized, was no prophet or even a radical reformer, never claimed to have a part in God's final plans for man, never claimed to be Messiah, and did not come to save.[23]

Based on the media attention surrounding the members of the Jesus Seminar and how they set up the Jesus Seminar to appeal to that same media, it isn't a far stretch to see them molding Jesus into what they themselves wish to be—popular sages to whom the public can run for "countercultural wisdom."[24]

In the end, the Jesus Seminar makes wide and radical assumptions based on outdated liberal ideas, leading them to disregard normal textual-critical arguments and evidence and to make logical fallacies. They seem to think they are more objective and have better insight than previous scholars. They use questionable methods that reveal their underlying skepticism and their desire for attention from the media.

THE JESUS OF *THE DA VINCI CODE*

In 2003 the writer Dan Brown released his fourth book, *The Da Vinci Code*. It is a novel, though Brown claims, "All descriptions of artwork, architecture, documents, and secret rituals in this novel are accurate," a claim that caused an uproar in the Christian community. Brown's assertions about Jesus were as radical as they were false. The well-documented errors in *The Da Vinci Code* led Sandra Miesel of *Crisis* magazine to quip, "So error-laden is *The Da Vinci Code* that the educated reader actually applauds those rare occasions where Brown stumbles (despite himself) into the truth."[25] Even Bart Ehrman, whom we will discuss later in this chapter, had disparaging words for Brown's lack of historical accuracy and his careless research.[26]

Unfortunately, many people may not have the discernment to separate truth from fiction in Brown's work. Although the upset over the novel has quieted down, some of the arguments made in the book continue to reverberate through society. The popularity of *The Da Vinci Code* has led to an upsurge in the popularity of finding alternatives to the orthodox view of Jesus. However, many claims that Brown makes are simply exaggerated retellings of current scholarly debates. We will limit our critique of Brown to his claims about Jesus, specifically His divinity, and Brown's mistaken interpretation of Gnostic versions of Jesus.

The Human Jesus of Dan Brown

Jesus is made God at the Council of Nicaea. At one point in the novel, one of Brown's characters is educating another on the "real" Jesus. He says, "At this gathering [the Council of Nicaea], many aspects of Christianity were debated and voted upon—the date of Easter, the role of bishops, the administration of the sacraments, and of course the *divinity* of Jesus." Later in a section of dialogue this character, Teabing, says to another,

> "My dear, until that moment in history, Jesus was viewed by his followers as a mortal prophet...a great and powerful man, but a *man* nonetheless. A mortal."

"Not the Son of God?"

"Right. Jesus' establishment as 'the Son of God' was offi-
cially proposed and voted on by the Council of Nicaea."

Brown goes on, through his character, to claim that it was a close
vote, and that it was Constantine who desired to make Jesus divine.
He says the church stole Jesus from His early followers, "hijacking his
human message, shrouding it in an impenetrable cloak of divinity,[27]
and using it to expand their own power."[28] He claims the "gospels" that
stressed Jesus' humanity were gathered and burned by Constantine,
but some escaped. Those who used them were called heretics, even
though they were using the "original" gospels. Among these "heretical gospels," Brown says, were the Dead Sea Scrolls and the "Coptic
Scrolls" found at Nag Hammadi.[29] Brown argues these documents
"speak of Christ's ministry in very human terms."[30]

Response to Brown's Claim

The biblical support for Jesus' deity. This outlandish claim about Jesus
is simply false, and easily proved so. First, the Gospels themselves testify
to Jesus' divinity. John 1:1 says, "In the beginning was the Word, and
the Word was with God, and the Word was God. He was in the beginning with God." John 8:58 says, "Jesus said to them, 'Truly, truly, I say
to you, before Abraham was, I am.'" Even if we accept the most liberal
scholarship, John's Gospel was written more than two centuries before
the Council of Nicaea. The apostle Paul in his letter to the Romans,
written AD 55-57, a little over 20 years after Jesus' crucifixion, clearly
indicates that Jesus was divine: "according to the flesh, is the Christ
who is God over all, blessed forever. Amen" (Romans 9:5).

The deity of Jesus in the post-apostolic church. Very early in the church,
the doctrine of Jesus' divinity was upheld and taught. The apostolic
Father Ignatius believed in the deity of Jesus, and wrote around AD
105, "God Himself being manifested in human form for the renewal
of eternal life."[31] Justin Martyr wrote in the first half of the second
century, "The Father of the universe has a Son; who also, being the

first-begotten Word of God, is even God."[32] Clement, working around AD 150, defended the divinity of Jesus and the Trinity when he said, "If it is thy wish, be thou also initiated; and thou shall join the choir along with angels around the unbegotten and indestructible and the only true God, the Word of God, raising the hymn with us. This Jesus, who is eternal, the one great High Priest of the one God, and of His Father, prays for and exhorts men."[33]

The deity of Jesus at the Council of Nicaea. Dan Brown doesn't seem to know what the Council of Nicaea was about. It wasn't the divinity of Jesus that was debated, but a new teaching by a man named Arius. The Council of Nicaea was convened not to solidify power by making up new doctrine, but to unify the church and defend the original teaching from new ideas. Arius believed

> *The Council of Nicaea was convened not to solidify power by making up new doctrine, but to unify the church and defend the original teaching from new ideas.*

Jesus was divine, but in a different or lesser way than the Father, because Arius claimed that Jesus was created by the Father. The vast majority of the bishops present at Nicaea were against this teaching. They only debated over what the wording of their creed should be to accurately describe the relationship between the Father and the Son.[34] In the end they came up with the familiar wording of the Nicene Creed:

> We believe in one God, the Father Almighty, Maker of heaven and earth, and of all things visible and invisible. And in one Lord Jesus Christ, the only-begotten Son of God, begotten of the Father before all worlds; God of God, Light of Light, very God of very God; begotten, not made, being of one substance with the Father, by whom all things were made.[35]

As for Constantine "gathering" all the "heretical gospels," the Nag Hammadi writings themselves prove this false. They are dated sometime in the fourth century, probably after AD 350, possibly even "a generation later,"[36] making their composition at least 25 years after the Council of Nicaea.

The humanity of Jesus in Gnosticism and in the canonical Gospels. Is the Jesus of the Gnostic gospels more human than the Jesus of the canonical Gospels, as Dan Brown argues?[37] As I discussed in a previous chapter, the word *Gnostic* is an umbrella term for a system of philosophy based on "secret knowledge" (*Gnostic* is derived from the Greek word for *knowledge*). Gnostics believed they had the correct knowledge of what was reality, which was not visible to everyone else.

There were some basic beliefs among Gnostics. The original divine essence produced other divine essences, but some sort of failing took place in the spiritual realm. As a result, matter came into existence. This matter then was produced out of evil. However, some of the original, pure, spirit nature was placed in some souls. These souls pass through the material world on their way back to the divine, but become trapped in their material "shells." A "redeemer," namely Jesus, came to reveal the way of escaping the material world for this bit of the divine nature.[38]

However, since material is inherently evil in Gnosticism, the Gnostic Jesus ranged anywhere from being a human vehicle for the divine spirit of the Son, to a simple apparition who had no material form at all. Far from emphasizing His humanity, the Gnostic gospels all but exclude it.

THE JESUS OF BART EHRMAN

The Journey of Bart Ehrman

Bart D. Ehrman is the department chair of Religious Studies at the University of North Carolina at Chapel Hill. Although he was "saved" in high school and attended Moody Bible Institute, he later lost faith while studying at Princeton.[39] During his studies he began to doubt "just about everything," not just the Bible, but "everything the Bible talks about." Ehrman's faith was rooted in the words of the Bible, but when he came to believe the words we have now are not the originals, those words were no longer trustworthy for him.

He now describes himself as an agnostic.[40] He says he is a "happy agnostic" because he's not worried about the problems in the Bible. He no longer has to try to believe something he thinks is false. He says that basing something on words we don't know are even true is not the best way to live. For Ehrman, the Bible is simply a book of some good morals to live by, an example.[41] He has written several books, his most famous being *Misquoting Jesus*.[42] Ehrman has also become an outspoken critic of conservative views of the Bible, specifically the orthodox view of Jesus.

Misstating Facts in *Misquoting Jesus*

Variegated Christianities and the new testament manuscripts. Ehrman's book *Misquoting Jesus* was released on November 1, 2005, just in time for the renewed interest in Jesus around Christmas. The title is a misnomer, because it really has little to do with what Jesus actually *said,* and more with proving that *we can't know* what he actually said. Within a few weeks it had climbed toward the top of Amazon.com and the New York Times' Best-seller List.

Ehrman appeared on *Fresh Air* and the Diane Rehm show, both on National Public Radio. Within three months *Misquoting* had sold more than 100,000 copies. He became a media sensation, an overnight celebrity. Following the popularity of *Misquoting Jesus,* Ehrman's other releases, *Lost Christianities* and *Lost Scriptures,* to name two, have gained popularity. *Lost Scriptures* claims the early church hotly debated which beliefs were right. Eventually the victors "rewrote the history of the conflict" so that it appeared their views were those of the earliest Christians, "all the way back to Jesus himself." Those who didn't support the victors were branded "heretics." Their works were "suppressed, forgotten, or destroyed."[43]

Lost Christianities goes over much of the same ground from the perspective of the various "losers" in the debates over orthodox Christianity, arguing that the early church was much more diverse than even today's "variegated phenomenon" of modern Christianity, making the differences between "Roman Catholics, Primitive Baptists, and Seventh-Day Adventists pale by comparison."[44]

Response to Ehrman's Textual Analysis

Why variants occur in the manuscripts. According to Daniel B. Wallace, Ehrman's book was written for "the skeptic who *wants* reasons not to believe, who considers the Bible a book of myths."[45] It is mostly "NT textual criticism 101."[46] Unfortunately, Ehrman goes beyond the field of textual criticism without letting the reader know he has done so.

The beginning of the book lays out a well-done explanation of the field of textual criticism. However, there are a few places where Ehrman strays from the majority of scholars. In chapter 2, Ehrman discusses the world of New Testament copyists. Wallace says of this chapter,

> Here Ehrman mixes standard text-critical information with his own interpretation, an interpretation that is by no means shared by all textual critics, nor even most of them. In essence, he paints a very bleak picture of scribal activity, leaving the unwary reader to assume that we have no chance of recovering the original wording of the NT.[47]

Ehrman argues that the process for copying books in the ancient world—a slow, handwritten copying of the texts—is "open to mistakes," either accidentally or intentionally.[48]

> Far and away the most changes are the result of mistakes, pure and simple—slips of the pen, accidental omissions, inadvertent additions, misspelled words, blunders of one sort or another. Scribes could be incompetent: it is important to recall that most of the copyists in the early centuries were not trained to do this work but were simply the literate members of their congregations who were more (or less) able and willing.[49]

He lampoons ancient scribes, saying, "sometimes they just couldn't be bothered to give their best effort."[50] He says these errors build through the history of the texts. An error is made and the next scribe copies it, thinking it correct, and adds his own errors. The next copyist includes the errors of the other two and adds his own, and so on. He claims that in the 5700 or so Greek manuscripts in existence, there may be over 400,000 variants.[51] In addition, Ehrman avers, "It would be wrong...to say—as people sometimes do—that the changes in our text have no real bearing on what the text means or the theological conclusions that one draws from them."[52]

> "I came to think that my earlier views of inspiration were not only irrelevant, they were probably wrong." Apparently, this view eventually led Ehrman to agnosticism.

With this sort of thinking, it is little wonder why Ehrman thinks it is impossible to have the original words of Jesus.

Are Ehrman's facts correct? Kurt Aland, the pre-eminent textual critic of our age, has studied the issue exhaustively. He contends the New Testament Greek texts "exhibit a remarkable degree of agreement, perhaps as much as 80 percent!" He says,

> Textual critics themselves, and New Testament specialists even more so, not to mention lay persons, tend to be fascinated by differences and to forget how many of them may be due to chance or normal scribal tendencies, and how rarely significant variants occur—yielding to the common danger of failing to see the forest for the trees.[53]

He goes on to argue that 63 percent of the New Testament verses are "variant-free."[54]

Character of textual variants. Further, Darrell Bock and Daniel B. Wallace, both respected scholars in Greek studies, discuss the character of these variants. They argue that because of the nature of the Greek language, the possibility for variants in the text is potentially infinite.[55] However, the vast majority of the variants in the Greek New Testament are minor, such as a change of a letter, changes involving synonyms, changes in pronoun use, and word order changes, and none affect major theology (for example, that Jesus is God or that salvation is by grace through faith).

Contradicting his statement cited above, even Ehrman admits that, "To be sure, of all the hundreds of thousands of textual changes found among our manuscripts, most of them are completely insignificant, immaterial, and of no real importance."[56] Despite this confession, it doesn't stop him from saying, "I came to think that my earlier views of inspiration were not only irrelevant, they were probably wrong."[57] Apparently, this view eventually led Ehrman to agnosticism.

As an anecdote showing why the number of variants can outnumber the actual words in the text, we can use Ehrman's own book *Misquoting Jesus.* In his discussion of Luke 3:22 (page 159) the text instead says, "Luke 3:23." That means this error occurs in *every single copy* of *Misquoting Jesus.* As of February 2005, *Misquoting Jesus* had sold 100,000 copies. Using the methods of textual criticism and assuming the error went uncorrected to that point, this means there are 100,000 errors in *Misquoting Jesus.*[58] Should subsequent editions of his book correct this mistake and those sell 100,000 copies, that means there would be 200,000 "variants" in *Misquoting Jesus.*[59] This is for a mistake in only one number. There may be even more errors, leading to more possible variants.

Should we doubt the trustworthiness of *Misquoting Jesus* because it has 100,000 errors, and possibly exponentially more variant readings? According to Ehrman's argument, yes. Suddenly, claiming "the New Testament is unreliable" because it has 400,000 variants isn't so convincing. This is especially so when one remembers that the Greek New Testament contains approximately 140,000 words. This means that among the approximately 5735 New Testament manuscripts, granting Ehrman's 400,000 variants (which I am not promoting), that would be an average of about 70 variants per manuscript, and most of these are insignificant to any teaching of the Bible. The case against the reliability of the biblical text doesn't look so devastating in this light. Other ancient sources are far more error-ridden, and yet scholars put trust in these works of antiquity.

Why Ehrman Is Wrong

Although Ehrman discusses several textual issues throughout his book, we will limit our study to two of them. We will show why Ehrman's conclusion that we can't trust the New Testament is simply wrong.

An example of how Ehrman's beliefs affect his view of the Gospels is evident when he discusses Luke's narrative of the Passion and crucifixion of Jesus.[60] Ehrman argues that Luke's "original" narrative in chapter 22 was so vastly different from the one in Mark (and others) that scribes later added verses 43 and 44 to make Luke fit with the rest of the Gospels. Ehrman goes on for ten pages with the arguments, concluding that verses 43 and 44 were probably not in the original.

What is troubling for a textual critic is the part of his argument *not* based on textual criticism. Ehrman assumes some key interpretive information: that Luke was written as "a story of Jesus' martyrdom" that instructs the faithful on how to "remain firm in the face of death."[61] He also assumes that Luke used Mark as a source "which he changed to create his own distinctive emphases."[62] Ehrman says, "It would be difficult to overestimate the significance of these changes that Luke made in his source (Mark) for understanding our textual problem."[63] These assumptions, similar to those made by the Jesus Seminar, reflect the notions that

- the later Gospel writers simply copied the earlier ones. In this case, Luke copied Mark. (Luke tells us he used a wide variety of sources, including eyewitness accounts—Luke 1:1-4.)

- there was no supernatural intervention in the writing of the Gospels that led the writers to put down what they did. It was *Luke* deciding what to include and leave out, not the Holy Spirit.

- there are new themes for the Gospels other than the ones widely accepted.

Normally textual criticism decides which reading of a text is most likely the original reading among textual variants, not the theological history of a text. But Ehrman is concerned about the latter in *Misquoting Jesus.* He argues that we should attempt to find theological errors, "not because they necessarily help us understand what the original authors were trying to say, but because they can show us something about how the authors' texts came to be interpreted by the scribes who reproduced them."[64]

What Ehrman means by an "error" may be seen in his discussion of Luke 3:22.[65] The reading of this passage in the most reliable manuscripts says, "You are my beloved Son; with you I am well pleased" (Luke 3:22). Ehrman, on the other hand, believes that when the voice comes from heaven at the baptism of Jesus, the text should read, "You are my Son, today I have begotten you."[66]

Ehrman's view reflects an adoptionist theology—namely, that Jesus was not the begotten Son of God from eternity, but was adopted as a Son at His baptism. Ehrman argues that the text was changed on theological grounds, even though he admits, "The vast majority of Greek manuscripts have the first reading (You are my beloved Son, in whom I am well pleased)."[67] His conclusion cannot be reached through normal textual critical methodology. In fact, only one Greek manuscript has the reading Ehrman favors, though he does not mention it.[68]

Usually this evidence would be enough to settle the argument in favor of the standard reading. This is not satisfactory for Ehrman, who argues that "the verse was quoted a lot by early church fathers in the period before most of our manuscripts were produced...And in almost every instance, it is the *other* form of the text that is quoted ('Today I have begotten you')."[69]

At first reading this sounds impressive. Though the majority of manuscripts say "with you I am well pleased," since the early Fathers say "today I have begotten you," it appears that we should agree with Ehrman and favor that reading. Or should we?

Ehrman is wrong at the most basic level because he does not understand that the Fathers are not quoting Luke 3:22 at all. Justin, Clement, Methodius, Hilary, and many others do have "You are my Son, this day I have begotten you," but they are citing an Old Testament passage, not the Gospel text. Justin, arguing with Trypho over whether Jesus is the promised Messiah, says,

> What, then, is Christ's inheritance? Is it not the nations? What is the covenant of God? Is it not Christ? As He says in another place: "Thou art my Son; this day have I begotten Thee. Ask of Me, and I shall give Thee the nations for Thine inheritance, and the uttermost parts of the earth for Thy possession."[70]

Because of the inclusion of the second phrase about the inheritance and the grammar of the Greek, we know Justin was quoting Psalm 2:7-8 in the Septuagint, the Greek translation of the Old Testament, not Luke 3:22 (3:23 in Ehrman). Justin was not discussing the baptism of Jesus, but His place as the promised Messiah to the nations. In almost all of the Fathers' use of this passage, they are quoting Psalm 2:7. We know this because of the context of the Fathers' writings, which Ehrman has apparently not consulted.

Ehrman's argument, then, that the copyists were affected by theology in altering their texts has really been turned back on him. The external evidence clearly supports the text that Ehrman rejects.

Ehrman...vastly overemphasizes the importance of the minor variants found in the Greek manuscripts.

But what about other textual-critical procedures of an internal nature, such as trying to figure how a particular error may have been introduced into a text? The alternate reading could easily have been introduced by the scribe of the Greek manuscript

Ehrman prefers (the codex labeled "D"),[71] who was familiar with the Septuagint's reading of Psalm 2:7 and introduced it in Luke 3:22, which starts out similarly.[72] In viewing the evidence, one wonders whether Ehrman has thoroughly studied the issue.

Ehrman concludes that there is no way to know what the original text was. He says, "The more I studied the manuscript tradition of the New Testament, the more I realized just how radically the text had been altered over the years at the hands of scribes, who were not only conserving scripture but also changing it."[73] He admits that as he began to see the "scribal text" was "a very human book," he also began to believe the *original* text (if we could find it) was a "very human book." After all, Ehrman argues, if God could not keep the copies of the Scriptures from error, how could He have inspired the originals? If God did not inspire the originals, how do we know they are actually teaching us about Jesus, let alone God?

Ehrman answers these questions with his agnosticism, and has launched a crusade to convince everyone else he is right.

There are, however, good reasons to doubt Ehrman's conclusions. He vastly overemphasizes the importance of the minor variants found in the Greek manuscripts. He uses the assumptions and presuppositions of higher criticism instead of limiting himself to textual criticism. Finally, he wrongly interprets data, overlooking or simply failing to look in depth at the information, arriving at an incorrect conclusion about the text. *Misquoting Jesus* "simply doesn't deliver what the title promises."[74]

Ehrman has lost his belief in the Jesus contained in the New Testament accounts. In his words, "These accounts that we have of Jesus' resurrection are not internally consistent; they're full of discrepancies, including the account of his death and his resurrection."[75]

When approaching Bart Ehrman's work, it is appropriate to paraphrase the old adage: *Let the reader beware.*

As we have seen, the Jesus of media scholarship is a far cry from the authentic Jesus of the New Testament. From the Jesus Seminar, we see Jesus as some kind of wandering dispenser of short and witty wisdom sayings. He comes off as a pacifist whom it is hard to imagine was crucified. Dan Brown's Jesus was only a human and did not die on the cross. It was the church who created the doctrine of His deity. Bart Ehrman isn't sure who Jesus is because we can know nothing that He originally said. A media hungry for controversy has popularized these versions of Jesus.

I have shown why all of these conclusions about Jesus are false. The Jesus Seminar uses outdated higher-critical methodology, much of it interdependent assumptions, to the exclusion of other forms of evidence. Dan Brown twists information or just makes it up (so much so that even Ehrman criticizes him). Bart Ehrman, while claiming to focus on textual criticism, allows higher criticism to obscure his analysis. He further fails to thoroughly examine all the information before making a conclusion.

◈

Chapter Twelve

THE JESUS OF POPULAR RELIGION

Since the very beginnings of the church, the physical image of Jesus Christ has been a powerful and important one. Until recently the only media for public expression were limited to artists, done in canvas and sculpture, and thus every representation of Jesus has reflected the culture of the artist,[1] whether it be Byzantine, Roman Catholic, or a variety of countries.

The physical images of Jesus little resemble what a Jewish man would have looked like in Israel 2000 years ago, but also His ideas, teachings, and life often have been distorted. Modern depictions of Jesus often have little to do with Jesus of Nazareth as He might have actually been. This has led to a wide cultural misunderstanding of who Jesus is, what He did, and how we should understand Him from a biblical standpoint.

Hollywood depictions of Jesus show Him as a mere human, some kind of cultural radical or even a comedic figure. Recent documentaries argue that the Bible's depiction of Jesus is wrong, even going so far as to claim to have found His grave. Popular culture, influenced heavily by relativistic postmodern philosophy, has taught that each individual determines what he or she believes to be true, including beliefs about Jesus. Our understanding of Jesus has unfortunately been hijacked by this "to each his own" philosophy to the point where people refuse to correct their belief even in the face of overwhelming evidence.

ANCIENT IMAGES OF JESUS

While we will focus on more recent depictions of Jesus, it is helpful to understand the history of depicting Jesus.

Images in the Eastern and Western Church

The Eastern Orthodox tradition. In the East, the tradition of icons, paintings depicting various biblical characters, has always been approached with reverence.[2]

The Orthodox icons are no mere portraits but the depiction of the "holy flesh" of Christ. The Eastern Orthodox Church believes grace can be transferred from the Holy Spirit, through the icon, to the faithful. For this reason icons are made to resemble the traits of the person as closely as possible. The church does not tolerate icons that are painted "according to the imagination of the artist or from a living model." In fact, the Church claims to have made icons of some saints immediately after their death, while their appearance was still fresh in the iconographer's mind. These images were then copied over and over, always striving to copy every feature exactly.[3]

The Roman Catholic tradition. In the West, images of Christ took more varied forms. Anyone who has been in a Roman Catholic Church has noted the crucified Christ at the front of the church, and there are often depictions of the Gospels painted on the church walls. Again, these works, being used in worship, were created with that purpose in mind. In the Roman Church images were not restricted to icons.[4]

Because of the Roman Catholic doctrine of the church being the center of all life, whether government, society, or culture, the images of Jesus used by the church permeated every level of life. Religious art was popular art. This trend continues to this day in areas that are heavily Roman Catholic.

There were images for every doctrine the Roman Church taught about Jesus:

1. *The earliest images.* The earliest depictions of Jesus are seen in the catacombs of Rome, and are of pagan origin. The figure of Orpheus was adopted by Roman Christians in the form of "Christ the Good Shepherd."[5]

2. *Jesus diversifies.* Gradually, as Christianity gained approval, then became the official religion of the Roman Empire, the catacombs were abandoned and along with them these depictions of Christ. As churches, basilicas, and cathedrals were built, they were adorned with a wide variety of depictions of Christ. Because of the Roman Church's focus on the suffering of Jesus, the most common is a depiction of the Passion Week, the week leading up to Jesus' crucifixion and resurrection. Often this depiction is painted on the walls, but sometimes is shown on the stained-glass windows.

> *Catherine of Siena believed that through the taking of the Eucharist she no longer needed any other food or drink.*

As mentioned above, another integral image in Roman Catholic churches is the crucifix.[6] Being an object so central to Catholic worship, utmost care is taken by the artist. However, this devotion was not governed by the same ideology as the Eastern Church. Artists were free to use their imaginations depicting Christ. Again, conforming to the centrality of Jesus' suffering on the Cross, crucifixes are shown with Jesus in intense agony. His face is strained in pain, and He is covered in blood.

Another tradition in the Roman Catholic Church has been intense personal devotion to Christ. Certain individuals throughout the Church's history have claimed special revelation or some kind of heightened spiritual state. As long as it conformed to Roman Catholic theology, these spiritual events were sanctioned and even encouraged, and these individuals serve as examples for personal devotion.

3. *The image of Jesus' blood and His torture.* The importance of

Jesus' blood is widespread in Roman Catholicism, stemming from the Church's doctrine of transubstantiation, the changing of the bread and wine of the Eucharist into the actual body and blood of Jesus. Catherine of Siena believed that through the taking of the Eucharist she no longer needed any other food or drink. For Catherine, the taking of the Eucharist to the exclusion of all other sustenance was to become like Christ in suffering and was a way of finding unity with Jesus. The Eucharist for her was akin to actually drinking Christ's blood from His side.[7] She believed it was what sustained her.

Catherine's devotion to the Eucharist was a theme that became very popular with Roman Catholic faithful, especially as the Reformation severely challenged their belief about the Eucharist. In 1648 Louis Cousin painted "Saint Catherine of Siena Drinking from the Side Wound of Christ." It shows a postresurrection Jesus offering His side to Catherine, who eagerly drinks the fluid that pours out.

4. *Jesus as bridegroom or lover.* The Roman Catholic doctrine of celibacy, imposed during the twelfth century, coupled with the teaching of intense devotion, has also led to the doctrine of the marriage of the Church to Jesus.[8] Saint Bernard saw the Song of Songs as a metaphor and said in a sermon that he wished Jesus would "kiss me with the kiss of his lips." The belief of Jesus as bridegroom was especially popular during the height of European chivalry, particularly among women. Margery Kempe, born in 1347, wrote devotionals that are laced with romantic visions of Jesus.[9]

5. *The "Sacred Heart of Jesus."* Saint Margaret Mary Alacoque is credited with formulating the modern Catholic doctrine of devotion to the Sacred Heart of Jesus. She lived in France from 1647 to 1690. Through fasting and self-inflicted lashing, she believed she was reliving the Passion of Christ. She is said to have had visions directly from Jesus, advising her of things He wanted for the Church.[10]

The Jesuit Order took up the cause of venerating the "Sacred Heart," and eventually the teaching was proclaimed official by Pope Pius IX. Since the time of St. Margaret, images of Jesus' Sacred Heart have been popular themes for Roman Catholics, especially in Latin America. Often pictures of the Sacred Heart or Jesus with the Sacred Heart are hung in churches and homes.[11] This picture has become one of the most popular images in the world. It is seen on everything from devotional candles to tattoos.

The Masters

Early popular images of Christ. The coming of the Renaissance brought a break from the artistic style in which Jesus had been depicted. Previously, images of Jesus were born from doctrine for the devotion of Roman Catholic faithful. From this point artists both continued this tradition, but also began to create works for popular consumption.[12]

The changing economic conditions of the Renaissance meant there was a growing upper-class society, composed of both the regal class and ordinary businessmen. Members of this class became patrons commissioning art for their own collections. The popular works began to include Christian, pagan, and nonreligious themes.

All this change had a tremendous impact on the way Jesus was portrayed. His image, and those of other biblical or Christian characters, began to take on more naturalistic features. The artist strove to portray Jesus as they thought He might have actually looked, albeit from a European perspective.

Soon artists of unusual giftedness began to emerge. Today we know them as the Masters. Mainly from Italy, these men are widely considered to be the geniuses of their time, and indeed are included among the most gifted men of any time. Many of them were artists, engineers, and early scientists. They are responsible for formulating the image of Jesus that has been popular ever since their time.[13]

The Reformation

Martin Luther. October 31, 1517, marked a sea change in Europe, with Martin Luther's 95 Theses. No longer would the Catholic Church hold a monopoly on religion. Luther, a theologian, not an artist, was nonetheless responsible for a shift in art, especially in the depictions of Jesus. One of his books, *The Passion of Christ and the Antichrist,* written in 1521, was illustrated by Lucas Cranach, a German artist who was a neighbor and friend of Luther. His illustrations depict Jesus as a powerful figure who is shown militantly dealing with the authorities, who look conspicuously like Roman Catholic priests and monks.[14]

The image of Christ suffering was de-emphasized. Gone from these works are the typical depictions of a young, often soft-featured and gaunt Jesus. Images of Jesus created for Luther's works are sometimes less literal than those in the Roman Catholic Church. For instance, Luther's Jesus became an actual lamb, emphasizing the sacrificial nature of the crucifixion rather than the suffering. However, he continued to teach the actual presence of Christ's blood in the Eucharist. The front page of one of Luther's Bibles shows a lamb holding a cross, bleeding into the chalice cup. This image was repeated often throughout Lutheran art.[15]

Other Protestant art depicting Jesus. One of the most fascinating studies of the changes taking place in Reformation Europe, especially with reference to Jesus, is the work of Albrecht Dürer. Born in Germany in 1471, he was active during the middle of the Protestant Reformation. In 1510 he created an etching of the Last Supper that is full of Roman Catholic teaching. The traditional sacrificial Passover lamb is on the table, signifying Jesus. There is no cup on the table.[16] Jesus has a halo that fills the room with beams of light. Thirteen years later, he recreated the scene. Now the lamb is gone but the cup is present. Jesus' halo is much smaller and muted, and Jesus is depicted as a more personal figure, embracing the apostle John.

John Calvin rejected the notion that images were helpful when it came to informing the masses about the Gospel.[17] Worship became a more personal activity so that "images necessarily played no role; in fact, they were usually perceived as a distraction from the inward focus on the preached (and sung) Word."[18]

From the Church to the Home: Jesus Moves In

Although art depicting religious themes had been, for the most part, removed from the church setting, some Protestant patrons still desired art containing religious images. An example is a painting by an unknown artist of the Last Judgment of Christ. It is a depiction of Jesus that is distinctly Northern European—Jesus has brown hair and a red beard. No other saints, such as Mary, are in the picture, giving evidence of the painting's Protestant nature.

A painting by Lucas Cranach the Elder[19] called "Christ and the Adulteress" further exemplifies Reformation art. Jesus is depicted saving the adulteress from her accusers. Above Him are the words, "Judge not lest Ye be Judged." This theme of refraining judgment was a popular one in Reformation Germany. A matching painting by the same artist shows Christ blessing infants gathered around Him. Especially poignant is one of His hands resting on an infant, another popular theme of the time.[20]

An even further change in form is shown by a painting called "Christ Blessing, Surrounded by a Donor and His Family," by Ludger tom Ring the Younger around 1580. The painting depicts a marriage with Jesus in the center of the wedding party.[21] Jesus at the center of the family gathering is a distinctly Protestant theme.

Probably the most influential Protestant artist of the period, and considered by some as the greatest European artist, was Rembrandt. The people of seventeenth-century Holland were a practical people. They did not care for "religious scenes imbued with grandeur and idealized figures."[22] They much preferred scenes of everyday life. Rembrandt's work perfectly reflects this cultural trend. Gone from his paintings are the images of a transcendent Jesus.[23]

Toward the end of his life, around 1669, he painted a series of portraits depicting Jesus, Mary, and the apostles. He used his Jewish neighbors as models to represent the apostles and Mary, and while

Jesus remained the typical fair, longhaired young man He had been shown as for hundreds of years, there are striking differences.[24] Another painting from the same time period shows the pre-crucified Jesus in a cloak, standing. He bears a contemplative look on His face. In these paintings, no surrounding contexts are given. He is shown in a much more personal and intimate way.[25]

The only indication this work is supposed to depict Jesus and Mary is a vase of white lilies, a symbol of virginity, in a window in the background, and the familiarity of the nativity story.

As mentioned above, even if they enjoyed religiously themed art, many Calvinists were not comfortable with actual depictions of biblical stories. Much of the art from this time displays only veiled references to biblical events. One example is a painting by Nicholas van Hoogstraten in the mid-seventeenth century titled "Firstborn Son." It is a scene of a bedroom where a young woman tends a baby in a bassinet while an elderly matron looks on with approval. The figures are strikingly similar to those in Rembrandt's scene. However, the only indication that this work is supposed to depict Jesus and Mary is a vase of white lilies, a symbol of virginity, in a window in the background, and the familiarity of the nativity story.

Counter-Reformation Art

The Roman Catholic Church mounted a reaction to Protestantism, and art by Catholics of this period reflects this. Around 1630, Peter Paul Rubens, a Flemish artist, painted a scene featuring the resurrected Christ.[26] Jesus is pictured crushing the head of a serpent with one foot and a skull with the other, representing sin and death, respectively. What makes this image of Christ stand out, however, is that Jesus is holding the elements of the Eucharist, the cup and the wafer, in His hand. This is clearly meant to support the Catholic Mass. The vast majority of Rubens's works show Christ either on the cross or coming down off the cross dead, reflecting the Catholic emphasis on the suffering Christ.

Another Catholic, Jean-Baptiste Marie Pierre, of eighteenth-century France, used his painting of the nativity scene to reinforce Roman teaching. It also reflects the popular trend of molding Jesus into whatever culture He is being represented in. It shows Mary as a blonde French woman of some means, strangely out of place in a stable. Jesus is a blond, blue-eyed infant. He is gesturing toward the angels who are gathered around, who are also infants and very French. Jesus is haloed and glowing, illuminating the entire stable.

It was at this time that Margaret Mary Alacoque, mentioned before, began having her visions. The Roman Catholic Church under the guise of the Franciscans took up the cause of the Sacred Heart, using it as a powerful anti-Protestant tool.

Post-Reformation Art

The return to the classics and the expulsion of religious iconography from the church during the Renaissance and Reformation had a great impact on art. Jesus was no longer the sole property of religion and religious activity. As was shown above, private financiers commissioned works depicting Jesus based on personal taste. This newfound freedom would lead to much more variety in the manner in which Jesus was displayed, but until the nineteenth century, His image remained largely the same as it had for centuries.

MODERN IMAGES OF JESUS

Art has experienced a revolution in the last 200 years. As modernism and then postmodernism burst onto the cultural scene, artists and later the media began to challenge the traditional view of Jesus. Artists began to push social limits, seeming to strive for ever more attention and controversy. Jesus began to be used as a tool for social criticism and individualistic perceptions. Congruent with the Enlightenment's effect on theologians (see chapter 9), during the last two centuries historians and philosophers have questioned every aspect of Jesus, even

His very existence. With the advent of movies and television, people were unleashed to display Jesus as anything imaginable, from hero to victim, from liberator to suppressor, from serious to comedic. Even within Christianity, Jesus' image changed radically. To put it mildly, "Modern artists…treat the theme [Jesus] frequently with independence and imagination."[27]

Jesus in Modernist Art

The modernist movement "eschewed the niceties of drawing correct proportions, [and] realistic color, for the forms that are flat and quickly read, and colors that are strong and direct."[28] As it became more and more acceptable to challenge social norms, artists began to portray social issues as they saw them. They also attempted to connect with audiences on a personal level.

Jesus used as social, political, and cultural metaphor. An early example of Jesus being employed to criticize culture is the works of a Frenchman, Édouard Manet. His subjects are typical of the modernist movement. In his "Christ Mocked," he portrays Jesus in a somewhat traditional style, but the accusers surrounding him are depictions of French socialites. Manet exhibited this painting along with another, showing a scandalous French courtesan, causing an uproar.[29]

A work done by German Hermann Clementz seems to display subtle anti-Semitism. The boy Jesus is pictured in the temple. The work is striking in its contrasts. Jesus is distinctly German, while the priests and rabbis around Him are eastern-looking in appearance and dress. Jesus glows, while those around Him are dark in the shadows. The priests are shown being confounded by Jesus. The high priest stands at a podium with a prominent star of David carved into the side and looks at Jesus quizzically.[30]

In a work done by Fritz von Uhde in the late 1800s, Jesus is shown being welcomed to the table of a peasant family for dinner. The house is simple and the food is scarce; the wife scoops some sort of gruel into bowls. Nonetheless the husband bids Jesus to sit down, and the wife seems joyful that Jesus has come to dine with them. The work seems to be arguing that Jesus is a man of the common folk, that it doesn't matter that they are poor. Other than His distinct tunic, Jesus is shown looking like an ordinary man.[31]

Pablo Picasso exemplified modernism. He is considered the father of cubism, creating works that attempt to analyze a subject by taking it apart piece by piece and reforming it in an almost random pattern. Though an atheist, Picasso nevertheless interacted with Jesus in his art. In one work he shows Jesus on the cross as a matador in the ring, fighting a bull. Later, as his cubism bloomed, he shows Jesus as a collection of randomly placed bones on the cross.[32]

A man who was "a caustic social critic," Max Beckmann used Jesus as a symbol of social injustice. "His personal mission was to uncover the hypocrisy, hatred and lust of modern society and let it scream out in his art."[33] He pictured the story of the woman caught in adultery several times. In these works he portrays Jesus defending women against oppressive men. Jesus is much older than usual, bald and clean-shaven. He is dressed simply, in a tunic that harkens to the traditional garb of Jewish men of the period. His grave look and threatening gestures make it clear that he is physically defending the woman from the men gathered around. They are priests, rabbis, merchants, and soldiers, seemingly representing a cross-section of society.

During the middle of World War I, Beckmann painted a moving picture of Jesus being taken off the cross.[34] The work is clearly in reaction to the horrors being experienced in the deadliest war the world had seen to that point. Showing Jesus' death in this manner could be trying to evoke the utter despair the people of Europe were experiencing, as if to say there was no hope. Beckmann never created a work showing Jesus' resurrection.

Later in his life, near the beginning of the Cold War, he drew a piece showing Jesus before Pilate. It is a simple work. Jesus' head is stretched vertically into grotesque proportions. He is dark, as if dirty. The figure of Pilate looks similar to cartoon drawings of Lenin. Perhaps Beckmann means to show Jesus being accused by Communism, reflecting the militant antireligious stance of the philosophy. The figure of Pilate almost smirks at Jesus. In contrast to Pilate's cartoonish features, Jesus is a stark figure, very serious and dignified despite His circumstances. It is as if Beckmann wanted to show that Christ was impervious to being mocked by this pseudo-Lenin, Pilate.

The sympathetic Jesus. As the wars and social upheaval of the nineteenth and early twentieth century wreaked havoc on traditional society, artists began to explore the pain and emotional suffering this unrest was causing. They began to show figures who displayed the characteristics of people downtrodden and emotionally traumatized.

Georges Rouault was a later modernist who worked at the beginning of the twentieth century. His characters often look sad or emotionally distressed. He depicted Jesus several times, both in traditional stories, such as on the cross or being flogged, and also in contextually ambiguous settings. For Rouault, Jesus always looks sad or downtrodden. In fact, one of his paintings is titled *Infinite Sadness.* Jesus looks dejected, almost resigned.

> *Chagall...pictures Jesus being crucified in the center of the work. All around Him are scenes of violence and oppression against Jews.*

In *Jesus and the High Priest,* Jesus and the high priest are shown alone in a nondescript room. Jesus doesn't face the priest but is instead turned toward the viewer, as if Rouault is asking those viewing the piece to judge Jesus, rather than His priestly accuser. In one titled, *The Flagellation,* Jesus is shown being whipped by the Roman soldiers. Despite being covered in blood, He is pictured as melancholy rather than in severe pain. It almost looks as if Rouault saw Jesus in some sort of depression, rather than the agony of torture.[35] He also portrayed sympathetic figures who were suffering that were similes of Jesus and His suffering.[36] All these depictions point to Rouault portraying the emotional problems of his time through the image of Jesus.

Sometimes Jesus is shown in situations that the viewer would be able to relate to directly. Diego Rivera, an artist working in the early twentieth century, shows Jesus receiving a vaccination. Although Jesus is clothed in His traditional linen tunic, the giver of the vaccine is a Roman Catholic priest. Rivera, a painter of social issues in Mexico, perhaps wanted to relieve the people's fear by showing Jesus bravely receiving his shot.[37]

Another artist, Richard West, painted thousands of pictures featuring the American Southwest and Native Americans. In some of these, he portrayed Jesus as a Native American.[38] Being a Native American himself, he seemed to be trying to contextualize biblical stories into Native American culture, something familiar to him, perhaps in order to help other Native Americans understand the stories themselves.

A Jewish artist, Marc Chagall, portrayed Jesus from the perspective of Judaism in late 1930s Europe. Anti-Semitism had been brought to a new fervor by Hitler and the Nazi party in Germany. In *Jesus the Eternal Jew*[39] he pictures Jesus being crucified in the center of the work. All around Him are scenes of violence and oppression against Jews. Houses burn, men flee, and soldiers march. Jesus is illuminated from above in Chagall's painting, rather than being self-illuminated. Perhaps Chagall means to show Jesus as a Jew, exemplifying Jewish suffering in their long history of persecution.[40]

The end of World War II, with the destruction of Germany and the rise of Communism, has been the backdrop for several German artists' renditions of Jesus. Michael Ell typified the social condition of Germany post–World War II. His rendition of the Last Supper shows Jesus as the savior of the common people in the aftermath of the terrors of war. The apostles are dirty, malnourished, and tired-looking peasants. The room is dark and gloomy except for the illuminating light of Jesus.[41]

E. Koch takes an opposite view. His work *The Collapse on the Way to the Cross* shows Jesus having stumbled carrying the cross. He is dressed in a white tunic and sandals. A featureless line of people march off into the distance in the background. They carry their belongings, while two are being carried in a cart. They march on heedless of Jesus. Koch lived in newly Communist East Germany in the late 1940s. To him the plight of the people went on without Jesus, as if He had never made it to the cross and had ultimately failed the people.[42]

Jesus in Postmodernist Art

Postmodernism came to signify a new philosophy in art (among many other things). It was an offshoot of modernism, and "like modernism before it, works to see just how much it can get away with. It strains to test all limits and to call all things into question."[43] As culture progressed through the postwar years, people looked ever more fervently for the next big thing. "The search for the new had become an end in itself," William Dyrness says. "As a result, the public, being open to anything provided no inertia against which artists could react."[44]

Postmodern artists seem to fall over one another striving for the public's attention. They try to shock the viewer, thereby generating interest. Obscenity, vulgarity, violence, and offensive images are all an integral part of most postmodern art. Adhering to the philosophical teachings of Existential Relativism, anything and everything is open game to the postmodernists, from the creating and building of something to even the object's destruction. From a picture of something, to the audience's reaction to the picture of something. Even the artist and their activities themselves are sometimes considered art. Many postmodern artists openly question whether their work is even art at all! Yet postmodern "art" is wildly popular.

Unfortunately, Jesus hasn't escaped postmodernism's attention. More often than not, postmodern images of Jesus are sacrilegious. One of the more controversial depictions is a picture of a crucifix in a jar of urine,[45] "created" by Andres Serrano.[46] He claims, "Religion depends largely on symbols, and as an artist, my job is to explore the possibilities in deliberate manipulation of that symbolism."[47]

Even secular critics see through Serrano's attempt to justify his work. James Gardener, a New York art critic, says, "If Serrano sincerely believes that he was merely examining symbols, he has some very serious problems communicating, which is what his real job is—'as an artist.' *Piss Christ* certainly looked like an attack on Christianity itself."[48] Serrano later claimed that the work was a reaction to the commercialization of religion in America and didn't have anything to do with his view of Jesus.[49]

Jesus in Christian Music

Since the very beginnings of the church, Jesus has been sung about. Some of the earliest passages in the New Testament are thought to be Christian hymns declaring attributes of Jesus.[50] For most of the history of the church, music was used in this way. In modern times, musicians have taken greater liberties in conveying their view of Jesus. Christian musicians have made use of allegory and have been influenced to a great degree by culture, while secular artists have used Jesus in much the same way other artists have—as a liberator, buddy, or a metaphor for oppression.

Hymns. Hymns are differentiated from "praise songs" in that hymns generally have stanzas and a short chorus and are often sung from a hymnal that is notated. Although hymns can be about any topic, Jesus figures prominently in most. Originally, hymns were designed to teach theology, such as the Trinity, Jesus as Savior, salvation by faith, and Jesus' atonement on the cross. Often hymns use text taken directly from Scripture. Although the theology of some hymns could be called into question, the image of Jesus portrayed in hymns is usually taken from Scripture.

Praise songs. In modern times, music for church has changed in structure and content. Churches moved from singing hymns to more modern musical forms. Church music began to reflect contemporary music with shorter stanzas and long choruses. Songs began to focus on the individual and their response to Jesus. "Jesus, Lover of My Soul" (the praise song, not the hymn by Charles Wesley) is an example. The songwriter says he is in love with Jesus because of what He has done for him. Jesus is the lover of the singer's soul and his closest friend, and he will never let Him go.

The theology expressed is most often simple, such as in "Lord, I Lift Your Name on High." Its chorus says Jesus came to earth to show the way, He went from the earth to the cross, and finally back to "the sky." Following popular culture's changing view of Jesus, praise songs have begun to reflect secular pop music, as in Steve Fee's "I'm Madly in Love with You." The song speaks of dancing for Jesus,[51] and it says that Jesus' love is "big" and "wild."

The lyrics hark back to the medieval view of Jesus as a bridegroom. Because this view is especially popular among young women, some have criticized these songs as "Jesus-is-my-boyfriend" music. Indeed, there is a resurgence among Evangelical Christians of views similar to that of Margaret Mary Alacoque.

In *Christianity Today*, Agnieszka Tennant relates a story about someone she knows who took the bridal theme literally.[52] At the website of the International House of Prayer, we find, "To understand Jesus as a passionate Bridegroom is to soon see ourselves as a cherished Bride. Intimacy causes our hearts to be lovesick for Jesus (inflamed; enraptured; overcome by His love)."[53] Beth Jones, in the prologue of her book *Jesus in Blue Jeans*, uses this language of infatuation when she says she "fell in love with Jesus."[54]

A current trend is to blur the line between popular Christian music and church worship music. Christian pop songs are used in church service, mostly without any change to lyrics or music. In fact, church music ministers listen to contemporary Christian music to find new songs to be used in church worship.

Contemporary Christian music. During the late 1970s and 1980s there was a debate within Christianity over whether Christians could make and listen to music that was distinguishable from secular music only in its lyrics. Many said that it did not matter if the words were "Christian," the music itself was evil. Supporters of what came to be called "contemporary christian music" accused the opposition of thwarting the work of spreading the Gospel.[55]

This argument proved to be persuasive to the general Christian public. Soon contemporary christian music, or CCM, became its own industry, with several recording studios opened in Nashville and a magazine titled *CCM* growing in popularity. "Christian" radio stations and later entire networks began to play CCM.[56] As CCM gained popularity, the industry has evolved to look more and more like the secular pop music culture. *Billboard* magazine now includes a chart covering "Hot Christian Adult Contemporary" music.

Recently, songs produced for secular audiences have received airplay on Christian radio stations. A remake of LeAnn Rimes's "I Need You" is one example. The only allusion to anything of Christ is a line that mentions needing someone.[57] An album featuring Christian artists singing U2 songs was also made, some of which receive airplay.[58]

Even if the song is not a copy from a secular artist, many CCM song lyrics are ambiguous to the point that it is confusing who the song is about. Tennant says, "And who among us hasn't detected an eerie resemblance between a contemporary Christian song and a pop diva's breathy rendition of a sensual love ballad?"[59]

Darlene Zschech's song "Kiss of Heaven" is one of these. Jesus is her "dream maker," and she feels she is "under the kiss of heaven." Jesus has "lit a fire inside" her. Zschech is the music pastor of Hillsong Church in Sydney, Australia, illustrating the close tie between CCM and church music today. This close relationship and the increasingly secular nature of CCM have led some to question CCM's influence on church music and worship.[60]

Jesus in Non-Christian Music

Counterculture visions of Jesus. Jesus has been a figure in secular music for many years. He was used by various groups to promote their message or strengthen their resolve or discuss social issues.

A song used by those involved in the early labor movement talks of the church losing its way: "She follows not the path of old; / And the cross has lost its sway. / They follow not the laws of Christ, / That lowly Nazarene."[61]

The 1960s and 1970s saw a surge in the use of Jesus in music critical of culture and politics. Bob Dylan is considered one of the most influential musicians and songwriters of American folk music. Many of his songs from the era refer to Jesus. One he wrote called "Property of Jesus" talks about the oppressed having something the oppressors never will, that they are "the property of Jesus."[62]

Joan Baez was another influential musician of the era. Her song "The Bells of Gethsemani" talks of belief in Jesus ending war, and that we might become the "brothers of God" and know the Christ of "burnt men."[63]

A slightly less famous but influential songwriter of the time was Phil Ochs. His song "The Ballad of the Carpenter" reflects the theological changes in academia and the rise of popular views of Jesus. He rewrites biblical history to make Jesus a political revolutionary. Jesus "was a working man" who "noticed how wealth and poverty live always side by side." He puts words in Jesus' mouth, having Him call working men to take over the world by standing together. He says that rich men got the Roman commander to put Jesus to death as a "menace to God and man." In Ochs's story, Jesus is offered bribes by the rich men to "work for the rich men's tribe." Jesus refuses, so they crucify Him.[64]

> U2 used imagery of the crucifixion for a political message in "Bullet the Blue Sky." The song pictures America as the crucifiers and the "orphans and widows" of the third world as Christ being sacrificed.

More recent artists have carried on the tradition. Jackson Browne wrote "Rebel Jesus." More than a social-justice song, it criticizes the church in America.[65] Ray Stevens sang "Would Jesus Wear a Rolex?", criticizing a familiar figure in American religion, the televangelist.[66] The Dead Kennedys picked up the "Jesus as rebel" theme in their song, "Jesus was a Terrorist."[67]

The group U2 has been controversial because some see the group as Christian, while others see them as secular. Robert Vagacs argues that U2 discusses issues of faith from a Christian perspective. However, their lyrics show they have a mistaken view of Jesus. In "Until the End of the World" Judas is in a ship called "Sheol." A figure (unnamed, but presumed to be Jesus), shows up and has a conversation with him. Judas asks if there is any forgiveness, but he receives no answer. Judas then tries to justify his actions by accusing the figure of leading him on.[68]

U2 used imagery of the crucifixion for a political message in "Bullet the Blue Sky." The song pictures America as the crucifiers and the "orphans and widows" of the third world as Christ being sacrificed. The group prays that "the cup of suffering" would be taken away from them. America, they say, burns crosses because of our hate of those in the third world.[69] In "I Still Haven't Found What I'm Looking For," U2's Bono addresses Jesus, asking how long the suffering on Earth will continue, as if to accuse Jesus of standing by and doing nothing.[70]

Some musicians identify Jesus as belonging to a particular group. Jill Sobule sings in "Jesus was a Dreidel Spinner" that Jesus was Jewish, so Christians should "light a menorah" and thank the wise men and "maccabis."[71]

Jesus in pop music. During the late '60s and into the '70s, Jesus became a popular topic in mainstream music. The Doobie Brothers sang "Jesus Is Just Alright with Me" in 1971. Reflecting the growing trend of personal identification with Jesus, they sang that Jesus was their friend, that He was "alright with me."[72] Around the same time Norman Greenbaum wrote a popular song that has been performed by many artists titled, "Spirit in the Sky." The lyrics also reflect the "Jesus is my friend" theology becoming ever more popular. He says we have to have a "friend in Jesus" to "recommend" us when we go before the "spirit in the sky."[73]

Today there are countless examples of Jesus in pop music. A popular country-and-western song by Carrie Underwood asks Jesus to "take the wheel" as her car spins out of control on a wintry Christmas Eve.[74] Mariah Carey, taking advantage of the popularity of Christmas songs, sang, "Jesus, Oh What a Wonderful Child." It speaks of her love for the "wonderful child" Jesus, who was born in a manger to the Virgin Mary and that Joseph "was his earthly father."[75] Jon Bon Jovi pokes fun at Christians in his song, "I Talk to Jesus," equating those who claim to do so with those who believe that Elvis and John Lennon are still alive and that aliens "control our lives."[76]

The Jesus of popular music is whatever the artist wants Him to be, or whatever serves their purpose. He can be a social revolutionary, a cultural critic, a friend, a member of one's own group. More often than not, He has little to do with the Jesus of the Bible.

Jesus in the Movies

Jesus has been a popular figure in cinema since the invention of the movie camera. His image has, however, radically changed over the decades. As cultural views of Jesus evolved, the image of Jesus evolved along with it.

Early movies. The first movie to show Jesus on film was *The Horitz Passion Play,* filmed in 1897. In 1900, Herbert Booth, son of Salvation Army founder William Booth, produced a program featuring short films, slides, hymns, sermons, and prayers. One of the short films showed Jesus suffering on the cross.

At least 70 films depicting biblical themes were produced before World War II, many featuring Jesus. The original *Ben Hur, From the Manger to the Cross,* and an Italian film, *Quo Vadis,* are among them.[77] These early films were reverent and true to the biblical text. Some clergy even encouraged their Sunday school teachers to use these films for "evangelical outreach, social ministry to the needy and sermons, as well as in providing entertainment for their parishioners."[78]

After World War I films began to change. This coincided with the general change in culture experienced in the 1920s. Movies became more and more licentious as movie studios reacted to the public's desires. These were the days before any government imposed decency laws or rating systems, so there was nothing to hold producers or studios back from portraying anything they thought would sell tickets.[79]

Cecil B. DeMille produced the most popular films of the period, and many portrayed Jesus. In *The King of Kings* (1927), Mary Magdalene owns a "lavish pleasure palace" and laments the loss of her boyfriend, Judas. Judas has "forsaken" her and followed Jesus. Becoming more and more distraught, Mary finally rides off to find Judas, and eventually becomes a follower of Jesus as well. The story ends the same as the biblical text, but the details are completely rewritten.[80]

The Hollywood epic. During World War II, few movies featured Jesus. However, the 1950s brought the Bible and Jesus back to the big screen. *Ben-Hur* (1959) is the quintessential Hollywood epic.[81] Although not directly about Jesus Christ, Jesus does have a prominent part in the film. He is shown giving a drink to the title character, Ben-Hur, and encouraging him to hang on to life. The next time we see Jesus, He is being crucified. Two characters are healed of leprosy by some of Jesus' blood that inadvertently washes into a cave where they are hiding. Ben-Hur ends up believing in Jesus after remembering His words of forgiveness. The film ends with a view of the empty crosses on Calvary, and a shepherd with his flock picturing Jesus as the Good Shepherd.

The first Hollywood epic to actually depict Jesus and His life was *King of Kings,* released in 1961. The movie shows Jesus as a preacher and healer of the people, contrasting Him with Barabbas. Jesus is shown as a stereotypical blue-eyed, white young man. He preaches a message composed of the various synoptic Gospels, woven together to show Him as a peacemaker and a giver of hope to the downtrodden masses. The people ask questions of Jesus, and He answers with words from the Gospels.

The movie *The Greatest Story Ever Told* was filmed in 1965. It was another portrayal of the life of Jesus. Jesus is again shown as a white man and is presented as a more personal figure than in some earlier depictions. The film ends with Jesus' ascension, and as He floats skyward He says,

> "Go now, and teach all the nations. Make it your first care to love one another, and to find the Kingdom of God. And all things shall be yours without the asking. Do not fret then over tomorrow. Leave tomorrow to fret over its own needs. For today's troubles are enough. And lo, I am with you always."

The words Jesus says here are an amalgam of made-up sayings and what Jesus actually said in the Gospels. In *The Greatest Story Ever Told*, Jesus' last words on earth leave out the important message of preaching the Gospel in all the nations, making disciples and baptizing them in the name of the Father, Son, and Holy Spirit, and teaching people to observe everything He has commanded.[82] *The Greatest Story Ever Told* was a box-office flop, costing an estimated 20 million dollars and making back only 12 million.

Because of this failure, biblical epics lost favor in Hollywood for a time. During the 1970s no new ones were filmed. However, Jesus did not completely disappear from the film screen. An independent project under the direction of Bill Bright, the founder of Campus Crusade for Christ, produced the film *Jesus*. Bright wanted a film that, unlike *The Greatest Story Ever Told* and *King of Kings*, was true to the biblical account. *Jesus* mostly follows the account of Luke's Gospel. While the movie was a box-office failure, Bright created the Jesus Film Project to promote the translation of *Jesus* into other languages. The project was a huge success, the film being translated into over 1000 languages.

> The Last Temptation of Christ...explores... *Jesus' temptations. Though He is without sin, His temptations cause Him to imagine all manner of sin, including fear, doubt, depression, and lust.*

In 2004 the latest film about Jesus created a national uproar. Mel Gibson's *The Passion of the Christ* was said to be anti-Semitic, too graphic, and focused too much on Jesus' torture and death, while giving only a glimpse of the resurrection. Despite these criticisms, *The Passion of the Christ* was wildly popular, grossing over 600 million dollars worldwide. The film begins in the Garden of Gethsemane and ends with Jesus walking out of the tomb. It follows the New Testament to a great extent, but there are significant differences. For example, Gibson shows Jesus crushing a serpent's head in the garden. Jesus was beaten before He was brought before Pilate. Also, on the way to the cross, Gibson shows the traditional Roman Catholic story of Veronica, who wipes Jesus' face, leaving an impression on a cloth that was thought to exist as a relic.

Question everything. Along with the later film epics, other movies began to be made that portrayed a version of Jesus different from the biblical account. These movies questioned the very core of orthodox Christian beliefs about Jesus' divinity, His resurrection, and even His message and purpose.

Two such films were released in 1973. *Godspell* was a film adaptation of a musical in which Jesus and the disciples are pictured in modern day New York City. Jesus is a "wandering minstrel"[83] dressed as a clown. He joins a group in Central Park, brought together by John the Baptist. John summons chosen people around the city by blowing on a magical instrument. They meet in a fountain, where they are baptized. Once Jesus, John the Baptist, and their followers are together, they move to a brightly colored junkyard where they outfit themselves. They dance their way through the streets of New York, reenacting biblical parables with "great enthusiasm and flamboyance."[84]

The other Jesus movie released in 1973 is more famous. It is Andrew Lloyd Webber's *Jesus Christ Superstar.* The film is a rock opera portraying the last week of Jesus' life from the perspective of Judas Iscariot. *Jesus Christ Superstar* denies Jesus' divinity, claiming "he's just a man," as well as His resurrection. Jesus' message is about ending poverty, not bringing salvation.

Martin Scorsese's *The Last Temptation of Christ* was filmed in 1988. It goes further than *Superstar,* even including the disclaimer that the film doesn't follow the biblical account. The film explores, as the title alludes to, Jesus' temptations. Though He is without sin, His temptations cause Him to imagine all manner of sin, including fear, doubt, depression, and lust. *The Last Temptation of Christ* shows Jesus as a confused and easily fooled human, almost on the verge of schizophrenia. He is not divine, nor does He exhibit the characteristics of the biblical Jesus. His message is misinterpreted in the film as well. At the Sermon on the Mount, the crowd disperses before Jesus has even finished speaking, leaving Him in doubt and uncertainty. Although Scorsese shows Jesus as being tempted but without sin, in *The Last Temptation* He is nonetheless required to redeem Himself through His suffering on the cross. (This theme of redemption is a common one throughout Scorsese's films.)[85]

Jesus the straight man. Only in recent times have movie producers taken the liberty of portraying Jesus as a comedic figure. Perhaps the culture was not yet secular enough to accept these portrayals in earlier times.

The first film of this type was Monty Python's *Life of Brian* (1979). Even in this film, Jesus is shown as a different character named Brian. It intimates that Jesus was merely one of many other messiahs running around during that time and that He was reluctant to have people follow Him. In the end Jesus (Brian) stumbles into situation after situation and is accidentally crucified. While the film accurately portrays the general desire for a messiah in first-century Palestine, it shows Jesus in a completely unbiblical way.

A little-known movie from 1998 called *The Book of Life* shows Jesus as a modern-day businessman who arrives at JFK with his assistant, Magdalena. He is supposed to be sent from the Father to initiate the final seals of the Apocalypse and bring the final judgment upon humankind. He begins to rethink this plan, sympathizing with his human "half." Seeing no need for "petty retribution," He makes a deal with Satan so man can continue on in the next millennia. Jesus is shown as a personal acquaintance of Satan. Jesus calls him on a cell phone, greeting him with, "It's me..." The film seeks to be humorous through irony. Jesus is half divine, half human. Despite His command from God, Jesus chooses to follow His humanity, ironically showing that humans have more persuasive power than God.

Jesus on TV

The image of Jesus on television paralleled that of the movies for many years. However, with the rise in popularity of alternative (most often unbiblical) depictions of Jesus, a wider variety of television shows have featured Jesus. Many of these have been documentaries using popular scholarship to find "fresh insights into the life and times of" Jesus. Others have been irreverent portrayals of false images of Jesus.

Documentaries. With the rise of educational cable networks such as the Discovery Channel and the History Channel, Jesus has seen significant airtime. The History Channel in particular has explored Jesus in programs such as *Beyond the Da Vinci Code,* which examines "both sides of the story—the conventional view of Christianity and the 'alternate history' proposed by Brown."[86] Another program purports that it "pieces together circumstantial evidence and tantalizing clues looking for a clearer picture of Christ's final days" in an effort to show why "many of the world's most distinguished biblical scholars insist that what the Bible has to say about the event cannot be correct."[87]

The Discovery Channel has also devoted many programs to examining the person of Jesus. Most focus on looking into contrabiblical stories. *Jesus in the Himalayas* explored the "popular legend of the Indian subcontinent that claims Jesus spent part of his life traveling through the Himalayas."[88]

Another recent program caused a great deal of controversy. *The Lost Tomb of Jesus* claimed that Jesus' family tomb had been discovered. The documentary argued that a tomb near Jerusalem contained ten ossuaries that were inscribed with names all found in the Gospels, one of them being "Jesus."

The Discovery Channel called it "one of the most important archeological finds in human history" with "potentially historic consequences."[89] As scholars, including Dan Bahat from Bar-Ilan University in Israel, began to pick apart the so-called evidence for this radical claim, the Discovery Channel pulled back its ambitious airing schedule. In the end, the program aired on the network only once.

At a conference held in Jerusalem in January 2008, "fifty archaeologists, statisticians and experts" debated the arguments made in *Lost Tomb.* The group left the conference deeply divided. The most positive opinion about the program's claim was that it was "very possible." None believed the arguments *proved* the tomb was that of Jesus.[90]

Other Popular Images

WWJD. In 1993, Garrett Sheldon updated his great-grandfather's book *In His Steps* and called it *What Would Jesus Do?* It is a fictional account of people who live out Jesus' teachings in their lives. It became a sensation among youth through the '90s. Soon merchandisers were producing items featuring the acronym "WWJD?" The phrase challenged people to think about what Jesus would do if He were in their situation. Theoretically this would encourage believers to follow Jesus more closely. Unfortunately this requires imagining Jesus living in today's world, rather than studying what He actually did and told us to do. To really know what Jesus would do would require the person desiring to follow Jesus to be thoroughly versed in the Gospel accounts to see what Jesus did do, and to extrapolate from Jesus' words and actions to what we should do. The church has hardly moved to that level of training its youth or adults, so that WWJD is nothing more than an empty slogan.

> *The Jesus that emerges is...one that falls into our culture's perception of Him...He is just as weak as we are, so much so that we could almost pity Him.*

The movement soon outgrew the Christian subculture, becoming a fad in the general society. Many people purchased the merchandise having no idea what it meant. While the movement is still around, its popularity has died down. Other Christian movements latched onto the popularity of using a short acronym. "FROG" (Fully Relying on God) is an example.

Anne Rice. Anne Rice began her literary career writing gothic fiction about vampires as well as adult novels under pseudonyms. The books were sexually explicit and intensely graphic. She was a self-described atheist from age 15 until her late 50s, when she began to read the works of John A.T. Robinson, St. Augustine, D.A. Carson, and Craig Blomberg. She began to believe in the historical validity of the resurrection. Soon she returned to Catholicism and decided to write a book about Jesus.[91]

But this book would be radically different from what had gone before. She decided to write it as a first-person narrative from the perspective of Jesus Himself. Drawing on early noncanonical, and sometimes heretical, works of the Patristic era, she portrays Jesus being part of a large extended family. Joseph is a widower who has children from the previous marriage (so Jesus has half-siblings, following Catholic tradition). Also following tradition, an eight-year-old Jesus is bullied by an older boy. He strikes him down, and then feeling regret, He raises him from the dead. He also makes a dove from clay and causes snow to fall. The boy Jesus has nightmares and finds Himself afraid and crying. He also knows nothing of His miraculous birth (His parents forbid Him to speak of it). He disobeys His parents and lies to them. Rice portrays Him as quite forgetful. He says He can't remember stories of Old Testament figures told Him repeatedly.

The Jesus that emerges from *Christ the Lord: Out of Egypt* is not the one from the biblical account, but one that falls into our culture's perception of Him. Rice embodies the sympathetic view of Jesus that is popular today. He is just as weak as we are, so much so that we could almost pity Him.

Everybody Loves Jesus!

It seems everyone today has his own view of who Jesus is. Politicians use Jesus as a supporter of a particular bit of legislation, or cite Him as their favorite "political philosopher or thinker."[92] Celebrities love Jesus. He is thanked many times during Hollywood award shows. Environmentalists ask, "What would Jesus drive?"[93] He is a buddy, a best friend we can take along with us anywhere we go. Jesus is found in popular phrases on T-shirts and bumper stickers: "Jesus is my copilot"; "Got Jesus?"; "Jesus died for my sins and all I got was this lousy bumper sticker"; and "Jesus is tribal."

Due in large part to postmodern existentialism, our culture believes each person's beliefs are valid, including those about Jesus. This has led many individuals to think that Jesus has nothing to do with Christianity. Dan Kimball from *Outreach* magazine conducted short interviews with college students and asked two questions: "What do you think of when you hear the name Jesus?" and "What do you think when you hear the word Christian?" [94] According to Kimball, the answers were quite varied.

> When they answered the first question, the students smiled and their eyes lit up. We heard comments of admiration such as, "Jesus is beautiful," "He is a wise man like a shaman or a guru," "He came to liberate women." One girl even said, "He was enlightened. I'm on my way to becoming Christian."

These responses were strikingly different from the answers to the second question.

> However, when we asked the second question, the mood shifted. We heard things like, "Christians and the Church have messed things up," and "The Church took the teachings and turned them into dogmatic rules." One guy said, "Christians don't apply the message of love that Jesus gave," then jokingly added, "They all should be taken out back and shot."

Kimball has traveled across the country and has come up with six reasons people "liked Jesus but did not like the church."[95] People see the church as 1) an organization with a political agenda, 2) judgmental and negative, 3) being dominated by males and oppressing females, 4) homophobic, 5) claiming all other religions are wrong, and 6) full of fundamentalists who take the whole Bible literally. Kimball concludes that the church needs to radically change its perception among unbelievers.

Both his findings and his conclusion may have some merit, but he fails to take into consideration the "elephant in the room." Kimball mentions only in passing the possibility that people completely misunderstand *Jesus*.[96] Their perceptions have little or nothing to do with who Jesus really is, so it is little wonder they don't understand the church.

One blogger argued that people like Jesus but not the church because people are far more interested in celebrity than in what they do or believe. He contends that people like the idea of opposites, seeing Jesus in opposition to the church. This conclusion succeeds where Kimball fails. In truth, Jesus and His church are inseparable.

People misunderstand Jesus' teachings. They say that He was "the guy who opposed unjust authority," "said to be nice to people even if they aren't nice to you," "cared about people no one else cared about," "defended people the religious authorities wanted to condemn." One commenter said he "lost faith in the Church" and it led him to lose faith in Jesus.[97] This is the sad truth.

As debate rages over the "real Jesus" in scholarly circles, the general culture is affected. The media focuses almost exclusively on proving the New Testament wrong in its portrayal of Jesus, molding Him into a more palatable image. Couple that with people's general ignorance of the New Testament, and the general perception of Jesus is bound to be faulty.

⊞

For hundreds of years the image of Jesus has been used in popular religion. During the Middle Ages, the church controlled His image, but individuals could see Him in myriad ways. His suffering and death were powerful images used to reinforce church teaching. During the height of chivalry He was sometimes even seen as a lover or husband.

As modern thought started to question everything, Jesus began to be used to convey popular ideas. He became a sympathetic figure, a liberator of the oppressed, a peacemaker, a philosopher, a buddy, a guru, and even "just a man."

Modern scholarship (see chapter 11) presented through the popular media has led to a radical misconception of Jesus among popular culture. He has been molded into whatever image people want Him to be.

Part Three

Finding
the
Real Jesus

Chapter Thirteen

WHO IS THE REAL JESUS?

Thus far we have looked at centuries of distortions, misrepresentations, and fabrications of Jesus, such as messianic sects in Judaism, the Gnostics of the first centuries of the church, world religions, skeptical biblical scholars, and existential Christians. All of these visions of Jesus are wrong. The only Jesus who ever lived is the one who came to Israel over 2000 years ago to reveal Himself as the Son of David and Son of God, the Savior of the world. All other Jesuses are false messiahs and fakes.

We will find our most important information about Him in the pages of the Bible, particularly the Gospels. We discover there that He came in fulfillment of the Hebrew Scriptures and proved Himself to be who He claimed by His words and works, as well as by the testimonies of His Father; His forerunner, John; the confession of His disciples; and last, from His testimony of Himself. Our attention, therefore, now turns to the real Jesus portrayed in the Bible, beginning with how He fulfilled the Law and the Prophets (Luke 24:27).

THE PROMISE OF THE MESSIAH
Will the Real Messiah Please Stand Up!

The human desire for a Messiah goes all the way back to Genesis 3:15, when Yahweh promised to send someone who would crush the head of the serpent who was the instigator of mankind's rebellion against God. Though there have been many messiahs throughout history, even before the coming of Jesus, He is the only one whose life and teachings conform to the promised Messiah of the Old Testament.

Jesus, when reading from the scroll of Isaiah at his home synagogue in Nazareth, indicated that He fulfilled the messianic proof of healing the sick, proclaiming good news to the poor, and liberty to the captive (Luke 4:17-21).

How exactly will people identify the Messiah when He comes? What will He be like?

After He read the text of Isaiah 61:1-2, Jesus said that the acceptable year of Yahweh had happened that day. However, He chose not to read the remainder of the verse concerning the coming time of God's judgment, revealing that the messianic fulfillment has two phases, with only one occurring when Jesus came in the first century.

Messiah in the Old Testament

What begins as a kernel in Genesis 3:15 finds culmination in the promise of Malachi 4:5 that Elijah would prepare the way of Yahweh. Jesus claimed to have fulfilled all the Law and the Prophets (Matthew 5:17). This is tantamount to saying that He fulfilled the entirety of the revelation of God in the Hebrew Scriptures.

How exactly will people identify the Messiah when He comes? What will He be like? The Old Testament presents the Messiah as a king (He is the son of David, Psalm 2), a prophet (Deuteronomy 18:15-18; see Acts 3:19-26), and priest (Psalm 110:4). Additionally, the Messiah is revealed to be God coming in the flesh, who would live forever, though He would also die for His people (Isaiah 52:13–53:12). For anyone to claim to be Messiah, He must be able to satisfy these revelatory components.

Before launching into the discussion about whether Jesus, in fact, satisfies these requirements, as the New Testament authors argue, we need first to examine the manner in which prophetic fulfillment was understood by the apostles.

FULFILLING THE LAW AND THE PROPHETS

The Nature of Prophetic Fulfillment in the New Testament

Only people who are willing to grant that there is a God and that He works in supernatural ways in His world will be able to accept that Jesus came in fulfillment of Old Testament prophecies. Prophecy is the foretelling of future events, certain knowledge of what has not yet happened. It is not unhistorical, but history known in advance. Prophetic knowledge of events such as the reign of Cyrus king of Persia (Isaiah 44:28; 45:1,13), the rise of kingdoms revealed in the book of Daniel, and the destruction of Jerusalem (Matthew 24) are proofs that God gave for His existence and supremacy in His universe—in contrast to false gods, who are not able to declare the future (Isaiah 44:9-20).

Rejection of this supernatural element causes some scholars to declare that the portions of Isaiah, Daniel, and the Gospel accounts that speak of historical events must be considered to have been written after the fact. Yet Peter says that prophecy comes from God (2 Peter 1:20-21), including those about the Messiah.

But what methodology was used by the New Testament authors to understand the Old Testament prophecies in such a way that they believed Jesus was the fulfillment of them? To this we now turn.

Interpretative Methods Used by New Testament Authors

The apostles used biblical materials in four different ways in their interpretation of prophetic texts, methods that they shared with the rabbis in the first century. This is important to understand because it is common for some biblical critics to question the legitimacy of messianic prophecies, especially in the nativity narratives of Matthew and Luke. Not imposing on the first-century interpreters the methodology of the twenty-first century does away with the alleged problems. Emil

Schürer identifies four rabbinic interpretive methods to develop four prophetic categories that are refined by David Cooper:[1]

1. *Pshat*, or literal interpretation. Prophecies in this category were literally fulfilled.[2] This category is prevalent in the New Testament, as we will see below. The prophecy of the Messiah being born in Bethlehem in Micah 5:2, then its fulfillment in Matthew 2:5-6, is an example of *pshat* prophecy.[3]

2. *Remez*, literally, "suggestion." This involves a literal interpretation of the text but also typological prophetic interpretation. Bible scholar Arnold Fruchtenbaum gives Matthew 2:14-15 as an example of *remez*. Here the apostle says, "When he arose, he took the young Child and His mother by night and departed for Egypt, and was there until the death of Herod, that it might be fulfilled which was spoken by the Lord through the prophet, saying, 'Out of Egypt I called My Son'" (NKJV). Matthew was quoting Hosea 11:1, which says, "When Israel was a child, I loved him, and out of Egypt I called my son." Hosea 11:1 was not actually a prophecy but a historical event, and Matthew would have understood this. Nonetheless, the fact that Israel was brought out of Egypt by God is a picture, or type, of God calling His firstborn son Jesus out of Egypt, who is "the more ideal Son of God."[4]

3. *Drash*, or "exposition." In this type of prophecy there is a literal event, and the "fulfillment" is an application of the truth in the original event. Fruchtenbaum gives Matthew 2:17-18 as an example of this category. Here, Herod has murdered all male children under age two in Bethlehem. There would have been great mourning in Bethlehem, so Matthew sees the similarity to Jeremiah's prophecy of the Babylonian captivity of Israel in Jeremiah 31:15. Jeremiah pictures the mourning of the Jewish mothers as Rachel weeping over her children. There is no similarity other than in *one* area, the mourning of the Jewish mothers, so the fulfillment is an application, not a literal fulfillment of a prophecy.[5]

4. *Sod*, a Hebrew term meaning "mystery" or "secret." This approach

to the biblical text is a summarization of biblical truth found in different texts in the Old Testament rather than referring to one particular passage. Fruchtenbaum argues that Matthew 2:23 is an example of *sod*.[6] Here, Matthew says, "And he went and lived in a city called Nazareth, that what was spoken by the prophets might be fulfilled: 'He shall be called a Nazarene.'" This is not said anywhere in the Old Testament. However, a survey of messianic prophecies shows that the Messiah would be rejected and hated by his own people. By studying the historical context of the New Testament we find that "Nazarenes were a despised people."[7] Being called a "Nazarene" was a term of reproach. Hence, Matthew is showing that Jesus, by being rejected and despised, is the fulfillment of the Old Testament promise, conveyed in terms that readers of his Gospel in the first century would have been very familiar with.

The apostles demonstrate greater restraint in their use of the methods than what is sometimes found in rabbinic interpreters using these methods. Though the rabbis never denied the literal meaning of the Old Testament passages, "they sometimes overused their imaginations and went well beyond the biblical author's intent. The inspiration of the Holy Spirit kept the New Testament writers from doing so. Thus the New Testament writers, while using rabbinic methodology, never changed the meaning of the Old Testament text."[8]

Awaiting the Coming of the Messiah

Anticipation of Messiah in the time period around Jesus' birth was extremely high, and it took several forms. Some were Zealots, ready to raise a rebellion, such as the supposed Messiah Judah of Galilee in AD 6, or the warriors against Rome in AD 66–70, or at Masada in AD 71–73. Still others were like the Essenes, who lived as hermits near the Dead Sea at Qumran; in apocalyptic fervor they waited for the victory of the sons of light over the sons of darkness. Some even waited for a spiritual Messiah and looked to the Scriptures for signs of His coming. Bishop Alexander says,

The numbers of Hebrews that were spiritually prepared for the acceptance of the Messiah can be seen from the first chapters of the Gospel of St. Luke. There, the Holy Virgin Mary, the righteous Elizabeth, the priest Zechariah, the righteous Simeon, the prophetess Anna and many citizens of Jerusalem linked the birth of Jesus with the fulfillment of the ancient prophecies about the coming of the Messiah, of the forgiveness of sins, of the overthrow of the proud and the elevation of the meek, about the restoration of the Testament with God, about the service of Israel to God with a pure heart. After Jesus Christ began to preach, the Gospel witnesses the ease with which many sympathetic hearts of the Jews recognized in Him the promised Messiah, which they related to their acquaintances, for instance, the apostles Andrew and Philip, later—Nathaniel and Peter (John 1:40-44).[9]

The overwhelming number of people, however, had an incorrect idea of what Messiah was supposed to be. Bishop Alexander adds,

If Christ shunned referring to Himself directly as the Messiah when among people, and only cited prophecies about Him, He did this by reason of the coarse and distorted representations of the Messiah which had become established among the people. Christ in every way avoided worldly glory and interference in political life.[10]

Distorted Notions About the Messiah in the Time of Jesus

Many rejected Jesus of Nazareth not because He was a false Messiah, or because He failed to fulfill prophecy, but because they had a mistaken view of the timing of the Messiah and His role and purpose.

The differentiation between the first and second comings of Christ. As we will see below, the Messiah was to be a suffering servant. So why did most of the Jews in the first-century look for a conquering Messiah? Were they wrong? The answer lies in the fact that Messiah was also supposed to be a conquering king. The first-century Jews simply had the wrong timeline. There is no way to get around the truth that there were to be two comings of the Messiah. The first would be to secure salvation. The second would be to usher in judgment and the Messiah's earthly kingdom.

Isaiah 61 shows this in clear detail. Verses 1-2 refer to the first coming:

> The Spirit of the Lord God is upon me,
> > because the Lord has anointed me
> to bring good news to the poor;
> > he has sent me to bind up the brokenhearted,
> to proclaim liberty to the captives,
> > and the opening of the prison to those who are bound;
> to proclaim the year of the Lord's favor,

Jesus Himself purposely claimed only to have fulfilled the first two verses (Luke 4:18-19), and did so in a literal manner. Verses 2b-7 refer to Christ's second coming, wherein He will establish a kingdom on earth, also literally:

> …and the day of vengeance of our God;
> > to comfort all who mourn;
> to grant to those who mourn in Zion—
> > to give them a beautiful headdress instead of ashes,
> the oil of gladness instead of mourning,
> > the garment of praise instead of a faint spirit;
> that they may be called oaks of righteousness,
> > the planting of the Lord, that he may be glorified.
> They shall build up the ancient ruins;
> > they shall raise up the former devastations;
> they shall repair the ruined cities,
> > the devastations of many generations.
>
> Strangers shall stand and tend your flocks;
> > foreigners shall be your plowmen and vinedressers;

but you shall be called the priests of the LORD;
they shall speak of you as the ministers of our God;
you shall eat the wealth of the nations,
and in their glory you shall boast.
Instead of your shame there shall be a double portion;
instead of dishonor they shall rejoice in their lot;
therefore in their land they shall possess a double portion;
they shall have everlasting joy.

Clearly, the coming of Jesus in the first century involved the first part, but the second part of this prophecy has yet to come to pass.

The warrior-king. The Messiah the disciples expected, as portrayed by noncanonical literature written during the intertestamental period, would be a warrior-king. This is made clear in the seventeenth "Psalm of Solomon." According to this psalm, a Davidic Messiah, raised up by God, would overthrow the Gentile overlords, restore Israel's glory, gather the dispersion, reign from Jerusalem, and bring the Gentiles under his sway as he acted as God's viceregent on earth.

Michael Green says, "This was the hope most widely shared, no doubt: a political Messiah of David's stock, wielding the weapons primarily of spiritual power, but nevertheless ridding the holy soil of Israel from foreign domination, and ushering in the days of glory of which the prophets had spoken."[11] This idea was born out of their mistaken timeline concerning the Messiah. The people of first-century Palestine were under the yoke of yet another foreign power, the mighty Roman Empire. But memories of the Maccabean revolt and the brief period of independence lingered. Bishop Alexander argues this is the reason so many of Jesus' own people refused to accept Him:

> *"Jesus...promised heavenly blessings, not earthly blessings, as a reward for a virtuous life. This was the reason why many Jews rejected Christ."*
> —BISHOP ALEXANDER

Due to their belittling dependence on Rome, many Jews wished the Messiah to be a mighty warrior-king, who would give them political independence, glory and earthly blessings. Jesus came in order to evince in people a spiritual rebirth. He promised heavenly blessings, not earthly blessings, as a reward for a virtuous life. This was the reason why many Jews rejected Christ.[12]

They did not see that this was to take place at a later time, so many of His followers fell away, and many others refused to accept Him.

The invulnerable Messiah. Another facet of the misperception of Jesus' coming was the widespread belief that the Messiah could not die:

No one anticipated that the Messiah would or could die. There are some references in rabbinic literature to a slain Messiah, but these are late, dating from AD 135 and after. In other words, by defining his messiahship in terms of death and resurrection, Jesus is forging new theological ground.[13]

The same problem that the disciples had with the idea of Jesus suffering and dying persisted even after these events actually took place. This was one of the issues that early Christian missionaries had to confront in evangelizing the Jews. According to Deuteronomy 21:22-23, anyone hanged on a tree is under God's curse. That Jesus, who was crucified on a treelike cross, could be the Messiah was therefore impossible in the view of many first-century Jews. This is evidenced by John 12:34: "The crowd answered him, 'We have heard from the Law that the Christ remains forever. How can you say that the Son of Man must be lifted up [crucified]? Who is this Son of Man?'"

First-century Gentiles had a similar problem. To them Jesus was simply a state criminal. That He was crucified meant He must have been a rebellious subject of the Roman Empire. Furthermore, His death pointed to His inherent weakness. The all-powerful God could not possibly work through such a person:

Indeed, "Christ crucified" is a contradiction in terms, of the same category as "friend ice." One may have a Messiah, or one may have a crucifixion; but one may not have both—at least not from the perspective of merely human understanding. *Messiah* meant power, splendor, triumph; *crucifixion* meant weakness, humiliation, defeat. Little wonder that both Jew and Greek were scandalized by the Christian message.[14]

These people missed the prophecies concerning His suffering and death, which will be shown below. There will be a time when Messiah, and indeed all people who believe in Him, will "not perish" (John 3:16). But this time is in the future, not at the first coming of the Messiah.

What Was the Messiah Supposed to Be, and How Did Jesus Fulfill This?

We have seen what people thought the Messiah was supposed to look like, why they rejected Jesus because He did not meet their expectations, and why they were mistaken. Jesus claimed to be the Messiah of Israel. What was this Messiah supposed to look like and do?

- He would be a prophet, like Moses (Deuteronomy 18:15-19).
- He would be a priest, like Melchizedek (Psalm 110:4).
- He would be a king, in the line of David (1 Chronicles 17:10-14).
- He would be a savior who would suffer for His people (Psalm 22:1-21; Isaiah 52:13–53:12).

These are the most important prophecies, but Jesus fulfilled many others.

Messiah in the New Testament

We will now examine some of the important prophecies about the Messiah and how Jesus fulfilled them.

The forerunner. Isaiah 40:3-5 (NKJV) predicts that there would be a forerunner for the Messiah,

> The voice of one crying in the wilderness:
>
>> "Prepare the way of the LORD;
>> Make straight in the desert
>> A highway for our God.
>> Every valley shall be exalted
>> And every mountain and hill brought low;
>> The crooked places shall be made straight
>> And the rough places smooth;
>> The glory of the LORD shall be revealed,
>> And all flesh shall see it together;
>> For the mouth of the LORD has spoken."

This prophecy was fulfilled in Matthew 3:1-3, "In those days John the Baptist came preaching in the wilderness of Judea, and saying, 'Repent, for the kingdom of heaven is at hand.' For this is he who was spoken of by the prophet Isaiah..."

The virginal conception and birth of Jesus. In Isaiah it was prophesied that the Messiah would be born of a virgin. In 7:14 we see, "The Lord himself will give you a sign. Behold, the virgin shall conceive and bear a son, and shall call his name Immanuel." The fulfillment of this prediction is found in Matthew 1:18-25. Matthew says Mary was betrothed to Joseph, but they had not yet consummated their marriage. When Joseph found her pregnant, he thought "to divorce her quietly" (verse 19). But an angel intervened, advising him that Mary had been with no man. The child was conceived of the Holy Spirit. Matthew says "all this took place to fulfill what the Lord had spoken by the prophet" (verse 22).[15]

His prophetic and saving work (His mission). Isaiah 61:1-2a, described on page 229, contains the mission of the Messiah's first coming. We see in verse 1 that he will "bring good news to the poor," "bind up the brokenhearted," "proclaim liberty to the captives, and the opening of the prison to those who are bound," and "proclaim the year of the Lord's favor." Jesus claimed to have fulfilled these words in Luke 4:16-22. He says, "Today this Scripture has been fulfilled in your hearing" (verse 21). Jesus proved this throughout His earthly ministry, as seen throughout the Gospels.

Time and place of birth. During the reign of Caesar Augustus (27 BC–AD 14), the first person to be declared as the Messiah, the Son of David, was born to a lowly young woman from Nazareth, in a humble village in Judea. The prophet spoke of this centuries before:

> But you, O Bethlehem Ephrathah,
>   who are too little to be among the clans of Judah,
> from you shall come forth for me
>   one who is to be ruler in Israel,
>   whose origin is from of old,
>   from ancient days.
>
> —Micah 5:2

One immediately observes in this Scripture that the newborn was to be no ordinary child because, though He is to be born in the community of Israel in insignificant surroundings, He preceded this birth "from ancient days." This depiction of Messiah is continued in Luke's account of Jesus' birth:

> Behold, you will conceive in your womb and bear a son, and you shall call his name Jesus. He will be great and will be called the Son of the Most High. And the Lord God will give to him the throne of his father David, and he will reign over the house of Jacob forever, and of his kingdom there will be no end (Luke 1:31-33).

Incredibly, a similar description of the coming Messiah is found among the Dead Sea Scrolls years before the birth of Jesus: "He will be called the Son of God, they will call him the son of the Most High" (4Q 246 f1ii:1).

In the scroll of the book. Some people did recognize that Jesus was the prophesied Messiah. As Jesus began His ministry, He called Philip to follow Him. Philip not only followed Jesus, but found his brother Nathanael and exclaimed to him these wonderful words, "We have found him of whom Moses in the Law and also the prophets wrote, Jesus of Nazareth, the son of Joseph"(John 1:45).

The Hebrew Scriptures lead to Jesus as the Messiah. This was Jesus' claim to His disciples after the resurrection:

> Then he said to them, "These are my words that I spoke to you while I was still with you, that everything written about me in the Law of Moses and the Prophets and the Psalms must be fulfilled." Then he opened their minds to understand the Scriptures, and said to them, "Thus it is written, that the Christ should suffer and on the third day rise from the dead, and that repentance and forgiveness of sins should be proclaimed in his name to all nations, beginning from Jerusalem" (Luke 24:44-47).

Jesus' teaching that He is found throughout the Old Testament is found in the Old Testament itself. Psalm 40:7 says, "Then I said, 'Behold, I have come; in the scroll of the book it is written of me.'" Further, the writer of Hebrews recognizes this and quotes from the psalm (Hebrews 10:7).[16]

A skeptic might simply believe that Jesus staged activities to fulfill prophecy. Certainly some could have been fulfilled in that way (for example, the riding of the donkey into Jerusalem during passion week), and even His being put to death might possibly have been preplanned to fulfill prophecy. Jesus *could not* have faked many other prophecies: the virgin birth, His place of birth, the slaughter of the infants, and the resurrection. It is a statistical impossibility that all of these prophecies in the Old Testament could have been literally fulfilled in the life of Jesus of Nazareth—unless He was who He claimed to be.

Conclusion

That Jesus of Nazareth is the fulfillment of Old Testament prophecies about the Messiah, there can be no doubt. We have seen just a portion of the prophecies Jesus fulfilled; there are many others.

EVIDENCE FROM HIS LIFE AND WORDS

It has been common for many critical scholars to say that Jesus did not see Himself as Messiah. If this were so, then why does Jesus explain to the two disciples on the road to Emmaus that the entirety of the Old Testament spoke of Him (Luke 24:25-27)? Moreover, that Jesus is the Messiah prophesied by the prophets of the Old Testament is fundamental to the faith of the early church, and even to Jesus' own self-identity. Not only the church shared this confidence, but the Jews before and during the time of Jesus held to the same hope.

But not only prophecies validated that Jesus was the one promised in the Old Testament as the Son of David and Son of God. The nature of this promised one is just as pivotal—that He be God and man.

The Deity of Jesus the Messiah

The claims of Jesus as to His deity. Jesus made many statements about His deity that shocked and enraged His Jewish contemporaries. One cannot read the Gospels, particularly the Gospel of John, without becoming acutely aware that Jesus understood Himself to be none other than God in human flesh. Theologian Millard Erickson has observed, "We should note that Jesus did not make an explicit and overt claim to deity. He did not say, 'I am God.' What we do find, however, are claims that would be inappropriate if made by someone who is less than God."[17]

Scriptural references to the deity of Jesus abound. Our task will not be to attempt to find every text, but to select just those verses among many that will be the best sampling for our limited scope.

Although some deny Jesus ever claimed to be divine, He did say things about Himself that only God could. Ultimately, these statements are what the Jewish rulers used as a pretext for plotting to kill Him. They thought He was committing blasphemy.

His Self-designations Declare Him to Be God

Son of Man. Jesus is the only one to refer to Himself as the "Son of Man," and it is a term of divinity. He uses it at least 80 times in the New Testament. In Matthew 9 Jesus encounters a paralytic. Jesus sees the faith of those who brought the paralyzed man to Him and says to the man, "Take heart, my son; your sins are forgiven" (verse 2). Some scribes watching Him discussed among themselves what He had said. For anyone to claim to forgive sin was tantamount to claiming divinity, which was blasphemous. Jesus, knowing what they were thinking, says to them, "But that you may know that the Son of Man has authority on earth to forgive sins [that is, the divine right to forgive sins]—" (verse 6). He then turns to the paralytic and heals him.

One cannot read the Gospels, particularly the Gospel of John, without becoming acutely aware that Jesus understood Himself to be none other than God in human flesh.

Jesus again calls Himself "Son of Man" (in addition to "Son of God") in John 5. Here Jesus is teaching about His authority. He says that the Son of Man has life in Himself, even as the Father, and that He has been given judgment (John 5:25-27). Notice that because Jesus is the Son of Man, evidenced through His performing of miracles, He has the authority to "execute judgment." This type of judgment is strictly reserved for divinity because it involves the ultimate fate of all people. When the Son of Man comes, He will decide those who "have done good" and are resurrected, and those who "have done evil" and will receive punishment for their evil (Matthew 25:31-46).

The last passage to be considered regarding Jesus' understanding of Himself as the Son of Man involves His appearance before the Sanhedrin. The high priest was the president of the Sanhedrin, the ruling body of the Jews, and the major antagonist against Jesus in His trial. The trial of Jesus before Caiaphas is of considerable importance to determine why Jesus was condemned to death by the Jewish authorities. What had He done that was so egregious that the leaders wanted Him dead? Was His teaching so far off base that He could be tolerated no longer? Did the favor He received from the people incur such jealousy as to bring matters to this end? Was the claim He was the Messiah sufficient to condemn Him to death?

The answer may lie in this trial before the Jewish leaders. When presented with the false witnesses about an alleged claim to destroy and rebuild the temple, He chose not to answer such meritless charges.

The attempt to frame the argument through false witnesses had failed. They had tried to find reason for the warrant of death, but they found none. What were they to do? Since the trumped-up charges would not stand, the high priest asked Him point blank, "Are you the Christ, the Son of the Blessed?" (Mark 14:61). To this Jesus was willing to respond, "I am" (verse 62), but He continued "and you will see the Son of Man seated at the right hand of Power, and coming with the clouds of heaven."

Did this admission in itself condemn Him? The answer appears to be no! Craig Evans says that in Jewish thought, the claim to be Messiah, by oneself or by others, was not considered to be blasphemy:

> Claiming to be Israel's Messiah was not considered blasphemous. Although disparaging them as impostors and opportunists, Josephus never accused any of the many would-be kings and deliverers of first-century Israel as blasphemers. Perhaps a more telling example comes from rabbinic tradition. Rabbi Aquiba's proclamation of Simon ben Kosiba as Messiah was met with skepticism, but not with cries of blasphemy...Even claiming to be *son of God* was not necessarily blasphemous, for there is biblical precedent for such an expression (Pss 2:7; 82:6; 2 Sam 7:14).[18]

If Jesus' response to the high priest's question is not what brought the charge of blasphemy, then what did? The answer comes in the understanding of the nature of blasphemy in first-century Israel and before, and what part of Jesus' answer was considered blasphemous.

Darrell Bock, in an important study on the nature of blasphemy in

Judaism, demonstrates that a person could commit blasphemy through improper use of the name of God, by claiming an association with God reserved only for certain persons (and then for limited purposes and for limited time), or by idolatry or "arrogant disrespect for God or toward his chosen leaders."[19]

Evans believes that Jesus may have even used the name of God, Yahweh, in saying "I am" in response to the question in which the high priest uses the euphemism "Blessed."[20]

The I AM. The belief that Jesus Christ is God and man comes from Christ's own claims about Himself and what was taught and passed on by His apostles to the church. The same Lord who conversed with Moses out of the burning bush in the Sinai Desert 3500 years ago stood before a hostile crowd of skeptical Jews 1500 years later and participated in a far different exchange.

Perhaps nothing else Jesus said gives more evidence to the fact that He claimed to be divine than the "I AM" statements. The Pharisees, who believed He was possessed by a demon, were questioning Jesus. Jesus says to them, "Truly, truly, I say to you, if anyone keeps My word he will never see death" (John 8:51 NASB). The Pharisees think they have just won the argument. They counter,

> Abraham died, as did the prophets, yet you say, "If anyone keeps my word, he will never taste death." Are you greater than our father Abraham, who died? And the prophets died! Who do you make yourself out to be?

Jesus isn't fazed by them. He claims "Your father Abraham rejoiced that he would see my day. He saw it and was glad." The Pharisees can't believe He has just said this. In their eyes, Jesus is claiming to be as old as Abraham. They ask how he could have seen Abraham, being "not yet fifty years old." Now Jesus makes it unequivocal, "Truly, truly, I say to you, before Abraham was, I AM" (John 8:58-59).

No one can say this but God Himself. Jesus is claiming to be eternal. But more than this, Jesus is using the term God used to name Himself. This is the statement God makes in Exodus 3:14: "God said to Moses, 'I AM WHO I AM.' And he said, 'Say this to the children of Israel, "I AM has sent me to you."' We know Jesus means to identify with this passage from Exodus because of the Greek construction used here. Jesus could have simply used the word *eimi* meaning "I am" or "I exist" to convey that He existed in eternity, but He adds *ego*. The Greek literally reads, "before Abraham was, I myself am." To the Pharisees gathered around, the message was clear. They knew Exodus

> *Jesus' manner of identifying Himself to the Jewish leaders as their God...was not direct. He did not speak pompously about Himself.*

by heart and did not miss what Jesus was saying. Previously in the discussion they thought he had a demon, which didn't necessitate punishment. Now they get ready to stone Him for blasphemy, a capital offense.

The message finally got through to the Jews with profound impact. When Jesus identified Himself as the I AM, there was no confusion over what His claim was. Since, in their view, Jesus was only a man, such a claim was blasphemy.

Jesus' manner of identifying Himself to the Jewish leaders as their God, the very same God who had led the nation out of Egyptian bondage to the Promised Land, was not direct. He did not speak pompously about Himself. Jesus portrayed a person fully aware of who and what He was. His attitude regarding His identity was as humble as were the circumstances of His birth.

He Claimed a Divine Relationship with the Father

He who sees Jesus sees the Father. Toward the end of Jesus' earthly ministry, He prepares the disciples for the events that are about to unfold. In John 14:1-11, Jesus once again claims divinity. He tells the disciples He is going to leave them to "prepare a place" for them. He tells them they already know the way. But Thomas argues, "Lord, we do not know where you are going. How can we know the way?" Jesus answers him,

> I am the way, and the truth, and the life. No one comes to the Father except through me. If you had known me, you would have known my Father also. From now on you do know him and have seen him (verses 6-7).

Jesus claims that looking at Him is looking at the Father. The two are equal.

But the disciples don't understand. Philip, completely misunderstanding the implications of what Jesus has just said, says to Him, "Lord, show us the Father, and it is enough for us." Jesus sets them straight, saying, "Whoever has seen me has seen the Father" (14:9). Jesus, as God's Son, shows what His Father's power, compassion, and holiness look like. Moreover, because Christ is God, His redemption is sufficient for all of our sins, for all who are called and believe. The One who did not have to die, died that we might live for eternity with Him. Jesus makes it crystal clear for them. He is God.

He and the Father are one being. Jesus makes other statements where He claims equality with the Father, and therefore to be God Himself.

In John 10:22-39 there is a lengthy interaction between Jesus and the Jewish leaders at the temple. Jesus had been performing miracles and confounding the Pharisees (it was not long before this that Jesus had made the "I AM" statement). Jesus goes into the temple compound. The Jews, seeing Him there, try to get Him to say something they can use against Him. They ask, "How long will you keep us in suspense? If you are the Christ, tell us plainly." Jesus, refusing to play their game, says that He already told them but they didn't believe. Moreover, His works revealed who He was. Then He said, "I and the Father are one." At this statement they pick up stones to stone Him, but once again He gets away from them.

By saying, "I and the Father are one," Jesus is clearly equating Himself with the Father. In the Greek text, He says, "I and the Father are one thing, or essence (*hen*)," not one person (*heis*). The underlying claim is that no one can be equal with God unless He is God Himself.

Jesus then says, "The Father is in me and I am in the Father" (verse 38). Again, the implication is impossible to miss. No one can be "in the Father" (that is, God) unless He Himself is God because nothing that is not God can be in God.

Later, in John 17:5, Jesus prays to the Father, "Now, Father, glorify me in your own presence with the glory that I had with you before the world existed." Here He is claiming eternal presence with the Father. Human beings certainly cannot make such a claim, because we were created after the world was. No one can claim this unless they are themselves divine.

He accepted worship. On a number of occasions after His resurrection, Jesus appeared in the flesh to different disciples and to His brothers, demonstrating that He had defeated death. But these appearances also affirmed His deity since He accepted worship as God.

Thomas had assured the other disciples that his incredulity over their claim that Jesus had risen from the dead knew no bounds: "Unless I see in his hands the mark of the nails, and place my finger into the mark of the nails, and place my hand into his side, I will never believe" (John 20:25). Eight days later, they were all together again with the doors shut, and Jesus comes and stands among them. "Peace be with you," He says, then immediately addresses Thomas: "Put your finger here, and see my hands; and put out your hand, and place it in my side. Do not disbelieve, but believe." Thomas did not hesitate, and he worshipped the man who stood before Him as God Himself: "My Lord and my God!"

This was not an exclamation, which would have been blasphemous and for which he would have been rebuked, but a statement of address. It would also have been blasphemy to ascribe deity to a man, and yet Jesus did not correct Thomas or rebuke him. Rather Jesus commends him for believing, adding a further blessing for those who will believe in Him without seeing Him.

His divine acts and His acceptance of divine status. The granting of forgiveness for sin is reserved for God alone because it involves a judgment of the person's soul. Jesus forgave many for their sins. One occasion is recorded in Luke 7:36-50, where a Pharisee named Simon asked Jesus to eat with him. As they are at the table, a "woman of the city, who was a sinner" comes to Him. She was probably a prostitute. She begins to weep upon Jesus' feet and to wipe them with her hair. She applies an ointment to His feet as well.

Simon is incredulous that Jesus would allow the "sort of woman" she is to touch Him. Jesus reprimands Simon, reminding him that he gave Jesus neither water to wash His feet nor oil for His head, while she had done these things out of love. "Therefore I tell you," Jesus says, "her sins, which are many, are forgiven—for she loved much. But he who is forgiven little, loves little." He then turns to the woman and says, "Your sins are forgiven. Your faith has saved you; go in peace."

Jesus would have had to know she had faith in Him to forgive her sins. Further, He had to have the authority to do so.

On several occasions Jesus not only does miraculous things, but He also accepts worship. Miracles by themselves don't prove His divine status, because the disciples also were given the ability to do miracles. But when combined with His receiving worship, the miracles give credence that the miracles were being done by God. Jesus says it is the Father who is dwelling in Him doing the works. So Jesus' accepting worship is appropriate.

In Matthew 8:1-3 Jesus is coming down from the mountain after delivering His Sermon on the Mount. Matthew says, "Behold, a leper came and worshiped Him, saying, 'Lord, if You are willing, You can make me clean.' Then Jesus put out *His* hand and touched him, saying, 'I am willing; be cleansed.' Immediately his leprosy was cleansed" (NKJV, italics in original). Notice that Jesus doesn't reprimand the leper for worshipping Him.

In Matthew 14:22-33, the disciples are in the middle of the Sea of Galilee, fighting bad weather, when they see what they think is a ghost. It is actually Jesus walking across the water. Peter, apparently speaking before thinking, asks the Lord to command him to walk out to Him. This Jesus does. Peter gets out of the boat, but gets distracted by the wind and the waves and begins to sink. Jesus has to rescue him, then gets in the boat and calms the weather. "And those in the boat worshiped him, saying, 'Truly you are the Son of God'" (verse 33). Again, Jesus shows mastery over nature, then accepts the worship of His followers.

On another occasion Jesus performed a miracle for a woman in the region of Tyre and Sidon. The woman, though Gentile, had great faith and worshipped Jesus, which He accepted and rewarded (Matthew 15:21-28). Worshipping Jesus was not limited to those of Israel. Even the Gentiles recognized that He was worthy of worship. All that was required of the woman was faith.

John 9:1-41 tells the story of a man born blind whom Jesus heals. The healed man doesn't know who it is who healed him, but knows His name is Jesus. Since the man was healed on the Sabbath, he is brought before the Pharisees for questioning. The exchange between the man and the Pharisees becomes heated, and eventually they throw him out.

Jesus hears of this and finds the man. He asks, "Do you believe in the Son of Man?" The man, seemingly unaffected by his experience before the Pharisees, answers, "And who is he, sir, that I may believe in him?" Jesus reveals to him, "You have seen him, and it is he who is speaking to you." The man replies, "Lord, I believe." John adds, "and he worshiped him" (verses 35-38).

Claims by Others of Jesus' Deity

Jesus wasn't the only one to testify about who He was. The Father and the Holy Spirit also are involved in speaking about Jesus.

The testimony of the Father. In Matthew 3:15-17 (and also in Mark 1:11), Jesus goes down to the Jordan to be baptized by John, in order to "fulfill all righteousness." As He came up from the water, the Spirit descended on Him and a voice from heaven said, "This is my beloved Son, with whom I am well pleased" (verse 17).

Later, Jesus takes Peter, James, and John up a mountain (Matthew 17:1-8; Luke 9:28-36), and at the summit, the disciples see Jesus transformed. "The appearance of his face was altered [Matthew says, "shone like the sun"], and his clothing became dazzling white" (Luke 9:29). Moses and Elijah appear and talk with Jesus. All of a sudden clouds envelop them, and a voice calls out, "This is my Son, my Chosen One; listen to him!"

The Father Himself gives His approval and extends His authority to Jesus.

The testimony of the Spirit. Jesus told us that the Spirit would "bear witness about me" (John 15:26). When the Spirit came He would bear witness to Jesus and everything He had done. The Spirit would be sent from the Father by the Son to testify to the truth. This was seen later as the apostles preached the Gospel beginning in Jerusalem and spreading out across the world.

The testimony of His works. Jesus said in John 5:36,

> The testimony that I have is greater than that of John. For the works that the Father has given me to accomplish, the very works that I am doing, bear witness about me that the Father has sent me.

Jesus was explaining that His testimony about Himself wasn't enough. But He doesn't have to testify about Himself. John the Baptist also testified about Him. But more than this even, the works Jesus did testify that He is who He says He is, and that He was working on the Father's behalf.

The claims of His disciples after the resurrection. Immediately after Jesus was crucified, His disciples were distraught, afraid, and discouraged. But Jesus appeared to them following His resurrection, showing them He was alive and well. He promised He would send the Holy Spirit to encourage them (Luke 24:33-49). Suddenly these fearful men changed. Overnight they became bold preachers with great joy (Luke 24:52-53) and began to publicly proclaim Jesus as Messiah (for example, Peter's sermon at Pentecost, Acts 2:22-38).

Shortly afterward, a Pharisee who had been persecuting these new followers of Jesus encountered Him on the road to Damascus. He became a follower then and there, and when he reached Damascus, "he proclaimed Jesus in the synagogues, saying, 'He is the Son of God'" (Acts 9:20). At first everyone thought he was just setting a trap for the Christians there, but Acts 9:22 says, "Saul increased all the more in strength, and confounded the Jews who lived in Damascus by proving that Jesus was the Christ." Of course, Saul becomes Paul, the great missionary of the church.

These apostles, witnesses of everything Jesus said and did and all the events of the crucifixion, death, burial, and resurrection, believed Jesus to be the Lord and Savior and took His message to the world.

> *These apostles, witnesses of everything Jesus said and did...believed Jesus to be the Lord and Savior and took His message to the world.*

The claims of the New Testament writers. The apostle Paul became the church's first great missionary. He went all over the Roman Empire preaching Jesus as the Christ. But was it the same Jesus as is seen in the Gospels? Did Paul even know what Jesus said and did? Because Paul is responsible for much of the New Testament, this question is important if we are to claim we have the truth about who Jesus is.

Paul taught that Jesus was the Son of God. Remember that Jesus is called this throughout the Gospels. In Paul's letter to the Romans he says, "concerning His Son Jesus Christ our Lord…declared to be the Son of God…" (Romans 1:3,4 NKJV). In 2 Corinthians 1:19, Paul speaks of "the Son of God, Jesus Christ, whom we proclaimed among you."

Paul also taught the correct story of Jesus' birth, His keeping of the Law, and His stated purpose for giving His life. In Galatians 4:4-5 he says, "When the fullness of time had come, God sent forth his Son, born of woman, born under the law, to redeem those who were under the law, so that we might receive adoption as sons." Paul says he was taught what Jesus taught and did. We see this in 1 Corinthians 11:23, where he passes on what the Lord Himself had told him about the Passover night before His crucifixion.

Paul teaches that Jesus was crucified (1 Corinthians 2:2), died

(1 Thessalonians 4:14), and was resurrected (2 Timothy 2:8), just as it is told in the Gospels. Even more than this, Paul had an intimate knowledge of Jesus' character. Paul talks about and affirms Jesus' meekness and gentleness (2 Corinthians 10:1), His obedience to God (Romans 5:19; Philippians 2:6-9), His patience (2 Thessalonians 3:5), His grace (2 Corinthians 8:9), His love (Romans 8:35), His righteousness (Romans 5:18), and His sinlessness (2 Corinthians 5:21). Paul preached and taught the very same Jesus we see in the Gospels.

The apostle John gives a view of Jesus' deity in a manner clearly reflected in Paul's theology. John 1:1-4 says, "In the beginning was the Word, and the Word was with God, and the Word was God. He was with God in the beginning. Through him all things were made; without him nothing was made that has been made. In him was life, and that life was the light of men." Even before John's Gospel was written, Paul wrote to the Colossians about the deity of Christ:

> He is the image of the invisible God, the firstborn of all creation. For by him all things were created, in heaven and on earth, visible and invisible, whether thrones or dominions or rulers or authorities—all things were created through him and for him. And he is before all things, and in him all things hold together. And he is the head of the body, the church. He is the beginning, the firstborn from the dead, that in everything he might be preeminent. For in him all the fullness of God was pleased to dwell, and through him to reconcile to himself all things, whether on earth or in heaven, making peace by the blood of his cross (Colossians 1:15-20).

In this passage, Paul describes a Man who in every way shared in God's divine nature, unlike even the most godly man in the Old Testament. Neither Moses nor Abraham was given such accolades, such praise and worship as in this passage. Paul and the early church knew that Jesus was not merely a man, but God Himself in the flesh.

In John 1:1, given above, John refers to Jesus not only as "God" but also as "the Word" (Greek *logos*). John's Greek readers would have immediately recognized this word since, by the time John wrote his gospel, *logos* had already come to occupy a venerable place in Greek philosophy. To the Greek mind, *logos* referred to the organizing principle of the universe, the thing that held it all together and allowed it to make sense. To his Jewish readers, *logos* would have meant the creative, powerful word of God in the Old Testament by which the heavens and the earth were created (Psalm 33:6).

John deliberately identifies Jesus with both of these concepts: He is the creative and powerful word of God (Hebrew concept) and the organizing or unifying force of the universe (Greek concept) who became man: "The Word became flesh and dwelt among us, and we have seen his glory, glory as of the only Son from the Father, full of grace and truth" (John 1:14).

During the first four centuries of the Christian church, numerous heresies vied for the hearts and minds of Christ's followers. As Paul had warned us, these heresies sprang from within the church itself. If the theological understanding of the Person of Christ were altered or corrupted in any way, then the future of the Christian faith would be in jeopardy. Salvation would vanish as well, since what we believe about Jesus affects our view of God's work of redemption in Christ.

Much of the truth of Christianity hinged on the issue of the nature of Jesus. In what sense was He God and in what sense man? This is called the *hypostatic union,* something we discuss below (see also chapter 7).

The Humanity of Jesus the Messiah

Theological considerations. At first blush, one might think that the humanity of Jesus would not incur the same level of discussion, or produce the considerable heresies, as the deity of Christ. Yet this is one of the major controversies of the ancient church. One would think a fully human Jesus would be an accepted fact since it deals with the concrete world instead of the invisible God who cannot be seen. The idea that the Son became human has been at the forefront of theological debate from the late second century until the present. Millard Erickson has suggested that the debate "has in some ways posed a greater danger to orthodox theology."[21]

In view of this we cannot underestimate the importance of the incarnation of the Logos, particularly its impact on salvation. Since man is not able to elevate himself to God to expiate his own sin, God must somehow enter human existence to accomplish this. Some union of God and man, creator and creature had to occur. The sufficiency and validity of the death of Jesus requires a holy God to judicially bring upon a perfect human the guilt for fallen humanity, something that could occur only with the incarnation of God's Son, one person in two natures. He must be fully God and fully human with no mixture of the two; His death as a human depends on the genuineness of His deity.

If He was truly human, He was fully aware of our human experience, our trials and temptations, and He could understand our experience and empathize with our struggles. If He was only partly human, then He cannot effect the type of intercession that a priest might on behalf of those He represents.

As was the case for the evidence of Jesus' deity, there is abundant evidence in the Scriptures for the full humanity of Jesus, including His virginal conception and birth. Why do I mention the virgin birth? God could not have brought His Son into human existence, connected to the humanity that is from Adam, without a human mother. In Matthew's Gospel we read, "Now the birth of Jesus Christ took place in this way. When his mother Mary had been betrothed to Joseph, before they came together she was found to be with child from the Holy Spirit" (Matthew 1:18). In Luke's Gospel, we are filled in on some important details not found in Matthew. Mary is clearly stated to be a virgin, very pleasing to God. She would give birth to a Son who would be the Son of the Most High and reign on the throne of David forever (Luke 1:26-33).

To unite both deity and humanity in one person, there really was no other way God could have sent His Son into the world. It would have been possible for God to create a human creature and send Him into the world, but He would not have been fully identifiable with us because He would not truly have been a part of the human race descended from Adam.

Moreover, the problem of inherited sin is solved when Jesus descends from Adam through His mother and not through a human father. As the eternal Son of God, Jesus retained His entire divine nature but assumed His human nature through His mother Mary. However, sin could not be transferred to Jesus from Mary because "The Holy Spirit will come upon you... *therefore* the child to be born will be called *holy—the Son of God*" (Luke 1:35, emphasis added).

> *The problem of inherited sin is solved when Jesus descends from Adam through His mother and not through a human father.*

Biblical Evidence for Jesus' Humanity

Jewish. We must never forget when discussing Jesus' humanity that He was Jewish. This is shown throughout the New Testament.

He was born to a woman of Jewish lineage. We know this from His genealogy (Matthew 1:1-17). He was circumcised according to the Law as all male Jews were (Luke 2:21). He was consecrated to the Lord as was required by the Law (Luke 2:22-24). He was raised keeping the Jewish feast days (Luke 2:41-42), and He continued to keep the feasts during His ministry (Matthew 26:18; John 2:13; 7:2; 10:22-23). He was taught according to Jewish tradition, learning Scripture from a young age (Luke 2:40). He went to synagogue on the Sabbath and taught Scripture in them according to Jewish tradition (Matthew 4:23; Mark 1:21; Luke 6:6). He regularly visited the temple in Jerusalem (Matthew 21:12; Mark 11:11, Luke 19:47; John 7:14). He was buried according to Jewish custom (Luke 23:53). He continued to keep Jewish customs even after His resurrection, performing the blessing of the bread before a meal (Luke 24:30).

For all people. Although Jesus was thoroughly Jewish, He also taught that He came on behalf of the Gentiles as well. He fulfilled God's promise of hope for the Gentiles (Matthew 12:15-21). He ministered in Gentile regions, healing and teaching (Mark 7:24-37). He recognized the faith of Gentiles (Matthew 8:5-13) and promised there would be people from the whole earth in the kingdom (Matthew 8:11). He foretold that the gospel would be preached to the "whole world" (Matthew 24:14) and told His disciples to "proclaim the gospel to the whole creation" (Mark 16:15).

Limitations in His humanity. The fact that Jesus was fully human is evident throughout the Gospels. Many times He demonstrated human limitations. He was not faking them or somehow voluntarily limiting Himself in order to seem more human. To do this would be to deny His full humanity and His perfect substitutionary sacrifice in our place. He was born in the normal human way (Luke 2:6-7). His body grew over time as a normal human body does (Luke 2:40,52). He was hungry at times (Matthew 4:2) and ate food (Mark 2:15-16; Luke 11:37). He got tired from walking and had to rest (John 4:6). At times He did not have knowledge of something (Mark 13:32). He had human emotions of awe, compassion, anger, sadness, and unrest (Matthew 8:10; 9:36; Luke 19:41; John 2:13-17; 11:33-35; 12:27).

Died and rose again as a man. Finally, Jesus' humanity is vividly portrayed in the events leading up to His crucifixion, in His death, and His resurrection. Here we see that Jesus was put to death and rose again as a real human being. He was flogged with a whip (John 19:1), and was beaten by the Roman soldiers (John 19:3). He was hung on a cross, one of the most excruciating ways to die (Luke 23:33; John 19:18). He actually died; He did not swoon or lose consciousness, only to revive later (Luke 23:46; John 19:30). His actual, physical body was resurrected, proven by the fact that there was no body when the women came to the tomb on the morning of the third day (Luke 24:1-3). His body was still human after the resurrection because the disciples could touch Him, and He could eat (Luke 24:36-43).

Just who is Jesus, really? The biblical text presents one portrayal, but there are many others as we have seen. Considerable confusion persists as to Jesus' identity and even whether He actually ever lived. Popular books and a hostile and often anti-Christian media challenge cherished views held by Christians for nearly two millennia. Liberal churchmen and other world religious leaders portray Jesus as a good man, maybe even a prophet, but far short of God manifest in the flesh.

In the end every one of us must decide, in the words of C.S. Lewis, whether the real Jesus is liar, lunatic, or Lord. The Old Testament declares His coming, and the Gospels make plain who the early disciples understood Him to be. This puts each of us in the position of making a decision as to who Jesus is, a decision that has eternal consequences.

JESUS CHRIST IS THE FOCUS OF CHRISTIANITY

In other religions of the world, the moral teachings of the religion provide the essence of the religion. As has been noted, Buddhism would continue if Buddha never lived. Islam could still have a vital belief in Allah even if Muhammad were not his prophet.

This is not true of Christianity. It is doubtful that Christianity would have survived the persecutions of the early centuries or blossomed to its magnitude today apart from belief in the special nature and work of Jesus Christ. Jesus is not merely appreciated for His teachings or respected for His high moral standards. He is worshipped, adored, and obeyed as the sovereign God and creator of the universe, the Savior of His people.

Lots of men throughout history have put themselves forward as a messiah (or others have done this for them). But none qualified for this position under the requirements set by the prophecies about the true Messiah. World religions and religious scholars have tried to revise the Jesus spoken of in the Gospel accounts, the letters of the apostles, and the teaching of the church, but the result has been a weak substitute for the Jesus who truly lived.

Though contemporary novelists and media sensationalists never tire of trying to find some new angle about Jesus to attract an audience, serious historians and biblical scholars are impressed with the evidence in the Gospels for the Jesus who lived, taught, performed miracles, died, was buried, and rose again from the dead.

In chapter 1 I said that the most important question in the world came from the mouth of our Lord to the fisherman Peter: "Who do you say I am?" The disciples had already conveyed the honorable but wrong evaluations of the people that Jesus was John the Baptist, Elijah, Jeremiah, or another prophet. But Peter gave Jesus a succinct and enlightened response: "You are the Christ, the Son of the living God." That response, revealed to Peter from heaven, was the only possible correct answer.

There are myriad Jesuses who never lived...who lead people away from the one who is the truth, the way, and the life.

To have given an incorrect answer would have put Peter's eternal destiny in doubt. Ideas have consequences. Not only is our eternal destiny at stake, but also the quality of our earthly existence is diminished if we follow a theological system that rejects the Jesus of the Bible.

The word *orthodoxy* is derived from two Greek words that mean "right" and "honor." To be orthodox is to be in right relationship with God through right doctrine and living. To be a heretic is to be opposed not only to right doctrine but to God Himself. In 2 Corinthians 11:4 Paul confesses his fear that the Corinthian believers will be led away all too easily to "another Jesus than the one we proclaimed." In Galatians Paul hurls the *anathema,* a curse,[1] at anyone who would pervert the true gospel of Christ. The end might be God's judgment, but the earthly life of one opposed to orthodoxy is clearly slavery, continually bound by the chains of sin and guilt. The gospel of Christ faithfully communicates the true essence of Christ's person and mission. Pervert His person and you have destroyed your only hope for salvation in this life and the next.

There are myriad Jesuses who never lived, created in the minds of individuals who are deluded or devious, who lead people away from the one who is the truth, the way, and the life. Along with Peter and millions of the faithful across the ages, we need to affirm the Jesus who really did live—the Jesus of history and the God of eternity—and by believing in Him we might have life in His name (John 20:30-31).

This is the true Jesus the Messiah, our Lord, the one who said,

> Truly, truly, I say to you, whoever hears my word and believes him who sent me has eternal life. He does not come into judgment, but has passed from death to life (John 5:24).

Appendix

✠

A SUMMARY OF
EARLY HETERODOX
PERSPECTIVES OF JESUS

HERESY	DATE	VIEWPOINT
Ebionism	First to fourth centuries AD	A Jewish philosophy most active in the first and early second century that believed Jesus was the Messiah spoken about in the Hebrew Scriptures but that He was only a human, not God.
Cerinthianism	c. AD 100	Cerinthus believed that the *Logos* descended on the human Jesus at His baptism and departed before His death on the cross.
Gnosticism	Second to fourth centuries AD	Gnosticism took a variety of forms, but in general argued for a god different from the God of the Old Testament. It believed that Jesus gave only the appearance of being a human being.

HERESY	DATE	VIEWPOINT
Valentinianism	c. AD 100 to c. 160	Most sophisticated of the Gnostic views, arguing for a number of emanations from the Supreme Father. Jesus was an *aeon* who appeared to be in bodily form but was actually an immaterial being from outside the world. The Savior was to bring enlightenment rather than forgiveness.
Marcionism	c. AD 110 to 160	Most well known of the heretics of the early church. Marcion was anti-Semitic, and he believed in a god of the Old Testament and a god of the New Testament who were in conflict with each other. Jesus was a spiritual entity sent to the earth. Marcion developed a canon of Scripture that excluded the Old Testament and included only Luke, Acts, and the Pauline letters.
Manichaeism	AD 210 to 276	Mani considered himself the prophet of the final religion, in the line of other prophets, including Jesus. He was influenced by Gnosticism and believed in two spheres of existence: light and darkness (the former ruled by God and the latter by Satan).

Heresy	Date	Viewpoint
Monarchianism	Second century AD	Monarchianism appeared in two forms. The first is *Dynamic* Monarchianism, in which God is unipersonal (one person) and Jesus only a man. *Modalistic* Monarchianism said that the *Logos of God* manifested Himself in three different forms—Father, Son, and Holy Spirit—but was only one person.
Arianism	Fourth century AD	View of Arius, a bishop in Alexandria, that the *Logos* was a being created by the Father, and although he had divine aspects, was not of the same essence as the Father.
Apollinarianism	Fourth and early fifth centuries AD	Apollinarianism argued that the *Logos* indwelt a human Jesus, so that Jesus was not a fully human being.
Eutychianism	Late fourth to middle of fifth century AD	Eutychianism believed that Jesus did not have two distinct natures, but His divine and human natures were blended into a new, third nature.
Nestorianism	Late fourth to middle of fifth century AD	Nestorius said that the divine and human natures were entirely separate from each other, resulting in two persons and two natures.

Notes

Chapter 1—What's It All About?

1. This alleged relationship has been exploited in recent days by authors such as Dan Brown in *The Da Vinci Code* (New York: Doubleday, 2003).

2. Judas also introduces this statement, "he's just a man," in the play—in the lyrics to "Judas' Death."

3. This is not to suggest that there were not other groups that vied for adherents even after several fell by the wayside with the destruction of Jerusalem or evolved to other forms.

4. Charles W. Hedrick and Robert Hodgson, eds., *Nag Hammadi, Gnosticism, and Early Christianity* (Peabody, MA: Hendrickson, 1986), 1-2.

5. H. Wayne House, ed., *Israel: The Land and the People* (Grand Rapids, MI: Kregel Publishers, 1998); Ray A. Pritz, *Nazarene Jewish Christianity: From the End of the New Testament Period Until Its Disappearance in the Fourth Century* (Jerusalem: The Magnes Press, 1992); Oskar Skarsaune and Reidar Hvalvik, eds., *Jewish Believers in Jesus* (Peabody, MA: Hendrickson Publishers, 2007).

6. "In Hinduism, a manifestation of Brahman, who descends into the realm of mortals, usually when there is widespread ignorance about the path to enlightenment." From H. Wayne House, *Charts of World Religions* (Grand Rapids, MI: Zondervan, 2006), 316. See chapter 8.

7. R. Pierce Beaver, et al., eds., *Eerdman's Handbook to the World's Religions* (Grand Rapids, MI: Wm. B. Eerdmans Publishing Co., 1994), 311, 315.

8. Maulana Muhammad Ali, trans., *The Holy Qur'an*, 7th ed. (Columbus, OH: Ahmadi-yyah Anjuman Isha'at Islam, 1963), Sura 3:45-47; Sura 19:18-19; 19:31, Sura 5:110; Sura 3:55; Sura 43:61.

9. Ali, trans., *The Holy Qur'an*, Sura 3:144; 18:110.

10. For images of these inscriptions, see www.islamic-awareness.org/History/Islam/Inscriptions/DoTR.html (last visited on January 15, 2008).

11. Ben Witherington III, *The Jesus Quest: The Third Search for the Jew of Nazareth* (Downers Grove, IL: InterVarsity Press, 1997), 42-57.

12. Gary Habermas, *The Historical Jesus: Ancient Evidence for the Life of Christ* (Joplin, MO: College Press, 1999), 143-243.

13. For a thorough summary of the evidence for the early belief in the resurrection, see N.T. Wright, *The Resurrection of the Son of God*, vol. 3 of *Christians and the Question of God* (Minneapolis, MN: Fortress, 2003).

14. Larry W. Hurtado, *How on Earth Did Jesus Become a God? Historical Questions About*

Earliest Devotion to Jesus (Grand Rapids, MI: Wm. B. Eerdmans Publishing Co., 2005), 134-51.

15. See Habermas.

16. Adapted by an unknown source from the original by James A. Francis, found in *The Real Jesus and Other Sermons* (Philadelphia: The Judson Press, 1926), 123.

17. Marcus J. Borg, *Jesus: A New Vision* (San Francisco: Harper San Francisco, 1991), 1.

18. Jaroslav Pelikan, *Jesus Through the Centuries: His Place in the History of Culture* (New Haven: Yale University Press, 1985), 1.

19. See D. James Kennedy and Jerry Newcombe, *What If Jesus Had Never Been Born?* (Nashville: Thomas Nelson Publishers, 1994); and Dinesh D'Souza, *What's So Great About Christianity?* (Washington, DC: Regnery Publishing, Inc., 2007).

20. Dan Kimball has written a book concerning this phenomenon, *They Like Jesus but Not the Church* (Grand Rapids, MI: Zondervan, 2007).

21. I say Messiah rather than Christ here because it is highly doubtful in the Gospels, and even in most of the New Testament, that the Greek term *christos* was a name rather than the title for the promised anointed one of Israel. The translators have done us a disservice by not using Messiah in all of those instances. See the statements of W.F. Albright and C.S. Mann, "Matthew," *The Anchor Bible* (Garden City, NY: Doubleday & Company, Inc., 1971), 194, at his discussion of Matthew 16:16. It does appear that in the letters of Paul, Christ at times became more like a last name, though in the Jewish world in the time of Jesus people did not use last names.

22. The apostle John speaks about this kind of relationship with Jesus and uses it as a proof for His true humanity against the incipient Gnostics at the end of the first century (1 John 1:1-3).

23. D.A. Carson, *Matthew,* 1-599 (Expositor's Bible Commentary; Grand Rapids: Zondervan, 1984), 337.

24. Albright and Mann, 194.

25. Jesus is also like Elijah in that both were fed in the desert, Elijah by ravens (1 Kings 17:3-6) and Jesus by angels (Matthew 4:11), but it is doubtful that the people would have been aware of the latter.

26. Jesus even used this story of God's graciousness to non-Jewish people when He spoke in His home synagogue at Nazareth (Luke 4:24-26).

27. Donald A. Hagner, "Matthew 14:1–28:20," *Word Biblical Commentary,* 33B, Bruce M. Metzger, gen. ed. (Dallas: Word Books, 1995), 467.

28. For an explanation, see Carson, 365; and Henry Alford, *The Greek Testament,* vol. 1 (Chicago: Moody Press, 1968), 171-72.

29. Borg, 1.

Chapter 2—How Jesus' Family and Disciples Viewed Him

1. Some have also argued that Jesus had connection to the Jewish sect at Qumran, but there is no credible evidence that this is so. See Gerd Thiessen and Annette Merz, John Bowden, trans., *The Historical Jesus: A Comprehensive Guide* (Minneapolis, MN:

Fortress, 1998), 148, 352 (a comparison of Jesus' interpretation of the Law and that of the Essenes at Qumran).

2. We don't know anything about the brothers of Jesus but for James and Judas, usually called Jude. The latter is said to be the author of the letter Jude, but we know little more about him. The former is more well known, as he led the Jerusalem church for a number of years until, according to Josephus, he was killed in AD 62 under the direction of the high priest Ananus.

   James was the leader of the church at Jerusalem (Galatians 1:19; 2:9; Acts 12:17) and presided at the Council of Jerusalem that decided Gentiles were not under obligation to be circumcised or follow the law of Moses (Acts 15:12-23).

3. Several noncanonical gospel accounts written after the apostolic period speak of acts by Jesus as a child, such as the *Infancy Gospel of Thomas* (see at www.earlychristianwritings .com/text/infancythomas-a-roberts.html), the *Gospel of Pseudo-Matthew* (see at www .ccel.org/ccel/schaff/anf08.toc.html), and the *Gospel of the Nativity of Mary* (see at www.ccel.org/ccel/schaff/anf08.toc.html).

4. In seventeenth-century England, a cousin was a member of one's extended family, not the child of an uncle or aunt as today. See "Origins and Meaning of Names," www .mayrand.org/meaning-e.htm (last visited February 7, 2008).

5. The Greek word is *sungenis,* meaning "kinswoman or relative." Walter Bauer, *A Greek– English Lexicon of the New Testament and Other Early Christian Literature,* 3rd ed., rev. and ed. Fredrick William Danker (Chicago: University of Chicago Press, 2000).

6. All through the Gospel of John, the other disciples are called by their names (that is, Peter, James, and so on). John is always referred to as "the disciple whom Jesus loved."

7. This great love is shown by Jesus' tears at Lazarus's grave immediately before He raised him from the dead (John 11:35-36), and the danger He submitted Himself to by coming to the area at that time (John 11:8,16). This resurrection signaled the beginning of the official design of Jewish leaders to put Jesus to death (John 11:45-53) along with Lazarus (John 12:10-11).

8. Mary of Magdala began to be identified with the "sinful woman" in Luke 7:36-50 from Pope Gregory the Great's identification of her in that light in a homily in 591, but this has no warrant from the biblical text. See Carl E. Olson and Sandra Miesel, *The Da Vinci Hoax* (San Francisco: Ignatius, 2004), 82.

9. The Greek expression seems to indicate a night-time kind of encounter, relating to the secretive nature of the meeting. John B.W. Johnson, *The New Testament Commentary,* vol. 3 (Oak Harbor, WA: Logos Research Systems, Inc., 1999), 55. "He probably chose the night in order to escape observation. The radical act of Jesus in driving the cattle and the dealers, as well as the money changers, from the temple court had excited the wrath of the priests who derived gain from the desecration."

10. See discussion in H. Wayne House, "John 3:5" *Nelson's Illustrated Bible Commentary,* Earl D. Radmacher, Ronald B. Allen, and H. Wayne House, eds. (Nashville, TN: Thomas Nelson Publishers, 1999), 1318-19.

11. *New Bible Dictionary,* ed. D.R.W. Wood (Downers Grove, IL: InterVarsity Press, 1996), 624.

12. See chapter 7.

Chapter 3—How the People and Leaders Viewed Jesus

1. Matthew 13:55; the word *tektone* actually refers to someone who is more than a carpenter, who also works in masonry. See Ken M. Campbell, "What Was Jesus' Occupation?" *JETS*, vol. 48, no. 5 (S. 2005), 501-519.

2. Gamaliel says in *Mishnah Aboth* 2.2, "Beautiful is the study of the Law when conjoined with a worldly avocation, for the efforts demanded by both stifle all inclination to sin. But study which is not associated with some worldly pursuit must eventually cease, and may lead to iniquity" (Michael Levi Rodkinson, *New Edition of the Babylonian Talmud* [New York: New Talmud Publishing Company, 1900], 59.) See also John Witte Jr. and J.D. Van Der Vyer, eds., *Religious Human Rights in Global Perspective* (Grand Rapids, MI: Eerdmans, 1996), 329, citing from Babylonian Talmud, Tractate 29a, 30b: "Anyone who does not teach his children a profession, it is as if he has taught them robbery."

3. Josephus portrays them as exercising political power, and that some priests were Pharisees. Josephus, *Antiquities* and *Wars*, as quoted in *The New Bible Dictionary*, ed. D.R.W. Wood (Downers Grove, IL: InterVarsity Press, 1996), 914.

4. The Gospel accounts speak harshly of Pharisees as opponents of Jesus. De Lacey provides an explanation for this:

> An important factor in assessing their influence is the impression given by the synoptic writers that it was the Pharisees who took it upon themselves to vet Jesus' credentials and to seek to destroy his subversive new teaching. Hence they are portrayed as natural authorities in the community of faith, or at least in that part of most interest to the early Christian community. This coheres with both Josephus' report of their claims to "accuracy" in interpretation, and with what we know of the early life of the erstwhile Pharisee, Paul (Gal. 1:13-14; Phil. 3:5f). In Luke, in particular, they appear to regard Jesus as an equal, even while suffering his biting criticisms. In Acts they appear as a voice of moderation in the Sanhedrin. But in general "the Pharisees" quickly became a stereotype for the opponents of Jesus (D.R. de Lacey, "Pharisees," 914-15 in *The New Bible Dictionary*).

5. Note the words of the *Jewish Encyclopedia:* "According to Josephus, who desired to present the Jewish parties as so many philosophical schools, the Pharisees, Sadducees, and Essenes were divided on this question. The Pharisees held that not all things are divinely predestined, but that some are dependent on the will of man; the Sadducees denied any interference of God in human affairs; while the Essenes ascribed everything to divine predestination ("B. J." ii. 8, § 14; "Ant." xiii. 5, § 9)." Kaufmann Kohler and Isaac Broydé, "Predestination," in *The Jewish Encyclopedia*, Cyrus Adler, et al., eds., www.jewishencyclopedia.com/view.jsp?artid=503&letter=P (last visited April 6, 2008), pp. 181-82.

6. There are seven (types of) Pharisees [*perushim*]:

    (a) the superficial Pharisee [*sheikmi;* lit: "shoulders"];

    (b) the critical Pharisee [*nikphi;* lit: "knocking"];

    (c) the calculating Pharisee [*qitzai;* lit: "cutting"];

(d) the persistent Pharisee [*dukai;* lit: "pounding"];

(e) the Pharisee for whom existence is work;

(f) the Pharisee concerned with his (own) strengths; and

(g) the Pharisee from inclination or the Pharisee from fear.

Babylonian Talmud (supplement), Aboth de R. Nathan 37.4.

Seen at http://virtualreligion.net/iho/pharisee.html

Verbatim:

> The rabbis taught: There are seven sorts of hypocrites (who try to show themselves as if they were true Pharisees), and they are: Shichmi; Niqpi; Qoosai; Medukhai; "What more is my duty, and will I do it?"; Pharisee of love; and Pharisee of fear. *Shichmi*—i.e., who acts like Shechem (Gen. xxxiv.), (who allowed himself to be circumcised, not to please God but for his own benefit). *Niqpi*—i.e., one who walks tiptoe (so that he strikes his feet against stones or other obstacles in the way), in order to show his meekness and thereby attract attention. *Qoosai*—i.e., one who shows himself as walking with his eyes shut in order not to look upon women, and strikes his head against a wall and bleeds. Such is the interpretation of R. Nahman b. Itz'hak. *Medukhai*—i.e., who so bends his body while walking that he resembles a pestle. Such is the interpretation of Rabba b. Shila *"What more is my duty,"* etc. Why is this hypocrisy? It means that he is boasting of having done every possible good thing, and challenges that he shall be told what more there is to be done and he will do it. *"Pharisee of love,"* etc. Abayi and Rabha both said to the scholar who repeated this: "Do not place love and fear with the hypocrites, as R. Jehudah said in the name of Rabh: 'Always shall one occupy himself with Torah and merits even not for the sake of Heaven, for once he makes it his custom to do so he will finally come to do it for the sake of Heaven.'"

(Michael L. Rodkinson, ed., *The New Babylonian Talmud* [New York: Talmud Publishing Company, 1900], 123-24.)

7. Two basic derivations have been suggested for the word *Sadducees:* First, that it comes from the Hebrew *tsaddiqim,* meaning "righteous ones," or second, that it is based on "Zadok" (meaning "righteous"), high priest under David the king (1 Kings 1:26), since Sadducees often were the priests. (*A Hebrew and English Lexicon of the Old Testament* [abridged]. Based on *A Hebrew and English Lexicon of the Old Testament,* F. Brown, S.R. Driver, and C.A. Briggs [Oxford: Clarendon Press, 1907]. Digitized and abridged as a part of the Princeton Theological Seminary Hebrew Lexicon Project under the direction of Dr. J.M. Roberts. Used by permission. Electronic text corrected, formatted, and hypertexted by OakTree Software, Inc. This electronic adaptation ©2001 OakTree Software, Inc. Version 3.2.)

8. See the important study of Mason, *Flavius Josephus on the Pharisees* (Leiden, Netherlands: Brill, 1991).

9. See above discussion about the Pharisees' beliefs.

10. F.F. Bruce, "Herodians," in *The New Bible Dictionary,* 472.

11. The group wasn't initially restricted to the priests, the first probably being Ezra, who

was priest and scribe (Nehemiah 8:9). Feinberg believes that they did not develop as a distinct political party until the repressive regime of Antiochus Epiphanes. They were largely operating in Judea prior to AD 70, but were also in Galilee (Luke 5:17) and the Diaspora (C.L. Feinberg, "Scribes," in *The New Bible Dictionary*, 1068).

12. Apparently the scribes were the originators of the synagogue and some were members of the Sanhedrin (Matthew 16:21; 26:3). After AD 70 they were responsible for writing the oral law and transmitting the Hebrew Scriptures. Thus, the task of the scribes was threefold. They preserved the law of Moses and endeavored to apply this law to daily life by means of "unwritten legal decisions" called oral tradition. Second, they "gathered around them" disciples to train who in turn would transmit their law to others; the Scripture tells us that they lectured in the temple (Luke 2:46; John 18:20). Third, their designation as "lawyers" or "teachers of the law" is used because they administered the law as judges in the Sanhedrin (Matthew 22:35; Mark 14:43,53; Luke 22:66; Acts 4:5; Jos., *Ant.* 18:16f). Generally scribes adhered to the party of the Pharisees, but were an independent entity (Feinberg, "Scribes," in *The New Bible Dictionary*, 1068).

13. "Their opposition mounts as the claims and mission of Jesus become clear, for example, in his challenge to the Sabbath legislation (Mt. 12:1-7; Mk. 2:23-27; Lk. 6:1-5) and in his parables that censured the religious leaders (Mt. 21:45-46). This conflict to the death was anticipated immediately after Peter's confession at Caesarea Philippi (Mt. 16:21; Mk. 8:31; Lk. 9:22), was intensified at the Palm Sunday reception and the subsequent Temple cleansing (Mt. 21:15,23,45-46; Mk. 11:27; Lk. 19:47-48; 20:1), and reached its bitter climax in the arrest and trial (Mt. 26–27). The Fourth Gospel also bears witness to the conflict (Jn. 7:32,45; 11:47, where Pharisees are the partners in crime; 12:10, where the hostility focuses on Lazarus; 18:19,22,24,35, where Caiaphas' role in Jesus' trial is stressed; see 19:15" (D.A. Hubbard, "Priests and Levites," in *The New Bible Dictionary*, 960).

14. His statements indicated clearly that this was His intent:

> I tell you, something greater than the temple is here (Matthew 12:6).

> Jesus answered them, "Destroy this temple, and in three days I will raise it up" (John 2:19).

> For even the Son of Man came not to be served but to serve, and to give his life as a ransom for many (Mark 10:45).

The author of the letter to the Hebrews develops this theme throughout his work.

15. In John 11:45-57, the Jewish leaders came together to discuss Jesus: "What shall we do? For this Man works many signs. If we let Him alone like this, everyone will believe in Him, and the Romans will come and take away both our place and nation" (verses 47-48 NKJV). From then on they "plotted to put Him to death" (verse 53 NKJV).

16. D.W.B. Robinson, "Sons (Children) of God," in *The New Bible Dictionary*, 1122-23.

17. David Bercot, ed., "Enoch, Book of," in *A Dictionary of Early Christian Beliefs* (Peabody, MA: Hendrickson, 1998), 230-31.

18. "Teacher, we know that You speak and teach correctly, and You are not partial to any, but teach the way of God in truth. Is it lawful for us to pay taxes to Caesar, or not?" (Luke 20:21-22 NASB). It may even be that they associated Jesus, as a prophet and messianic contender from Galilee, with Judas the Galilean Zealot. The question on taxation to Caesar would particularly cause difficulty with one having Zealot leaning,

because he would not likely deny his feeling in this matter, thus revealing that he was a political revolutionary.

We should remember that when they came to arrest Jesus, He questioned their manner of apprehending Him, as though against a robber (Greek, *lesten*), since He daily taught in the temple (Mark 14:48; John 18:20). Certainly this was the type of caricature they desired to portray of Jesus before Pilate: an enemy of Rome. In fact, He was crucified between two "robbers," likely those with whom Barabbas was to be crucified until he was released as a substitute for Jesus (Mark 15:7). Hengel says, "All this would suggest that Barabbas was a member of the Jewish freedom movement, towards which the people were to some extent sympathetic. Political murder was frequently committed by the Zealots, who are also repeatedly mentioned as causing disturbances. The author of the Fourth Gospel characterizes Barabbas simply as a robber (Jn. 18:40), in so doing using the name that was so often employed by Josephus for the Zealots and with the same meaning" (Martin Hengel, *The Zealots* [Edinburgh: T&T Clark, 1989], 341).

19. Hengel, 341.

20. E.M. Blaiklock, *The Archaeology of the New Testament* (Grand Rapids, MI: Zondervan, 1974), 70; for a photo and description of the inscription, see www.bible-history.com/archaeology/israel/pilate-inscription.html (last visited January 17, 2007).

21. James S. Jeffers, *The Greco-Roman World of the New Testament Era* (Downers Grove, IL: InterVarsity Press, 1999), 113-19.

22. Jeffers, 131.

23. Philo, *The Works of Philo: Complete and Unabridged,* trans. C.D. Yonge (Peabody, MA: Hendrickson Publishers), 784.

24. Tacitus, *Annals,* 15.44.

25. Eusebius Pamhilus, *Church History,* 2.7 (*NPNF* 2.1:110).

26. His wife Claudia Procula was made a saint by the Eastern Church, which celebrates a feast in her honor on October 27 (Marcus Benjamin, ed., *Appleton's New Practical Cyclopedia* [New York: Appleton], 1910, 117).

27. They set forth indictments against Jesus different from the one that condemned Him in the Sanhedrin, that of blasphemy, since the latter would have no standing before the Roman governor.

Chapter 4—What Roman and Jewish Sources Said About Jesus

1. Pliny says "Sir…I have never been present at the examination of Christians, on which account I am unacquainted with what used to be inquired into, and what, and how far they used to be punished; nor are my doubts small, whether there be not a distinction to be made between the ages?…whether there be not room for pardon upon repentance? Or whether it may not be an advantage to one that had been a Christian that he forsake Christianity?…In the meantime, I have taken this course about those who have been brought before me as Christians. I asked them whether they were Christians or not? If they confessed that they were Christians, I asked them again, and a third time, intermixing threatenings with the question. If they persevered in their confession, I ordered them to be executed; for I did not doubt but,…this positiveness and inflexible obstinacy deserved to be punished…(Some) denied that they were Christians, or ever had been. They called upon the gods, and supplicated to your image…they also

cursed Christ…(Some) assured me that the main of their fault, or of their mistake was this—That they were wont on a stated day, to meet together before it was light, and to sing a hymn to Christ, as a god" (Pliny, *Epistle to Trajan* 10.96 [Radice, LCL]).

2. "My Pliny:

"…These people are not to be sought for, but if they be accused and convicted, they are to be punished; but with this caution, that he who denies himself to be a Christian, and makes it plain that he is not so by supplicating to our gods, although he had been so formerly, may be allowed pardon, upon his repentance" (Pliny, *Epistle to Trajan*).

3. "I therefore adjourned the proceedings, and betook myself at once to your counsel. For the matter seemed to me well worth referring to you, especially considering the numbers endangered. Persons of all ranks and ages, and of both sexes are and will be involved in the prosecution. For this contagious superstition is not confined to the cities only, but has spread through the villages and rural districts; it seems possible, however, to check and cure it.

"It is certain at least that the temples, which had been almost deserted, begin now to be frequented; and the sacred festivals, after a long intermission, are again revived, while there is a general demand for sacrificial animals, which for some time past have met with but few purchasers. From hence it is easy to imagine what multitudes may be reclaimed from this error, if a door be left open to repentance" (Pliny, *Epistle to Trajan*).

4. "In our case no such procedure is followed, although there was an equal necessity to sift by investigation the false charges that are bandied about, how many slaughtered babes each had already tasted, how many times he had committed incest in the dark, what cooks, what dogs had been present. Oh, what fame would that governor have acquired if he had ferreted out someone who had already eaten up a hundred infants! But we find that in our case even such inquiry is forbidden. For Pliny Secundus, when he was in command of a province, after condemning some Christians and having dislodged others from the stand they had taken up, was nevertheless greatly troubled by their very numbers, and then consulted the emperor Trajan as to what he should do in future, stating that, apart from the obstinate refusal to sacrifice, he had found out nothing else about their mysteries save meetings before dawn to sing to Christ and to God, and to establish one common rule of life, forbidding murder, adultery, fraud, treachery, and other crimes. Then Trajan replied that such people were not indeed to be sought out, but that if they were brought before the court they ought to be punished" (Tertullian, *Apology*, 2.5.7. [Rendall, LCL]).

5. Suetonius, *The Lives of the Twelve Caesars: Tiberius Claudius Drusus Caesar, XXV,* tr. Alexander Thomson (New York: George Bell & Sons, 1893), 318.

6. The expulsion by Claudius is referred to in Acts 18:2, where Paul's companions, Aquila and Priscilla, had been part of the group of Jews expelled from Rome (H. Wayne House, *Charts of the New Testament* [Grand Rapids: Zondervan, 1981], 78).

7. Suetonius, 347.

8. "For what benefit did the Athenians obtain by putting Socrates to death, seeing that they received as retribution for it famine and pestilence? Or the people of Samos by the burning of Pythagoras, seeing that in one hour the whole of their country was covered with sand? Or the Jews by the murder of their Wise King, seeing that from that very

time their kingdom was driven away from them? For with justice did God grant a recompense to the wisdom of all three of them. For the Athenians died by famine; and the people of Samos were covered by the sea without remedy; and the Jews, brought to desolation and expelled from their kingdom, are driven away into every land. Nay, Socrates did 'not' die, because of Plato; nor yet Pythagoras, because of the statue of Hera; nor yet the Wise King, because of the new laws which he enacted" (Mara, Son of Serapion, *Letter* [*ANF* 8.737]).

To read the entire letter of Serapion, see www.earlychristianwritings.com/text/mara .html (last visited February 4, 2008).

9. Catherine M. Chin, "Rhetorical Practice in the Chreia Elaboration of Mara bar Serapion," *Hugoye: Journal of Syriac Studies,* http://syrcom.cua.edu/Hugoye/Vol9N02/ HV9N2Chin.html (last visited February 4, 2008).

10. See Farrell Till, "The 'Testimony' of Mara Bar-Serapion," *The Skeptical Review Online,* July-August 1995 (print version 1990–2002) (last visited February 4, 2008).

11. See the rebuttal by J.P. Holding, "Mara Bar-Serapion: Letter from a Near Eastern Jail: The Reliability of the Secular References to Jesus," www.tektonics.org/jesusexist/ serapion.html (last visited February 4, 2008).

12. "It was now that [Proteus] came across the priests and scribes of the Christians, in Palestine, and picked up their queer creed. I can tell you, he pretty soon convinced them of his superiority; prophet, elder, ruler of the Synagogue—he was everything at once; expounded their books, commented on them, wrote books himself. They took him for a God, accepted his laws, and declared him their president. The Christians, you know, worship a man to this day—the distinguished personage who introduced their novel rites, and was crucified on that account...

"You see, these misguided creatures start with the general conviction that they are immortal for all time, which explains the contempt of death and voluntary self-devotion which are so common among them; and then it was impressed on them by their original lawgiver that they are all brothers, from the moment that they are converted, and deny the gods of Greece, and worship the crucified sage, and live after his laws. All this they take quite on trust, with the result that they despise all worldly goods alike, regarding them merely as common property. Now an adroit, unscrupulous fellow, who has seen the world, has only to get among these simple souls, and his fortune is pretty soon made; he plays with them" (*The Death of Peregrine,* www.sacred-texts.com/cla/ luc/wl4/wl420.htm—last visited February 5, 2008).

13. Habermas, *The Historical Jesus* (Joplin, MO: College Press, 1999), 206.

14. Adolf Harnack, *The Mission and Expansion of Christianity in the First Three Centuries,* 2nd rev. ed., trans. James Moffatt (London: G.P. Putman's Sons, 1908), 266, 267.

15. Harnack, 290-311.

16. "About 250 AD, during the Emperor Decius' short but furious persecution, persons suspected of Christianity were evidently obliged to clear themselves by sacrificing to the old gods, then taking out a certificate to protect themselves against further legal proceedings" (William Stearns Davis, ed., *Readings in Ancient History: Illustrative Extracts from the Sources,* vol. 2 [Boston: Allyn and Bacon, 1912, 1913], 289).

17. *Foxe's Book of Martyrs,* ed. William Byron Forbush (Chicago: Winston, 1926), 11.

18. Quoted in Josh McDowell, *More Than a Carpenter* (Carol Stream, IL: Tyndale, 1987), 84, 85.

19. One such example may be found on an atheist site seeking to prove that Jesus did not live and that Josephus did not refer to Jesus. They quote the work of Rameus A., who argues that

    1. the *Testimonium* does not fit in the context of Josephus' works where it is found,

    2. no early Christian apologists quote from it; Eusebius in the fourth century was the first Christian to refer to it,

    3. it is absurd to think a Jewish Pharisee would say what the *Testimonium* says, and,

    4. early Christians had both opportunity and motive to create this spurious passage and they further were guilty of creating apocryphal documents.

    Such assertions do not address honestly the arguments of some researchers who, while admitting that there likely are some interpolations in the *Testimonium*, nevertheless find reasons to accept portions of it as authentic.

20. Christopher Price, "Did Josephus Refer to Jesus? A Thorough Review of the *Testimonium Flavianum*" (2004, 2007), www.bede.org.uk/josephus.htm.

21. Flavius Josephus, *Antiquities* 18.63, William Wiston, trans., *The Works of Josephus* (Peabody, MA: Hendrickson, 1987). For discussion on the wording see H. Wayne House, *Chronological and Background Charts of the New Testament* (Grand Rapids, MI: Zondervan, 2000), 76. See also C.K. Barrett, *The New Testament Backgrounds, Selected Documents* (New York: Harper and Row, 1961), 196-201.

22. Babylonian Talmud, Tractate Sanhedrin 43a. For discussion see House, *Charts,* 77.

23. Rabbi Michael J. Cook, "References to Jesus in Early Rabbinic Literature," www .bc.edu/research/cjl/meta-elements/text/cjrelations/resources/articles/cook_rabbis_ and_jesus.htm.

24. Dennis McKinsey, "Ancient Hebrew (Talmud) Account of Christ," http://skeptically .org/bible/id4.html 1-19-2008, 57 (last visited January 19, 2008).

25. John Patrick, *The Apology of Origen in Reply to Celsus* (Edinburgh: William Blackwood and Sons, 1892), 5; also William Turner, "Celsus the Platonist," in *The Catholic Encyclopedia*, www.newadvent.org/cathen/03490a.htm (last visited April 6, 2008).

Chapter 5—What the Early Church Believed About Jesus

1. Dan Brown, *The Da Vinci Code* (New York: Doubleday, 2003), 253.

2. Clement, *First Epistle of Clement to the Corinthians,* 1, 16, 20, 24, 36 (*ANF* 1.5, 9, 11, 14).

3. Ignatius, *Epistle of Ignatius to the Ephesians,* 7 (*ANF* 1.96).

4. Polycarp, *Epistle of Polycarp to the Philippians,* 2, 12 (*ANF* 1.33, 35).

5. Mathetes, *The Epistle of Mathetes to Diognetus,* 7 (*ANF* 1.27).

6. Mathetes, 7, 9, 10 (*ANF* 1.27, 1.28, 1.29).

7. Justin Martyr, *The First Apology of Justin,* 17, 4, 23 (*ANF* 1.168, 1.164, 1.170).

8. Justin Martyr, *The First Apology,* 63 (*ANF* 1.184).

9. Justin Martyr, *Dialogue With Trypho,* 36 (*ANF* 1.212).

10. Justin Martyr, *Dialogue,* 56 (*ANF* 1.223).

11. Justin Martyr, *Dialogue,* 61 (*ANF* 1.227).

12. Justin Martyr, *Dialogue,* 58 (*ANF* 1.225).

13. Irenaeus, *Against Heresies,* 1.10.1 (*ANF* 1.330).

14. Irenaeus, 2.23.4 (*ANF* 1.391).

15. Irenaeus, 3.6.1 (*ANF* 1.418).

16. Irenaeus, 3.8.3 (*ANF* 1.421).

17. Irenaeus, 3.11.6 (*ANF* 1.427).

18. Irenaeus,4.16.2 (*ANF* 1.440).

19. Irenaeus, 5.27.2 (*ANF* 1.556).

20. Theophilus, *To Autolycus,* 2.15 (*ANF* 2.100).

21. Theophilus, 2.22 (*ANF* 2.103).

22. Athenagoras, *A Plea for the Christians,* 10 (*ANF* 2.133).

23. Athenagoras, 12 (*ANF* 2.134).

24. Athenagoras, 24 (*ANF* 2.141).

25. Clement of Alexandria, *Exhortation to the Heathen,* 1 (*ANF* 2.173).

26. Clement of Alexandria, *Exhortation to the Heathen,* 10 (*ANF* 2.201).

27. Clement of Alexandria, *The Instructor,* 1.5, 6 (*ANF* 2.215, 216).

28. Clement of Alexandria, *The Instructor, A Hymn to Christ the Savior* (*ANF* 2.296).

29. Tertullian, *Against Praxeas,* 2 (*ANF* 3.598).

30. Tertullian, *The Prescription Against Heretics,* 13 (*ANF* 3.249).

31. Tertullian, *The Prescription Against Heretics,* 13 (*ANF* 3.249).

32. Tertullian, *Against Marcion,* 3.20 (*ANF* 3.338).

33. Tertullian, *Against Marcion,* 4 (*ANF* 3.345-423).

34. Tertullian, *Against Marcion,* 3 (*ANF* 3.328); 4 (*ANF* 3.345-423).

35. Origen, *De Principiis, Preface* 4, 1.2.10 (*ANF* 4.240, 250).

36. Origen, *De Principiis,* 1.3.4 (*ANF* 4.252).

37. Origen, *Commentary on the Gospel of John,* 1.11 (*ANF* 10.303).

38. Origen, *Commentary on the Gospel of John,* 2.6 (*ANF* 10.328).

39. Origen, *Commentary on the Gospel of John,* 2.6 (*ANF* 10.328).

40. Hippolytus, *Treatise on Christ and Antichrist,* 4 (*ANF* 5.204).

41. Hippolytus, 26 (*ANF* 5.206).

42. Hippolytus, 67 (*ANF* 5.219).

43. Cyprian, *Treatise XII,* 2.8 (*ANF* 5.515).

44. Cyprian, "The Seventh Council of Carthage Under Cyprian," Prooemium (ANF 567).

45. Cyprian, "The Seventh Council."

46. Novatian, *A Treatise Concerning the Trinity,* 10 (*ANF* 5.619).

47. Novatian, 21 (*ANF* 5.632).

48. Novatian, 12 (*ANF* 5.621).

49. Novatian, 30 (*ANF* 5.642); see John 20:28.

50. Jerald C. Brauer, ed. *The Westminster Dictionary of Church History* (Philadelphia: Westminster Press, 1971), 245.

51. The Old Roman Creed is a combination of a short Trinitarian confession and an early Christian kerygma that probably traced back to the Matthian baptismal confession and the message of the apostolic preaching (Brauer, ed., 246).

52. The Creed says, "And in one Lord Jesus Christ, the only-begotten Son of God, begotten of the Father before all worlds, God of God, Light of Light, very God of very God, begotten, not made, being of one substance with the Father" (*NPNF* 2.14.3).

53. The difference between the two words is in the one letter, the Greek letter *iota*, which is equivalent to our letter "i." Some have criticized the church for allowing such a bitter doctrinal dispute and division to develop over a "diphthong." The difference, however, is profound. Arius could agree to the word *homoiousios,* but the Council of Nicaea and the Council of Constantinople in 381 realized that this word did not go far enough in exactly describing the essence Christ shared with his Father. If Christ did not share this essence with the Father in every way, then He was not fully God. Therefore, both councils insisted that Christians confess Jesus to be *homoousios,* of the same essence as the Father, God of God, Light of Light, very God of very God. If this battle was not won, the difference of the Christian message from that of the pagan world would vanish, and Jesus would be reduced to just another semidivine deity typical to that of the ancient world.

    Wayne Grudem sums it up well when he writes, "But the difference between the two words was profound, and the presence or absence of the iota really did mark the difference between biblical Christianity, with a true doctrine of the Trinity, and a heresy that did not accept the full deity of Christ and therefore was nontrinitarian and ultimately destructive to the whole Christian faith" (Wayne Grudem, *Systematic Theology* [Grand Rapids, MI: Zondervan, 1995], 244-45).

54. Grudem, 245.

55. Grudem, 556. The Chalcedonian Definition refined theological refutations against the following errors regarding the person of Christ: 1) Against Apollinaris, who claimed that Christ had no human mind or soul: "*truly man,* of a *reasonable soul* and body... *consubstantial with us* according to his Manhood; in all things like unto us." 2) Against Nestorius, who claimed that Christ was two persons united in one body: "indivisibly, inseparably...concurring in *one Person* and one subsistence, not parted or divided into two persons." 3) Against Monophysitism (Eutychianism), which claimed that Christ had one nature, His human nature absorbed in union with the divine nature: "to be acknowledged in *two natures, inconfusedly, unchangeable*...the distinction of natures being by no means taken away by the union, but rather the property of each nature *being preserved.*"

56. *Consubstantial* means possessing the same "substance," essence, or nature of something else.

57. Sinclair B. Ferguson, David F. Wright, and J.I. Packer, eds. *New Dictionary of Theology* (Downers Grove, IL: InterVarsity, 1998), 180.

58. Ferguson et al., 180.

Chapter 6—The Prophecy of False Messiahs

1. See the words of Alberto Ferreiro, "Moreover, prophetic revelations do not follow any strict historical chronological order or perspective. A single prophecy may at times contain predictions about events in the immediate or distant future. We witness these same phenomena in the New Testament in prophecies attributed to Jesus. Matthew 24 is a clear example. Numerous scholars point out that immediate prophecy also served as types and figures of future events so that a single prophecy had potential application for a contemporary situation in the prophet's lifetime and the distant future. Most of the church fathers, with the exception of those who followed Theodore of Mopsuestia, who limited themselves to the prophecies singled out by the New Testament, were convinced that all of the prophecies, even the Psalter, spoke of Christ either in explicit or veiled ways" (Alberto Ferreiro, "The Twelve Prophets," *The Ancient Christian Commentary on Scripture, Old Testament,* vol. 14 [Downers Grove, IL: InterVarsity Press, 2003], xix).

2. Some have viewed the predictions of Jesus to refer to the destruction of Jerusalem a few years away, while others believe these are about the coming tribulation that will immediately precede the second coming of Jesus the Messiah in power and glory:

> Expositors are widely separated as to how far these signs were to extend. G. Campbell Morgan holds that the entire section up to Matthew 24:22 relates to the destruction of Jerusalem. Morgan states, "Everything predicted from verse six to verse twenty-two [in Matthew 24] was fulfilled to the letter in connection with the Fall of Jerusalem within a generation." (G. Campbell Morgan, *The Gospel According to Matthew* [New York, 1929], p. 286). In arriving at this conclusion, he agrees with Alfred Plummer, who takes Matthew 24:4-14 as *"Events which must precede the End,"* and Matthew 24:15-28 as *"Events Connected With the Destruction of Jerusalem,"* going further than Morgan in making even the second coming of Christ fulfilled in AD 70 (Alfred Plummer, *An Exegetical Commentary on the Gospel according to S. Matthew* [London, 1909], pp. 330, 332. Quotation in italics in original).

> What both Morgan and Plummer fail to comprehend, however, is that the events beginning with Matthew 24:15 clearly are identified with the "great tribulation" (Matt. 24:21), which in both the Old and New Testaments is related immediately to the second coming of Christ as a future glorious event. Further, it cannot be demonstrated with any reasonable exegesis of this or other passages that the second coming of Christ was fulfilled in AD 70. It is simply not true that the prophecy has been fulfilled to the letter. Accordingly, as will be brought out in later discussion, the interpretation regarding Matthew 24:15-31 as being specifically the end time and related to the second coming of Christ is far preferable and permits a literal interpretation of the prophecy. Significantly, both Morgan and Plummer avoid a detailed exegesis (quoted from John F. Walvoord "Christ's Olivet Discourse on the Time of the End; Part II: Prophecies Fulfilled in the Present Age," *Bibliotheca Sacra,* vol. 128 [1971], no. 511, 206-14).

3. There is considerable disagreement over whether or not these false christs are to be

equated with the antichrists or the Antichrist mentioned elsewhere in the NT. Stressing their distinction, the false christs are said to be those who make false claims to be the Messiah, impersonate Him, and allow others to proclaim them as such. Stressing their equality, it is argued that the false christs' very act of impersonating Christ is akin to the Antichrist's attempt to usurp His position and pervert His teaching. Like the antichrists, the false christs are active opponents of Christ, seeking to undo His work and teaching (1 John 2:18,22; 4:3; 2 John 7), like the supreme Antichrist of the last days (2 Thessalonians 2:1-12; Rev. 13:1-10). See also Colin Brown, ed., *New International Dictionary of New Testament Theology* (Grand Rapids, MI: Zondervan, 1979), 1:124-26; Duane F. Watson, "False Christs," in D.N. Freedman, ed., *The Anchor Bible Dictionary* (New York: Doubleday, 1992), 2:761.

4. "Another probable reference to the Antichrist is 'the man of lawlessness' (2 Thes. 2:3). The passage is difficult to interpret, but the person described seems to be the same person later designated by John as the Beast. Both the apostles Paul and John saw present events as leading up to the events of the future. Instructing the church at Thessalonica about the second coming of Christ (2 Thes. 2:1-12), Paul stressed that the appearance and rebellion of the man of lawlessness must occur beforehand. That man would oppose the worship of any gods or God and even proclaim himself to be God (2 Thes. 2:4). He would subsequently be destroyed by Christ at his return (2 Thes. 2:8)—an indication that those events are set in the final days of history" (W.A. Elwell and P.W. Comfort, eds., *Tyndale Bible Dictionary* [Wheaton, Il: Tyndale House Publishers, 2001], 65).

5. "In the book of Revelation, John's symbol for the Antichrist is probably 'the beast' (Rev. 13:1-18; 17:3, 7-17). The Beast is described, not only as an opposer of Christ, but more specifically as a satanically inspired Christ-counterfeit. Although the Beast (Antichrist) is clearly distinguishable from the Lamb (Christ), he receives worship from everyone except God's elect" (*The Tyndale Bible Dictionary,* 65).

6. "The term 'false Christs' is used only twice (Mt. 24:24; Mk. 13:22). Although it has obvious similarities to John's 'antichrist,' the Gospel passages do not refer to 'a deceiver' or 'false Christ' in the singular as do John's and Paul's writings" (*Tyndale Bible Dictionary*).

7. P.L. Tan, "False Christs," *Encyclopedia of 7700 Illustrations: A Treasury of Illustrations, Anecdotes, Facts and Quotations for Pastors, Teachers and Christian Workers* (Garland, TX: Bible Communications, 1979, 1996).

8. Quoted in Tan.

9. For a discussion of the meaning and nature of these signs and wonders, see N.L. Geisler, *Baker Encyclopedia of Christian Apologetics* (Grand Rapids, MI: Baker Books, 1999), 481.

10. I rely in my dating in general on an unpublished article by Eugene Mayhew, "A Common Jewish Argument on Messianism: Mirror or Mirage," Appendix Two: *Encyclopedia of Messianic Candidates,* pp. 9-12 (paper read at the Second Annual Meeting of the International Society of Christian Apologetics, June 1-2, 2007).

11. D.A. Hagner, "Judaism," *New Bible Dictionary,* D.R.W. Wood, ed. (Downers Grove, IL: InterVarsity Press, 1996), 624.

12. G.W. Bromiley, ed. *The International Standard Bible Encyclopedia,* rev. (Grand Rapids, MI: Wm. B. Eerdmans Publishing Co., 1988, 2002), 1:666.

13. Meaning of "son of a star," referring to the prophecy of Numbers 24:17: "a star shall come out of Jacob," an Aramaic name given to him by his supporter Rabbi Akiva. Oskar Skarsaune, *In the Shadow of the Temple: Jewish Influences on Early Christianity* (Downers Grove, IL: InterVarsity, 2002), 52.

14. Stanely E. Porter and Brook W. R. Pearson, *Christian–Jewish Relations Through the Centuries* (New York: T&T Clark, 2004); and James Orr, "Christs, False" in The International Standard Bible Encyclopedia, rev. ed., James Orr, et al. eds. (Grand Rapids, MI: Baker, c. 1915, 1979), 1:1666.

15. Doron Mendels, *The Rise and Fall of Jewish Nationalism: Jewish and Christian Ethnicity in Ancient Palestine* (Grand Rapids, MI: William B. Eerdmans Publishing Co., 1992), 388.

16. Referring to rabbinic text about Aqiva and bar Kochba, Schäfer says, "The most famous among them is R. Aqiva's dictum that bluntly and unmistakably proclaims Bar Kokhba as the Messiah. The version in the Jerusalem Talmud reads:

    R. Shimon b. Yohai taught: "My teacher Aqiva used to expound: 'A star shall step forth from Jacob' (Num. 24:17) [in this way:] Kozeba/Kozba steps forth from Jacob."

    When R. Aqiva beheld Bar Kozeba/Kozba, he exclaimed: "This one is the King Messiah."

    R. Yohanan b. Torta said to him: "Aqiva, grass will grow between your jaws and still the son of David will not have come!"

    Peter Schäfer, ed. "Bar Kochba and the Rabbis," *The Bar Kokhba War Reconsidered: New Perspectives on the Second Jewish Revolt Against Rome,* ed. Martin Hengel and Peter Schäfer (Tübingen, Germany: Mohr Siebeck, 2003), 2-3. Schäfer doubts that Aqiva was original in the Talmudic text, p. 3.

17. Martin Hengel, *The Zealots: Investigations into the Jewish Freedom Movement in the Period from Herod I Until 70 AD* (Edinburgh: T & T Clark, 1989), 294, f.n. 350.

18. Apol 1,31.6 = Eusebius, *Hist Ecc* 4,8.4. See also *ANF* 1.173.

19. Yigael Yadin, *Bar-Kokhba: The rediscovery of the legendary hero of the last Jewish Revolt against Imperial Rome* (London: Weidenfeld and Nicolson, 1971), 125. See further the discussion of the bar Kochba letters in Peter Schäfer, ed. "Bar Kochba and the Rabbis," 8-9.

20. N.N. Glatzer, *Geschichte der talmudischen Zeit* (n.p., Berlin 1937), 40, quoted in Hengel, *The Zealots,* 301.

21. Archelaus, *Acts of the Disputation with the Heresiarch Manes,* 36 (ANF 6.209).

22. See examples of this in "Matthew 14–28," *Ancient Christian Commentary on Scripture,* New Testament Ib, Thomas C. Oden, gen. ed. (Downers Grove, IL: InterVarsity Press, 2002), 197-99; also see the *Didache* 16:1-8.

23. Raphael Patai, *The Messiah Texts* (Detroit: Wayne State University Press, 1979), xliii.

24. *Ani Ma'amim,* Jerry Rabow, *50 Jewish Messiahs,* title page.

25. Rabow, 152.

Chapter 7—The Rise of Alternate Christs

1. See David G. Harrell, "Early Jewish Christianity," *The Early Christian World,* I, Philip F. Esler, ed. (New York: Routledge, 2000), 154. We don't have any Ebionite writings, but they are discussed in a variety of church fathers, including Ignatius (*Epistle to the Philadelphians* 6 [*ANF* 1.82]), Irenaeus (*Against Heresies* 1.26.2 [*ANF* 1.351]), Origen (*Commentary on John* 11.12 [*ANF* 10.440]), and Eusebius (*Church History,* 3.27.1-6 [*NPNF* 2.1.158-59]).

2. Philip Schaff, *History of the Christian Church,* Chapter XI, "The Heresies of the Ante-Nicene Age," (Oak Harbor, WA: Logos Research Systems, Inc., 1997), quoted in www .ccel.org/s/schaff/history/2_ch11.htm (last visited April 17, 2008).

3. Oskar Skarsaune, "The Ebionites," *Jewish Believers in Jesus,* eds. Oskar Skarsaune and Reidar Hvalvik (Peabody, MA: Hendrickson Publishers, 2007), 421: "This was not a sect-name and was not a derogatory designation by outsiders. In the Hebrew Bible, *ebion* and *ebionim* are very frequently occurring terms, and they generally refer to those in Israel who are looked down upon by the rich and powerful, and who expect to be delivered by the God of Israel in the present time or in the eschaton. The *ebionim* are those within the people of Israel who are the primary addresses of God's salvation, now and in the future."

4. Apparently Epiphanius ascribed the beginning of the Ebionites as a specific group of Jews to the destruction of the temple. Biggs, "The Clementine Homilies," *Studies in Biblical and Patristic Criticism,* ed. S.R. Driver, T.K. Cheyne, and W. Sanday, vol. 2 (Piscatussy, NJ: Gorgias Press, repr. 2006), 181.

5. Eusebius, *Ecclesiastical History,* 3.27 (*NPNF* 2.1.158).

6. Epiphanius, *Panarion* 30; see also 18, 19, 29, 53.

7. G.J. Reinink and A.F.J. Klijn, *Patristic Evidence for Jewish-Christian Sects* (Leiden, Belgium: E.J. Brill, 1973), 20.

8. Renan correctly sets forth their departure from what became orthodox Christianity:

   Their admiration for Jesus was unbounded: they described him as being in a peculiar degree the Prophet of Truth, the Messiah, the Son of God, the elect of God: they believed in his resurrection, but they never got beyond that Jewish idea according to which a man-God is a monstrosity. Jesus, in their minds, was a mere man, the son of Joseph, born under the ordinary conditions of humanity, without miracle. It was very slowly that they learned to explain his birth by the operation of the Holy Spirit. Some admitted that on the day on which he was adopted by God, the Holy Spirit or the Christ had descended upon him in the visible form of a dove, so that Jesus did not become the Son of God and anointed by the Holy Ghost until after his baptism. Others, approaching more nearly to Buddhist conceptions, held that he attained the dignity of Messiah, and of Son of God, by his perfection, by his continual progress, by his union with God, and, above all, by his extraordinary feat of observing the whole Law. To hear them, Jesus alone had solved this difficult problem.

   When they were pressed, they admitted that any other man who could do the same thing would obtain the same honour. They were consequently compelled, in their accounts of the life of Jesus, to show him accomplishing the fulfillment of the whole Law; wrongly or rightly applied, they constantly cited these words, "I am not come to destroy, but to fulfil." Many, in short, carried towards gnostic and cabbalist ideas, saw in him a great archangel, the first of those of his order, a created being to whom God had given power over the whole visible creation, and upon whom was laid the especial task of abolishing sacrifices.

(Ernest Renan, *The History of the Origins of Christianity,* book V, "The Gospels," 32-33.)

9. Eusebius, *Ecclesiastical History,* 3.27, 4(*NPNF* 2.1.158). For more discussion of their theology, see Reinink and Klijn, 19-43.

10. Jerome, *Letter* 112, 4, 13: www.newadvent.org/fathers/1102075.htm (last visited January 8, 2008).

11. Epiphanius of Salamis, *Panarion* 2.15.3.

12. Renan, 34: "It is probable that this sojourn was prolonged for many years after the siege. A return to Jerusalem was impossible, and the antipathy between Christianity and the Pharisees was already too strong to allow of the Christians joining the bulk of the nation on the side of Jabneh and Lydda. The saints of Jerusalem dwelt therefore beyond the Jordan."

13. On the other hand, the Jews were also repudiating Jewish believers in Jesus, partly due to their abandonment of the city and move to Pella.

14. Justin, in his *Dialogue with Trypho the Jew,* mentions two Jewish groups, one of which he could fellowship, since even though they practiced the law, did not believe that Gentiles needed to, in contrast to the other who believed the law of universal requirement. See Justin Martyr, *Dialogue with Trypho* 48 (*ANF* 1.219).

15. H. Wayne House, gen. ed., *Israel, the Land and the People* (Grand Rapids, MI: Kregel, 1998). Richard Bauckham speaks clearly of their orthodoxy: "The patristic evidence about the Nazarenes is unanimous in regarding their observance of the Tora as the only characteristic worth mentioning that distinguished them from Catholic Christians. Even Epiphanius, who is unequivocal in regarding them as a heresy, admits he has no knowledge of heretical beliefs held by them. As we know from Jerome's excerpts from their commentary on Isaiah, they even viewed Paul and his Gentile mission with full approval." Richard Bauckham, "The Origin of the Ebionites" in *The Image of the Judaeo-Christians in Ancient Jewish and Christian Literature,* Peter J. Tomson and Doris Lambers-Petry, eds. (Tübingen: Mohr Siebeck, 2003), 162.

16. Quoted in Alister McGrath, ed., *The Christian Theology Reader* (Cambridge, MA: Blackwell, 1995), 139-40.

17. Epiphanius in his *Panarion* gives a good overview of Sabellius's views. See McGrath, ed., 108.

18. *The Christian Theology Reader,* 137.

19. Quoted in *The Christian Theology Reader,* 137.

20. *The Christian Theology Reader,* 273.

21. *The Christian Theology Reader,* 273. Elaine Pagels and others have said that the *Gospel of Thomas* is not truly Gnostic (which may be correct) but builds on Judaism, as do the canonical Gospels, and may even precede them in recording traditions from

Jesus. This last assertion is almost certainly wrong. See "Incorrect Understanding About Extrabiblical Documents" in chapter 9 for an evaluation of *Thomas* and other noncanonical works.

22. Quoted in *The Christian Theology Reader,* 137.

23. *The Christian Theology Reader,* 134.

24. Irenaeus says Polycarp, a disciple of John, handed the story down. See *Against Heresies,* 3.3.4 (*ANF* 1.416).

25. After the Jewish orientation of the church changed, ultimately leaving the teachings of the apostles, specifically John, long behind, the millenarian view of Cerinthus also became joined with his (Cerinthus's) false teaching. For example, Gaius, a third-century theologian, who strongly opposed Montanism's view of the millennial kingdom, and consequently that of Cerinthus on this topic, also opposed Johannine literature that taught similar ideas. (Gunnar af Hällström and Oskar Skarsaune, "Cerinthus, Elxai, and Other Alleged Jewish Christian Teachers or Groups," *Jewish Believers in Jesus,* Oskar Skarsaune and Reidar Hvalvik, eds. [Peabody, MA: Hendrickson Publishers, 2007], 492-95.) Eusebius, also an anti-millenarian, quotes Gaius: "And he (Cerinthus) says that after the resurrection the kingdom of Christ will be set upon on earth, and that in Jerusalem the body will again serve as the instrument of desires and pleasures. And since he is an enemy of the divine Scriptures and sets out to deceive, he says that there will be a marriage feast lasting a thousand years" (Eusebius, *Hist. eccl.* 3.28.2 [*ANF* 1.160]).

26. Hällström and Skarsaune, 489. Simon Magus is said to be the "father of *all* heresy" by the Church Fathers.

27. Hällström and Skarsaune, 489.

28. Hällström and Skarsaune adroitly aver,

> One can hardly speak of an incarnation in connection with this doctrine; inhabitation is closer to the point. The Christ of Ebion was more coherent, since the man called Jesus remained the same single individual also in and after baptism, whereas Cerinthus taught that a new person from an unknown world took possession of Jesus.

Hällström and Skarsaune believe Cerinthus was similarly close to Gnosticism (Hällström and Skarsaune, 491).

29. Irenaeus, *Against Heresies,* 1.26.1 (*ANF* 1.352).

30. Tertullian, *Against the Valentinians,* 4 (*ANF* 3.505).

31. Irenaeus, *Against Heresies,* 3.11.9 (*ANF* 1.429).

32. Irenaeus calls it "The Gospel of Truth, *Against Heresies* 3.11.9 (*ANF* 1.429). Tertullian, *Against All Heresies* (ANF 3.652).

33. *A Field Guide to Heresies,* www.davnet.org/kevin/articles/heresy.html, pp. 2-3 (last visited January 10, 2008).

34. Marcion's Luke was different from the canonical Luke and did not have important Messianic elements regarding Jesus.

35. Harold O.J. Brown, *Heresies: The Image of Christ in the Mirror of Heresy and Orthodoxy from the Apostles to the Present* (Garden City, NJ: Doubleday, 1984), 61. See also Everett

Ferguson, *Church History, vol. 1: From Christ to Pre-Reformation* (Grand Rapids, MI: Zondervan, 2005), 86-89.

36. Robert L. Marrott, "A Collection of Isms," class notes for Rel. 352, BYU Idaho, http://emp.byui.edu/marrottr/352Folder/ism%20collection.html (last viewed January 10, 2008), 3.

37. Marrott, 6.

38. Marrott, 6.

39. Marrott, 6.

40. Augustine, *Confessions* 3.6-10.

41. *The Westminster Dictionary of Church History,* ed. Jerald C. Brauer (Philadelphia: The Westminster Press, 1971), 47.

42. Millard J. Erickson, *Christian Theology* (Grand Rapids, MI: Baker Academic, 1998), 715.

43. *The Christian Theology Reader,* 140-41.

44. Apollinaris writes, "We confess that the Word of God has not descended upon a holy man, which was what happened in the case of the prophets. Rather, the Word himself has become flesh without having assumed a human mind—that is, a changeable mind, which is enslaved to filthy thoughts—but which exists as an immutable and heavenly divine mind" (quoted in *The Christian Theology Reader*).

45. See Grudem, *Systematic Theology* (Grand Rapids, MI: Zondervan, 1994), 562-63.

Chapter 8—The Jesus of World Religions

1. Quoted in Carl E. Olson and Anthony E. Clark, "Are Jesus and Buddha Brothers?: If so, there's a serious family feud," www.catholic.com/thisrock/2005/0505fea1.asp (last visited January 15, 2008), 1.

2. Olson and Clark, 1.

3. Olson and Clark, 1.

4. Marcus J. Borg, "Jesus and Buddhism: A Christian View," *Buddhists Talk about Jesus, Christians Talk about the Buddha,* ed. Rita M. Gross and Terry C. Muck (New York: The Continuum International Publishing Group Inc., 2003, originally published as *Buddhist-Christian Studies* 19 [1999], University of Hawai'i Press), 79.

5. In an example of postmodern liberal thinking, Borg asserts, "All of the essayists cite problems generated by exclusivist and absolutist Christian claims about Jesus. I agree that the most prevalent forms of Christianity through the centuries have made such claims, and that they are (in Rita Gross's language) 'dangerous, destructive, and degraded.' But prevalent as these claims have been, I do not think they are intrinsic or necessary to Christianity" (Borg, 79).

6. "Raised in the flesh" was the wording of the early creeds, and is preferable since some have invented the idea of a human body that is not truly flesh but some kind of spiritual-material mixture, as though "spiritual body" (1 Corinthians 15:44) is the same as "spirit body," rather than the correct understanding of a physical body influenced by the Holy Spirit. See the important study of Robert Gundry in which he demonstrates that body, or *soma,* in the New Testament must be understood as

a physical body. Robert H. Gundry, *Soma in Biblical Theology* (Grand Rapids, MI: Zondervan, 1987).

7. V. Jayaram, "Did Jesus Live in India?" *Hinduism and Christianity,* www.hinduwebsite .com/hinduism/h_christianity.asp (last visited January 17, 2008).

8. See the Book of Mormon, 3rd Nephi 11 (1986 ed.).

9. Pandit Sutta, *Bhavishya Maha Puranan,* 3.3.17-31 (Bombay: Venkateshwar Press, 1917), 282. See also Holger Kersten, *Jesus Lived in India,* transl. T. Woods-Czisch (Longmead, Shaftesbury, Dorset, England: Element Book, 1986), 195-96; and K.N. Ahmad, *Jesus in Heaven on Earth,* 369, cited in James W. Deardorff, "Survival of the Crucifixion: Traditions of Jesus within Islam, Buddhism, Hinduism and Paganism," www.tjresearch.info/legends.htm (last visited January 16, 2008), 4-8.

10. Jawarharlal Nehru, *Glimpses of World History* (New York: John Day Co., 1942), 84, cited in Deardorff.

11. Ahmad's teachings on Jesus and Buddha are found in "Buddhism—Jesus and Buddha," www.tombofjesus.com/core/majorplayers/buddhism/buddhism-p3.htm (last visited January 15, 2008).

12. Kersten, *Jesus Lived in India,* 177-78; *The Talmud of Jmmanuel,* ed. Eduard Meier (Mill Spring, NC: Wild Flower Press, 2001), 237; and www.tjresearch.info/paulconv.htm, cited in Deardorff, 4-8.

13. Mir Khawand bin Badshah, *Rauza-tus-Safa (The Gardens of Purity)* (Bombay: reprinted in 1852) vol. 1 of 7, 132-36. See also the secondary source: Ahmad, *Jesus in Heaven on Earth,* 358, 404; *Jami-ut-Tawarikh,* vol. 2 (1836), p. 8, cited in Deardorff, 4-8.

14. Omar Michael Burke, *Among the Dervishes* (London: Octagon Press, 1976), 107, cited in Deardorff, 4-8.

15. "Linkages between two God-men saviors: Christ and Krishna," www.religioustolerance .org/chr_jckr.htm (last visited January 27, 2008).

16. The author of this article gives the Eusebius quote from Church History, Book IV, and the Augustine quote in the following words: "Exact original citation unknown. Copied from: Kersey Graves, 'The World's Sixteen Crucified Saviors,' Adventures Unlimited Press, Chapter 32, Page 280. (1875; Reprinted 2001)." This is commonly the practice of those advocating Jesus' contact with other religions, or dependence on them. A reference is made to some wording supposedly to prove the point, but there is no clarity regarding the location of the quote or its context.

Graves, mentioned here, wrote his book at the end of the nineteenth century. He provided little or no documentation for a variety of extravagant claims about Jesus. His amazing claims and dubious supporting evidence are freely cited by several specious books and websites about Jesus. The quote of Eusebius is actually from Eusebius's *Church History,* Book I.iv.15, not in Book IV, and is in the context of a discussion on the faith of Abraham and Moses, not Eastern or pagan religions. The reference to Augustine is from the *Retractations* I.xiii.3, in which Augustine seeks to demonstrate the truthfulness of Christianity and that it was the true religion from Adam to the present. Augustine says, "What we now call the Christian religion existed amongst the ancients, and was from the beginning of the human race, until Christ Himself came in the flesh; from which time the already existing true religion began to be styled Christian." (*Retract.,* I, xiii, 3.)

17. Kersey Graves, *The World's Sixteen Crucified Saviors* (Adventures Unlimited Press, 1875; reprinted 2001).

18. Others give dates of 1477, 3112, 3600, 5150, or 5771 BC for his birth. Linkages between two God-men saviors: Christ and Krishna, www.religoustolerance.org/chr_jckr.htm (last visited January 27, 2008). These alternate dates are said to be in Padmakar Vishnu Vartak, "The Scientific Dating of the Mahabharat War," found at www.hindunet.org; and Graves, p. 279.

19. For a distinction between the classical view of Krishna and Hare Krishna or ISKCON, see H. Wayne House, *Charts of World Religions* (Grand Rapids, MI: Zondervan, 2006), chart 65.

20. The following webpage provides a fairly balanced perspective of Jesus and Hinduism: "Hinduism and Jesus," www.franciscans.org.uk/2001jan-goswami.html (last visited January 27, 2008).

21. "Jesus as a Reincarnation of Krishna," http://near-death.com/experiences/origen047.html (last visited January 27, 2008).

22. Bhagavad-Gita, 10:20.

23. Bhagavad-Gita, 10:12-13.

24. Stephen Van Eck, "Hare Jesus: Christianity's Hindu Heritage," www.theskepticalreview.com/tsrmag/3hare94.html (last visited January 27, 2008).

25. The Bhagavad-Gita says, "Arjuna said: You are the Supreme Personality of Godhead, the ultimate abode, the purest, the Absolute Truth. You are the eternal, transcendental, original person, the unborn, the greatest. All the great sages such as Narada, Asita, Devala and Vyasa confirm this truth about You, and now You Yourself are declaring it to me" (BG 10:12-13). Nothing in this passage provides anything that is remotely similar to Luke 2:25.

26. Bhagavad-Gita, 2.72.

27. Vijay Kumar, "God," www.godrealized.com/god.html (last visited January 27, 2008).

28. Kumar, "God."

29. Vijay Kumar, "Hinduism Revelations Vedas," www.godrealized.org/hindu/hindu_revelations.html.

30. Vijay Kumar, "John 14:3: Interpretation," www.rgveda.com/john/john_chapter_14_verse_3.html.

31. Vijay Kumar, "John 14:1: Interpretation," www.bible-commentary.org/john/john_chapter_14_verse_1.html (last visited January 27, 2008).

32. "Jesus as a Reincarnation of Krishna." Also see statements of these comparisons, with little reference to primary sources, by Clinton Bennett, *In Search of Jesus: Insider and Outsider Images* (London: Continuum, 2001), 340-41.

33. In the seventh chapter of his book, speaking of Krishna's birth and gifts that were allegedly presented to him, Graves claims, "Other Saviors at birth, we are told, were visited by both angels and shepherds, also 'wise men,' at least great men. Chrishna, the eighth avatar of India (1200 B.C.) (so it is related by the 'inspired penman' of their pagan theocracy) was visited by angels, shepherds and prophets (avatars). 'Immediately

after his birth he was visited by a chorus of *devatas* (angels), and surrounded by shepherds, all of whom were impressed with the conviction of his future greatness.' We are informed further that 'gold, frankincense and myrrh' were presented to him as offerings," (Graves, 65).

34. Carl E. Olson and Sandra Miesel, "Christ, the Early Church, Constantine, and the Council of Nicaea," www.envoymagazine.com/PlanetEnvoy/Review-DaVinci-part2-Full .htm (last visited January 27, 2008). See also Daniel Morais and Michael Gleghorn, "Did Christianity Borrow from Pagan Religions?" www.probe.org/cults-and-world-religions/cults-and-world-religions/did-christianity-borrow-from-pagan-religions .html#text19 (last visited January 27, 2008).

35. A passage in the Bhagavad-Gita that resembles New Testament teaching apart from the words of Jesus is the reference in BG 8:17 to the Hindu God Brahma about a "thousand ages" being as "one day." The New Testament statement "one day is as a thousand years, and a thousand years as one day" (2 Peter 3:8) seems to carry a similar meaning. But this does not prove that Peter borrows from some Hindu scripture, or even vice versa; they may simply express a similar thought by coincidence.

36. See the chart in the appendix.

37. Quoted in Bennett, 316.

38. Edwin M. Yamauchi, "Jesus, Zoroaster, Socrates, and Muhammad," *Christianity Today,* October 17, 1971, 7-11.

39. Tashi Tsering, Geshe Tashi Tsering, and Gordon McDougall, *The Four Noble Truths: The Foundation of Buddhist Thought* (Somerville, MA: Wisdom Publishing, 2005), 8.

40. Bhikkhu Bodhi, *The Noble Eightfold Path: Way to End Suffering* (Kandy, Sri Lanka: Buddhist Publication Society, 1984), 63.

41. Bodhi, 66.

42. Bodhi, 56.

43. Bodhi, 63.

44. Bodhi, 66.

45. Bodhi, 79.

46. Bodhi, 97-98.

47. Mark Durie, "'Isa, the Muslim Jesus," www.answering-islam.org/Intro/islamic_jesus .html (last visited January 18, 2008).

48. Passages from the Qur'an are from Maulana Muhammad Ali, *The Holy Qur'an: Arabic Text, English Translation and Commentary,* rev. ed., 7th ed. (Columbus, OH: Ahmadiyyah Anjuman Isha'at Islam, 1991).

49. See Domenico Bettinelli Jr., *Is Allah the same as the God Christians invoke?* www .bettnet.com/blog/index.php/weblog/comments/is_allah_the_same_as_the_god_ christians_invoke/ (last visited January 15, 2008).

50. These include the three major codices—Sinaiticus (fourth century), Vaticanus (fourth century), and Alexandrinus (fifth century)—as well as numerous other manuscripts, all of which predate Islam and Muhammad by at least 200 years.

51. Many factual errors are present in the Qur'an. Muhammad relied on an alleged

book called the Injil, rather than the four gospels. There is no evidence for the Injil's existence.

52. For further discussion of the name *'Isa* in Islam, see "Jesus in Islam, A Christian Perspective of Islamic Thought, His Name and Its Significance," www.itl.org.uk/Jesus/name.html (last visited January 16, 2008).

53. Durie.

54. Quoted in "Jesus in Islam." See *The Encyclopaedia of Islam,* vol. IV, p. 82.

55. See 1 Samuel 24:7,11; 26:9,11,16,23; 2 Samuel 1:14,16; 19:22; 22:51; 23:1; Daniel 9:25-26.

56. "Jesus in Islam"; see *The Encyclopaedia of Islam,* vol. IV, p. 82. For example, Maulana Muhammad Ali, though acknowledging that *Masih* may mean "to anoint," favors the idea of "one who travels":

> The literal significance of Masih is either *one who travels much* or *one wiped over with some such thing as oil* (LL). It is the same word as the Aramaic *Messiah,* which is said to mean *the anointed.* Jesus Christ is said to have been so called because *he used to travel much* (Rz, R), or because *he was anointed with a pure blessed ointment with which the prophets are anointed* (Rz). It is, however, the first significance, viz., that *Masih* means *one who travels much* that finds the foremost acceptance with the commentators as well as the lexicologists, and this lends support to the evidence recently discovered which shows that Jesus traveled in the East after his unfortunate experience at the hands of the Syrian Jews, and preached to the lost ten tribes of the Israelites who had settled in the East, in Afghanistan and Kashmir.

(*The Holy Qur'an,* 142, n. 424.)

57. For example, "The commentators *al-Jalalayn* say that Jesus made for his disciples a bat, for it is the perfect bird in make (sic), and it flew while they looked at it; but when it had gone out of their sight, it fell down dead. That he cured in one day fifty thousand persons, and that he raised Lazarus from the dead; also Shem, the son of Noah, who had been dead 4,000 years, but he died immediately; also the son of an old woman, and the daughter of a tax collector" (see T.P. Hughes, "Jesus in Islam," *Dictionary of Islam* (London: n.p., 1895), 231.)

58. *The Holy Qur'an,* 1056, n. 2496.

59. *A Greek-English Lexicon of the New Testament and other Early Christian Literature,* 3rd ed., rev. and ed. Fredrick William Danker (Chicago: University of Chicago Press, 2000).

60. For example, one Muslim commentator argues on this verse that "Ahmad or Muhammad, the Praised One is almost a translation of the Greek word Periclytos. In the present gospel of John 14:16, 15:26 and 16:7, the word comforter in the English version is for the Greek word Paracletos, which means Advocate, one called to the help of another, a kind friend, rather than Comforter. Our doctors contend that Paracletos is a corrupt reading for Periclytos, and that in their original saying of Jesus there was a prophecy of our Holy Prophet Ahmad by name. Even if we read Paraclete, it would apply to the Holy Prophet, who is a Mercy for all creatures (21:107) and most kind and merciful to the Believers (9:128)" ("Jesus in Islam").

61. Henry G. Liddell and Robert Scott, "Perikletos," in *A Greek-English Lexicon* (New York: Oxford Univ. Press, c. 1843, 1996), 1377.

62. I owe points 5, 6, and 7 to "Jesus in Islam."

63. The reader may consult my books on world religions and cults/religious movements to examine the various ways these religions are in conflict with each other. See H. Wayne House, *Charts of World Religions* (Grand Rapids, MI: Zondervan, 2006); and H. Wayne House, *Charts and Cults, Sects, and Religious Movements* (Grand Rapids, MI: Zondervan, 2000).

Chapter 9—The Quest for the Historical Jesus Since the Enlightenment

1. Only fanatical atheists or anti-Christians would deny the historicity of Jesus, as exemplified in the following comment: "It is obvious that no serious researcher could claim the historicity of Jesus, unless it were the savior of the dominating religion of the prevailing culture. So there's nothing but Christian prejudice which keeps even secular researchers from admitting non-historicity, except of course the small minority of those who do." Klaus Schilling, "The Denial of the Historicity of Jesus in Past and Present Arthur Drews (1865–1935)," www.egodeath.com/drewshistorymythiconlyjesus.htm (last visited January 28, 2008).

2. Darrell L. Bock, *Studying the Historical Jesus: A Guide to Sources and Methods* (Grand Rapids: Baker Book House, 2002), 141.

3. H.S. Reimarus, *Fragments,* ed. C.H. Talbert, tr. Ralph S. Fraser, Lives of Jesus Series (Philadelphia: Fortress, 1970).

4. Carl Friedrich Bahrdt considered Nicodemus and Joseph of Arimathea to be Essenes who were able to keep their association a secret. Jesus, as well, was connected to the Essenes, and through their help was able to fake His miracles, with Luke assisting in the various healings. Luke was also involved with providing necessary drugs that enabled Jesus to survive the crucifixion. After Jesus was well again, He then made visits to His disciples (C.F. Bahrdt, *Ausführung des Planes und Zwecks Jesu* (Berlin: n.p., 1784–1793).

5. Venturini had a similar view to Bahrdt, believing that the Essenes trained Jesus in His youth. The miracles were not supernatural. Unlike Bahrdt, Venturini did not believe that the crucifixion was a plot; he believed that Jesus really expected to die on the cross. However, after they observed signs of life in Jesus as they were preparing Him for burial, Nicodemus and Joseph of Arimathea contacted the Essenes, who took away His body. After Jesus regained His health, He visited His disciples. K.H. Venturini, *Natürliche Geschichte des grossen Propheten von Nazareth* (3 vols., Bethlehem: n.p., 1800-1802).

6. Albert Schweitzer, *The Quest of the Historical Jesus* (New York: Macmillan, 1968), 38. See the works of Bahrdt and Venturini mentioned in notes 4 and 5.

7. Schweitzer, 38-47.

8. Many other scholars are important for this period, such as Christian Weisse, Bruno Bauer, and Ernest Renan, but space does not permit examination of each person's contribution.

9. David F. Strauss, *The Life of Jesus Critically Examined,* 2nd ed., trans. G. Eliot (New York: MacMillan, 1892).

10. Schweitzer, 51.

11. Strauss, 140-41.

12. Adolf Schlatter, *The History of the Christ: The Foundation of New Testament Theology*, trans. Andreas J. Köstenberger of *Die Geschichte des Christus* (Grand Rapids: Baker Books, 1997).

13. Alfred Edersheim, *The Life and Times of Jesus the Messiah*, updated ed. (Peabody, MA: Hendrickson Publishers, 1993). This work is still profitably used by students of the New Testament.

14. Martin Kähler, *The So-Called Historical Jesus and the Historic Biblical Christ*, trans. Carl E. Braaten (Philadelphia: Fortress, 1964).

15. Kähler, 92.

16. "I wish to summarize my cry of warning in a form intentionally audacious: *The historical Jesus of modern authors conceals from us the living Christ.* The Jesus of the 'Life-of-Jesus movement' is merely a modern example of human creativity, and not an iota better than the notorious dogmatic Christ of Byzantine Christology. One is as far removed from the real Christ as is the other" (Kähler, 43).

17. There have been a plethora of discussions on the messianic secret of Mark. Two helpful explanations have been offered. W.R. Telford has suggested that the claim of secrecy actually goes back to Jesus rather than being invented by Mark (W.R. Telford, *The New Testament, a Short Introduction* [Oxford, 2002], 139). Maybe this was done to deflect from the notion that Jesus would be the political Messiah often expected by the people. Or possibly His purpose was to provide for Himself and His disciples some measure of privacy. See James L. Blevins, *The Messianic Secret in Markan Research, 1901-1976* (Washington, DC: University Press of America, 1981).

18. Charles C. Anderson, *Critical Quests of Jesus* (Grand Rapids, MI: William B. Eerdmans Publishing Co., 1969), 73.

19. Charles Anderson, 72-73.

20. Charles Anderson, 74.

21. Hugh Anderson, *Jesus and Christian Origins* (New York: Oxford, 1964), 21-22.

22. Roth explains this tension in Strauss:

> Strauss wanted to harmonise faith and reason, and found himself unable to do so. Thus at the beginning of his *Life* he draws up a series of methods for detecting the unhistorical elements of the Gospels, searching for the impossible and inconsistent; at every turn he concludes that the unhistorical is no mistake, not the blindness of simple minds, but a calculated and cynical effort to construct rhetorically a Christ who would tally with messianic expectations from the Old Testament, so as to promote belief. Thus the narrated events become symbolic, or rather mythical, in the classical sense of the term. Strauss expends 700 pages accounting for every event of the Gospels in terms of this basic theory, and at the end of it, he still admits defeat at reconciling faith and reason, though he denies the success of those before him. Ultimately, Strauss' Christ can only be a useful fiction, propagated for the purposes of converting a primitive audience to a doctrine which would be historically beneficial.

Conrad H. Roth, "Varieties of Unreligious Experience," http://vunex.blogspot
.com/2006/05/lives-of-jesus-books.html (last visited January 28, 2008).

23. As Charles Anderson rightly concludes, "The liberals saw difficulties in places, but were
certain that through literary criticism they could arrive at an accurate picture of the
historical Jesus. As a result of the work of Wrede, German scholarship became much
more skeptical of the possibility of such an achievement" (Charles Anderson, 71).

24. More than 100 years before Schweitzer's pronouncements on the first quest, German
philosopher Gotthold Lessing, mentioned earlier, had declared that there was a "nasty
big ditch" between history and faith (N.T. Wright, *Who Was Jesus?* [Grand Rapids,
MI: William B. Eerdmans Publishing Co., 1992], 6-7).

25. Rudolf Bultmann, *Jesus and the Word,* trans. L.P. Smith and E.H. Lantero (New York:
Scribner, 1958), 8.

26. One may read Käsemann's essay in a collection of other essays edited by Craig A.
Evans, *The Historical Jesus: Critical Concepts in Religious Studies* (New York: Routledge,
2004), 8.

27. Evans, "Introduction," *The Historical Jesus,* 7.

28. James Robinson, *A New Quest for the Historical Jesus,* Studies in Biblical Theology, First
Series, 25 (London: SCM, 1959), summarized by Gary R. Habermas, *The Historical
Jesus: Ancient Evidence for the Life of Christ* (Joplin, MO: College Press Publishing
Company, 1996), 23.

29. Charles Anderson, 166.

30. Charles Anderson, 167.

31. Darrell Bock, *Studying the Historical Jesus* (Grand Rapids, MI: Baker Book House,
2002), 146.

32. Bock.

33. Norman L. Geisler, "The Quest for the Historical Jesus," *Baker Encyclopedia of Christian Apologetics* (Grand Rapids: Baker Books, 1999), 385.

34. Morna Hooker, "On Using the Wrong Tool," Evans, ed., *The Historical Jesus,* 443.

35. The perspectives of Jesus have been categorized under numerous rubrics:

   • Jesus the Myth: Heavenly Christ (Earl Doherty, Timothy Freke, and
     Peter Gandy)

   • Jesus the Myth: Man of the Indefinite Past (Alvar Ellegard and G.A.
     Wells)

   • Jesus the Hellenistic Hero (Gregory Riley)

   • Jesus the Revolutionary (Robert Eisenman)

   • Jesus the Wisdom Sage (John Dominic Crossan, Robert Funk, Burton
     Mack, Stephen J. Patterson)

   • Jesus the Man of the Spirit (Marcus Borg, Stevan Davies, Géza Vermes)

   • Jesus the Prophet of Social Change (Richard Horsley, Hyam Maccoby,
     Gerd Thiessen)

   • Jesus the Apocalyptic Prophet (Bart Ehrman, Paula Fredriksen, Gerd
     Lüdemann, John P. Meier, E.P. Sanders)

- Jesus the Savior (Luke Timothy Johnson, Robert H. Stein, N.T. Wright)

    See "Historical Jesus Theories," http://earlychristianwritings.com/theories.html (last visited January 29, 2008).

36. N.T. Wright says regarding this emphasis: "One of the most obvious features of this 'Third Quest' has been the bold attempt to set Jesus firmly into his Jewish context. Another feature has been that, unlike the 'New Quest,' the writers I shall mention have largely ignored the artificial pseudo-historical 'criteria' for different sayings in the gospels. Instead, they have offered complete hypotheses about Jesus' whole life and work, including not only sayings but also deeds. This has made for a more complete, and less artificial, historical flavour to the whole enterprise" (Wright, *Who Was Jesus?*, 14).

37. Habermas, 24-25.

38. Synthesized from Geisler, *Baker Encyclopedia of Apologetics,* and Bock, *Studying the Historical Jesus,* 149-50.

39. Geisler, *Baker Encyclopedia,* 386.

40. H. Cancik and P. Schafer, eds., *Geschichte-Tradition-Reflexion: Festschrift für Martin Hengel zum 70 Geburtstag, I, Judentum* (Tübingen: Mohr Siebeck, 1996), 27.

41. Geisler, *Baker Encyclopedia,* 386.

42. Wright.

43. Wright, 17.

44. Wright, 18.

45. Wright, 95-96.

46. Wright, 96.

47. Wright, 96.

Chapter 10—The Jesus of False Christianities

1. Millard J. Erickson, *Christian Theology* (Grand Rapids, MI: Baker Books, 1985), 738.

2. For a more in-depth look at various cults and sects of Christianity, see H. Wayne House, *Charts of Cults, Sects, and Religious Movements* (Grand Rapids, MI: Zondervan, 2000).

3. Francis J. Beckwith and Stephen E. Parrish, *See the Gods Fall: Four Rivals to Christianity* (Joplin, MO: College Press Publishing, 1997), 97.

4. For an excellent discussion on this topic see Jerald and Sandra Tanner's *Mormonism: Shadow or Reality?* (Salt Lake City: Utah Lighthouse Ministry, 1987).

5. For Mormons, "Christ is *Jehovah;* they are one and the same Person"; whereas "Elohim…is also used as the exalted name-title of God the Eternal Father" (Bruce R. McConkie, *Mormon Doctrine* [Salt Lake City: Bookcraft, 1977], 392).

6. "Jesus is greater than the Holy Spirit, which is subject unto him, but his Father is greater than he!" (Joseph Fielding Smith, *Doctrines of Salvation* [Salt Lake City: Bookcraft, 1954], 1:18).

7. Milton R. Hunter, *The Gospel Through the Ages* (Salt Lake City: Melchizedec Priesthood Course of Study, 1945–1946), 21.

8. James E. Talmage, *A Study of the Articles of Faith* (Salt Lake City: Church of Jesus Christ of Latter Day Saints, 1987), 472.

9. Hunter, 12-15.

10. Heber C. Kimball, *Journal of Discourses,* 8:211.

11. McConkie, p. 547.

12. Smith, 1:18.

13. *Jehovah's Witnesses in the Twentieth Century* (Brooklyn, NY: Watchtower Bible and Tract Society, 1989), 13.

14. *You Can Live Forever in Paradise on Earth* (Brooklyn, NY: Watchtower Bible and Tract Society, 1982), 58.

15. "Well, did Jesus ever say that he was God? No, he never did. Rather, in the Bible he is called 'God's Son.' And he said: 'The Father is greater than I am' (John 10:34-36; 14:28). Also, Jesus explained that there were some things that neither he nor the angels knew but that only God knew (Mark 13:32). Further, on one occasion Jesus prayed to God, saying: 'Let not *my* will, but *yours* take place' (Luke 22:42). If Jesus were the Almighty God, he would not have prayed to himself, would he? In fact, following Jesus' death, the Scripture says: 'This Jesus God resurrected' (Acts 2:32). Thus the Almighty God and Jesus are clearly two separate persons. Even after his death and Resurrection and ascension to heaven, Jesus was still not equal to his Father.—1 Corinthians 11:3; 15:28" (*You Can Live Forever,* 39-40).

16. *Should You Believe in the Trinity?* (Brooklyn, NY: Watchtower Bible and Tract Society, 1989), 15.

17. *You Can Live Forever,* 63.

18. *Reasoning from the Scriptures* (Brooklyn, NY: Watchtower Bible and Tract Society, 1985), 218.

19. *You Can Live Forever,* 58.

20. *You Can Live Forever,* 21.

21. *You Can Live Forever,* 138.

22. *Insight on the Scriptures,* vol. 1 (Brooklyn, NY: Watchtower Bible and Tract Society, 1988), 1189.

23. For a full discussion on this issue, refer to Roy B. Zuck, *Open Letter to a Jehovah's Witness* (Chicago: Moody Press, 2000), 8-11; or James W. Sire, *Scripture Twisting* (Downers Grove, IL: InterVarsity Press), 161-63.

24. Walter Martin, *The Kingdom of the Cults,* gen. ed. Hank Hanegraaff, rev. ed. (Minneapolis: Bethany House Publishers, 1997), 288. (Chapter on "The Theosophical Society" updated and edited by Gretchen Passantino.)

25. Martin.

26. Martin, 291-92.

27. Mary Baker G. Eddy, *Science and Health with Key to the Scriptures* (Boston: Trustees Under the Will of Mary Baker G. Eddy, 1934), 196, and the 1881 edition, 473.

28. Ernest Holmes, with Maude Allison Lathem, *The Science of Mind,* rev. ed. (New York: Dodd, Mead, 1938), 603.

29. Holmes.

30. Eddy, 332:19.

31. Holmes, 367.

32. *What Unity Teaches* (Lee's Summit, MO: Unity School of Christianity, n.d.), 3.

33. Others also claimed that Jesus was the Christ (John 20:31; Matthew 16:16-20; Acts 2:36; 9:22; 17:3; 18:5).

34. Erickson, 334.

35. Erickson.

36. Erickson, 335.

37. *The P.A.S.T.O.R.S. Course:* Theology, Book Two of Five, 114.

38. David K. Bernard *Meet the United Pentecostal Church International* (Hazelwood, MO: Word Aflame Press, 1989), 58.

39. Bernard, *Meet,* 59.

40. Bernard, *Meet,* 63.

41. David K. Bernard, *The Oneness of God:* Series in Pentecostal Theology, vol. 1 (Hazelwood, MO: Word Aflame Press, 1984), 66.

42. Bernard, *Meet,* 59.

43. David K. Bernard, *Essential Doctrines of the Bible* (Hazelwood, MO: Word Aflame Press, 1988), 8.

44. Bernard, *The Oneness of God,* 115.

45. Bernard, *The Oneness of God,* 57.

Chapter 11—The Jesus of Media Scholarship

1. Douglas Groothuis, *Jesus in an Age of Controversy* (Eugene, OR: Harvest House Publishers, 1996), 18-19.

2. www.westarinstitute.org/Jesus_Seminar/jesus_seminar.html (last visited April 17, 2008). Though the Jesus Seminar is the most famous of the Westar Institute projects, new projects such as The Jesus Seminar on Christian Origins, the Seminar on the Acts, and the Literacy and Liturgy Seminar are at various stages of progress today.

3. Ben Witherington III, *The Jesus Quest: The Third Search for the Jew of Nazareth* (Downers Grove, IL: InterVarsity Press, 1997), 43-45.

4. Robert W. Funk, et al. *The Five Gospels: What Did Jesus Really Say?* (San Francisco: Harper San Francisco, 1997), 2.

5. Funk, et al., 25. In practice, the seminar is 100 percent inclined, which indicates something far less than objectivity; it's a commitment to only one view.

6. Funk, et al., 7.

7. Funk, et al., 7.

8. Funk, et al., 27-33.

9. Funk, et al., 23.

10. Funk, et al., 27.

11. Funk, et al., 35.

12. Funk says, "Biblical scholars and theologians have learned to distinguish the Jesus of history from the Christ of faith...The distinction between the two figures is the difference between a historical person who lived in a particular time and place and was subject to the limitations of finite experience, and a figure who has been assigned a mythical role, in which he descends from heaven to rescue humankind and, of course, returns there" (Funk, et al., 7).

13. Funk, et al., 35.

14. Witherington, *The Jesus Quest*, 44.

15. Funk, et al., 2-3.

16. Funk, et al., 3.

17. Groothuis, 97. See also 41-50.

18. Funk, et al., 4.

19. As are all but one saying in the Jesus Seminar's version of John, John 14:26 was voted black (meaning they consider it inauthentic).

20. Jason Nightengale has memorized word for word several books of the New Testament, including John's Gospel, which is not a unique phenomenon. He makes a living reciting these books at churches and college chapels. See www.wordsower.org/index.htm.

21. Funk, et al., 5.

22. According to the Jesus Seminar, the story of the Good Samaritan teaches that we should expect help from unlikely places, especially from someone racially different than us (Funk, et al., 324).

23. Witherington offers this critique, "So we might ask how anyone as inoffensive as this could have generated so much hostility, much less get himself crucified. The Jesus of Jesus Seminar could never have ended up on Golgotha nailed to the cross. Yet the crucifixion of Jesus is one of the basic historical givens of what we know about Jesus... Since Jesus is characterized by the seminar as a man with a laconic wit given to exaggeration, humor, and paradox, he seems a much better candidate for a late-night visit with David Letterman or Jay Leno" (Witherington, 56-57).

24. Witherington, 57.

25. Sandra Miesel, "Dismantling the Da Vinci Code," *Crisis* magazine, July 8, 2004.

26. Ehrman says, "But like most historians who have spent their lives studying the ancient sources for Jesus and early Christianity, I immediately began to see problems with the historical claims made in the book. There were numerous mistakes, some of them howlers, which were not only obvious to an expert but also unnecessary to the plot. If the author had simply done a little more research, he would have been able to present the backdrop of his account accurately, without in any way compromising the story he had to tell" (Bart D. Ehrman, *Truth and Fiction in the Da Vinci Code* [New York: Oxford University Press, 2004], xiii).

27. Compare with the statements made by the Jesus Seminar above. Their factual errors are repeated in Dan Brown's novel.

28. Dan Brown, *The Da Vinci Code,* paperback ed. (New York: Doubleday, 2003), 253.

29. Brown is simply sloppy here. The Dead Sea Scrolls contain no Gospels, but are Jewish texts that make no mention of Jesus. Most were written between 50 and 100 years before Him. The "Coptic Scrolls" are Gnostic writings that include some "gospels" among many other works. They are usually referred to as the Nag Hammadi Library, and are not scrolls at all but bound books called *codices* (singular, *codex*).

30. Brown, 254.

31. Ignatius, *Epistle to the Ephesians,* 19 (*ANF* 2.205).

32. Justin Martyr, *The First Apology,* 43 (*ANF* 1.184).

33. Clement of Alexandria, *Exhortation to the Heathen* 12 (*ANF* 2.205).

34. Everett Ferguson, *Church History, Volume I: From Christ to Pre-Reformation* (Grand Rapids, MI: Zondervan, 2005), 191-95.

35. Rick Brannan, "Historic Creeds and Confessions" (electronic ed.; Oak Harbor, WA: Logos Research Systems, Inc., 1997), Article 12.

36. James M. Robinson, gen. ed., *The Nag Hammadi Library* (San Francisco: Harper San Francisco, c. 1978, 1999 ed.), 16.

37. Part of Jesus' "humanity" relates to Brown's claim that Jesus married Mary of Magdala and bore children through her. This demonstrates another example of Brown's "facts" being untrustworthy. He says it is a "matter of historical record" that Jesus was married, found in the Gospel of Philip: "And the companion of the Saviour is Mary Magdalene. Christ loved her more than all the other disciples and used to kiss her often on her mouth. The rest of the disciples were offended by it and expressed disapproval. They said to him, 'Why do you love her more than all of us?'" [Brown, 266]. The text that Brown, through Teabing, "quotes" *actually* says, "And the companion of the [...] Mary Magdalene. [...] more than [...] the disciples [...] kiss her [...] on her [...]. The rest of [...]. They said to him, "Why do you love her more than all of us?" The Gospel of Philip is in poor condition. All of the [...] marks are where the text has been destroyed. Some of those areas are actually missing *several* words. Dan Brown took the liberty of filling in the text to make it fit his plot. While the canonical Gospels don't mention Jesus being married, and there is no other evidence He ever was, this idea has gained popularity. From a theological perspective, it simply doesn't fit with Jesus' mission to preach the Gospel and be sacrificed on the cross.

38. Ferguson, 93.

39. See "Losing Faith," *Biblical Archaeological Review,* March/April 2007.

40. *Fresh Air* on National Public Radio, December 14, 2005.

41. *Fresh Air.*

42. Bart D. Ehrman, *Misquoting Jesus* (San Francisco: Harper San Francisco, 2005).

43. Bart Ehrman, *Lost Scriptures: Books that Did Not Make It into the New Testament* (New York: Oxford University Press, 2003), 1-2. Compare with discussion of Dan Brown previous.

44. Bart Ehrman, *Lost Christianities: The Battles for Scripture and Faiths We Never Knew* (New York: Oxford University Press, 2003), 1.

45. Daniel B. Wallace, "The Gospel According to Bart," online at www.bible.org/page .php?page_id=4000, 2007.

46. Wallace, "The Gospel…".

47. Wallace, "The Gospel…".

48. *Fresh Air.*

49. Ehrman, *Misquoting Jesus,* 55.

50. Ehrman, *Misquoting Jesus,* 54. Apparently, neither could Ehrman be bothered to give his best effort, since there are typos in his text. See note 86.

51. Ehrman, *Misquoting Jesus,* 89.

52. Ehrman, *Misquoting Jesus,* 207-8.

53. Kurt and Barbra Aland, *The Text of the New Testament,* trans. Errol F. Rhodes (Grand Rapids, MI: Wm. B. Eerdmans Publishing Co., 1981), 28-29.

54. Aland and Aland.

55. Darrell L. Bock and Daniel B. Wallace, *Dethroning Jesus: Exposing Popular Culture's Quest to Unseat the Biblical Christ* (Nashville: Thomas Nelson, 2007), 52-58.

56. Ehrman, *Misquoting Jesus,* 207.

57. Ehrman, *Misquoting Jesus,* 211.

58. In textual criticism, an error in one copy of the text is counted, no matter if it is the same error found in many, many other copies.

59. Again, in textual criticism, if there is a variant reading in one copy of the manuscript, it is counted, even if that same variant occurs in many, many other manuscripts.

60. Ehrman, *Misquoting Jesus,* 139-49.

61. Ehrman, *Misquoting Jesus,* 141.

62. Ehrman, *Misquoting Jesus,* 142.

63. Ehrman, *Misquoting Jesus,* 143.

64. Ehrman, *Misquoting Jesus,* 151.

65. Which, ironically, is where there is an error in Ehrman's book.

66. Ehrman, *Misquoting Jesus,* 159.

67. Ehrman, *Misquoting Jesus.*

68. This manuscript is the "Codex Bezae Cantabrigiensis" (also labeled D), so called because it once belonged to Theodore Beza and is now housed at Cambridge University. It was written by someone who is thought to have been a native Latin speaker but was writing Greek, who worked in Alexandria, Egypt, sometime in the fifth century. Kurt Aland, the premier textual critic of our age, describes this manuscript as "the most controversial of the New Testament uncials." He says D exhibits the "touch of a significant theologian" (Aland and Aland, 109, 110).

69. Ehrman, *Misquoting Jesus,* 159.

70. Justin Martyr, *Dialogue with Trypho,* 72 (*ANF* 1.260).

71. Greek manuscripts are labeled for identification purposes. See www.earlham.edu/~scidti/iam/interp_mss.html for a chart listing the manuscripts, their dates, and contents.

72. Metzger comments, "The Western reading, 'This day I have begotten thee,' which was

widely current during the first three centuries, appears to be secondary, derived from Ps 2.7" (Bruce Metzger and United Bible Societies, *A Textual Commentary on the Greek New Testament, Second Edition: A Companion Volume to the United Bible Societies' Greek New Testament*, 4th rev. ed. [New York: United Bible Societies, 1994], 112).

73. Ehrman, *Misquoting Jesus*, 207.

74. Wallace, "The Gospel…".

75. Bart Ehrman, from "Is There Historical Evidence for the Resurrection of Jesus?" a debate between William Lane Craig and Bart D. Ehrman, March 28, 2006, at College of the Holy Cross, Worcester, MA.

Chapter 12—The Jesus of Popular Religion

1. For the Byzantine Church, Jesus took on the features of an Eastern, Greek figure. When the Roman Church commissioned artists to produce images of Jesus, He became Roman. As the Roman Catholic Church moved into Northern Europe, Jesus took on the look of a German, Dutch, French, or English man.

2. In a short hymn honoring the triumph of Orthodoxy, written sometime around AD 900, we find an example of this reverence: "No one could describe the Word of the Father; But when he took flesh from you, O Theotokos (God-bearer), He consented to be described, And restored the fallen image to its former state by uniting it to divine beauty. And we proclaim our salvation in words and images." Leonid Ouspensky, "The Meaning and Content of the Icon," in *Eastern Orthodox Theology: A Contemporary Reader*, ed. Daniel B. Clendenin (Grand Rapids, MI: Baker Books, 1999), 34.

3. Ouspensky, 48.

4. Charles G. Herbermann, et al., eds., "Ecclesiastical Art," in *The Catholic Encyclopedia*, online version, www.newadvent.org/cathen/05248a.htm (last visited on January 21, 2008).

5. Geoffrey Miles, ed., *Classical Mythology in English Literature: A Critical Anthology* (Milton Park, UK: Routledge, 1999), 64.

6. "The crucifix is the principal ornament of the altar. It is placed on the altar to recall to the mind of the celebrant, and the people, that the Victim offered on the altar is the same as was offered on the Cross. For this reason the crucifix must be placed on the altar as often as Mass is celebrated" (Herbermann, et al., eds. "Altar Crucifix").

7. "Catherine completely objectifies Christ when she describes him as 'an open, overflowing font of blood: as a banquet table rich with sumptuous blood: as a bridge to the divine that consists of and brims over with blood…' This flow of fluids from the wound in Christ's side—the mixture of blood and water—is the concoction that shapes Catherine's soteriology" (Amy M. Indyke, *Saint Catherine of Siena: Permutations of the Blood Metaphor in Written Text and Painted Image*, unpublished thesis, April 23, 2007, Department of Religion, Harvard College).

8. Roland H. Bainton, *Behold the Christ, A Portrayal in Words and Pictures* (New York, Harper and Row: 1976), 200-201.

9. She has Jesus say to faithful young women, "Daughter, thou mayest boldly, when thou art in thy bed, take me to thee as thy wedded husband, as thy dear worthy darling… Therefore thou mayest boldly take me in the arms of thy soul and kiss my mouth, my

head, my feet, as sweetly as thou will" (James Clifton, *The Body of Christ in the Art of Europe and Spain: 1150-1800* [New York: Prestel, 1997], 19-20).

10. He made known to her His "burning heart" of love, His ardent desire to be loved by men, and His design of manifesting His Heart with all its treasures of love and mercy, of sanctification and salvation. He appointed the Friday after the octave of the feast of Corpus Christi as the feast of the Sacred Heart; He called her "the Beloved Disciple of the Sacred Heart" and the heiress of all its treasures (Herbermann, et al., eds. "St. Margaret Mary Alacoque").

11. In the late 1700s José de Páez painted a picture for devotion that featured a disembodied heart ringed with the familiar crown of thorns, and a cross protrudes out of the top. The heart is shown surrounded by angels. The pierce wound of the spear is shown as well (Clifton, 148).

12. "Religious scenes treated as gorgeous pieces of sumptuously coloured decoration, began to be seen" (Herbermann, et al., eds. "Ecclesiastical Art").

13. See Peter and Linda Murray, *The Art of the Renaissance* (New York: Thames and Hudson, 1963); and Richard Muhlberger, *The Bible in Art: The New Testament* (New York: Portland House, 1990), for various works and descriptions of the Masters.

14. On one page Jesus is shown chasing the money changers out of the temple with His whip. On the next page, the authorities are shown complaining to a figure looking very much like the pope. The book ends with Jesus shown being raised up to heaven while the pope figure is being thrown into hell (Muhlberger, 84).

15. Bainton, 196.

16. The medieval Roman Catholic Church did not allow laity to receive the chalice cup of the Eucharist. Dürer could be portraying this practice with the absence of the cup.

17. While he never banned images of Jesus in the worship setting, he changed "the way the mind grasps and articulates reality" (William A. Dyrness, *Visual Faith: Art, Theology, and Worship in Dialogue* [Grand Rapids: Baker Books, 2001], 53).

18. Dyrness, 54.

19. www.metmuseum.org/toah/hd/refo/ho_1982.60.35.htm.

20. It is speculated that it was a distinctly Lutheran theme supporting infant baptism, which was being challenged by the Anabaptists at the time. If so, this would be among the first uses of the image of Jesus for the purpose of one denomination arguing against the theology of another.

21. The bride and groom stand on either side of a table, surrounded by family. There are several people holding Luther's version of the Bible, and passages from that Bible hang on the walls behind the gathering (www.metmuseum.org/TOAH/ho/08/euwc/ho_17.190.13-15.htm).

22. Muhlberger, 23.

23. In *Holy Family with Angels* the scene is set in Joseph's workshop, where he is busily working away at a piece of carpentry. Mary is shown with a book in one hand (presumably the Bible) while she attends to Jesus in a crib with the other. It is a scene of tenderness and intimacy. There is a warm fire glowing in the fireplace, and the infant Jesus is bundled up in rabbit fur and blankets. He bears no outward indication of His

divinity; no halo or gestures of "the sign of blessing." It is a thoroughly humanized scene (Muhlberger, 23).

24. Jesus is shown looking directly at the viewer. He is also not on the cross, but is shown after the resurrection. His torso wound is barely visible. The look on His face is one of fatigue but also hopeful expectation. Also, Rembrandt is not depicting any specific biblical story.

25. Muhlberger, 23. For paintings, see www.nga.gov/exhibitions/2005/rembrandt/flash/index.shtm (last visited January 21, 2008).

26. Seen at www.metmuseum.org/toah/hd/rvd_p/ho_37.160.12.htm# (last visited January 21, 2008).

27. Bainton, 44.

28. Muhlberger, 123.

29. Muhlberger, 123-24.

30. Cynthia Pearl Maus, *Christ in the Fine Arts* (New York: Harper and Brothers, 1938), 106.

31. Maus, 137.

32. Bainton, 154.

33. Muhlberger, 85.

34. The landscape surrounding the cross is dismal and barren, replicating the battlefields of the war. Jesus, the men taking Him down, and the individuals around Him are gaunt and pale. Jesus almost looks as if He has begun to decompose already. His face and body are all but a skeleton with a covering of skin (Beckmann's *The Descent from the Cross* was seen at www.moma.org/collection/provenance/items/328.55.html [last visited on January 24, 2008]).

35. Bainton, 157.

36. Muhlberger, 122.

37. Bainton, 77.

38. In one painting that West called *Native American Supper,* Jesus and the apostles sit in a tepee around a campfire. There is a jug and a small plate representing the wine and bread. In another, West shows Jesus as an Apache, praying with a pained look. Even though surrounded by southwestern desert, it is an obvious representation of the Garden of Gethsemane (Bainton, 123).

39. Bainton, 157.

40. Chagall himself fled the rise of Communism in Russia (although he was a devout supporter of the party, Russian Communists were anti-Semitic), then the rise of Nazism in Germany, finally ending up in America.

41. Bainton, 119.

42. Bainton, 142.

43. James Gardener, *Culture or Trash?* (New York: Birch Lane, 1993), 170.

44. Dyrness, 116-17.

45. Eventually the photograph met its end when it was taken to Australia. Two youths

destroyed it with a hammer. Seen at www.museum-security.org/97/oct181997.html#2 (last visited January 18, 2008).

46. A storm of controversy surrounded Serrano and his work when it came to light that part of the funding for the exhibit containing Serrano's art came from public grants. The Southeastern Center for Contemporary Art, a recipient of National Endowment for the Arts funding, granted Serrano a $15,000 fellowship in April of 1989. It was at this time the work was done. See Philip Brookman and Debra Singer, "Chronology," in *Culture Wars: Documents from the Recent Controversies in the Arts,* ed. Richard Bolton (New York: New Press, 1992), 343.

47. Gardener, 190.

48. Gardener, 190.

49. Gardener, 190.

50. For a short discussion of one example, see D.A. Carson, *New Bible Commentary: Twenty-first Century Edition* (Downers Grove, IL: InterVarsity Press, 1994), Phil. 2:6.

51. The song never actually mentions the name *Jesus,* but is implied.

52. These women "took part in a 'tea with the Lord,' during which she and the other women wore their wedding gowns—those, at least, who managed to squeeze into them—and fancied themselves as brides of Christ" (Agnieszka Tennant, "Dating Jesus" in *Christianity Today,* December 6, 2006).

53. Seen at www.ihop.org/Publisher/Article.aspx?ID=1000010559 (last visited on January 25, 2008).

54. She says, "Many years ago I dreamed that I was standing in a meadow. Suddenly I saw a man approaching me. As he got nearer I gasped to realize that it was Jesus in Blue Jeans. When he saw the expression on my face he said, 'Why are you surprised? I came to them in robes because they wore robes. I come to you in blue jeans because you wear blue jeans.' I fell in love with him at that moment. There is something so familiar—and so powerful—about a man in jeans" (Laurie Beth Jones, *Jesus in Blue Jeans* [New York: Hyperion, 1998], xi).

55. Steve Lawhead argued that Christians should embrace any form of music because that is how Jesus would have it. Those who were critical he labeled "Pharisees" (Steve Lawhead, *Rock Reconsidered: A Christian Looks at Contemporary Christian Music* [Downers Grove, IL: InterVarsity, 1981], 95, 97).

56. Examples include K-LOVE and Air 1.

57. See www.klove.com/lyrics/lyrics.asp?2177 for Kristy Starling's version of Rimes's song.

58. See www.artistunitedforafrica.com/.

59. Tennant.

60. Paul Jones, in *Singing and Making Music,* says,

> In the past few decades we have witnessed the downward spiral of principle and excellence of church music whereby musical integrity has been abandoned more often from ignorance than by intention. Pragmatism, relativism, narcissism, and popular culture have invaded the church subtly masked

as stewardship, "progressive" thinking, and cultural relevance…They have taken a toll on church music and worship in the process. Much of this has come into play through the Contemporary Christian Music movement which, irrespective of taste, cannot be categorically separated from the secular cultural forces and mediocre music ideals that inform it, no matter how Christianized the texts may be.

(Paul S. Jones, *Singing and Making Music: Issues in Church Music Today* [Phillipsburg, NJ: P and R Publishing Co., 2006], 199-200.)

61. Richard W. Fox, *Jesus in America: Personal Savior, Cultural Hero, Natural Obsession* (San Francisco: HarperSanFrancisco, 2004), 292.

62. www.lyrics007.com/BobDylanLyrics/PropertyofJesusLyrics.html (last visited on February 15, 2008).

63. www.joanbaez.com/lyrics.html (last visited on January 28, 2008).

64. http://web.cecs.pdx.edu/~trent/ochs/lyrics.html (last visited on January 28, 2008).

65. http://artists.letssingit.com/jackson-browne-lyrics-the-rebel-jesus-ftmb6bf (last visited on January 28, 2008).

66. http://artists.letssingit.com/ray-stevens-lyrics-would-jesus-wear-a-rolex-4t5fdlx (last visited on January 28, 2008).

67. www.lyricsdownload.com/dead-kennedys-jesus-was-a-terrorist-lyrics.html.

68. Robert Vagacs, *Religious Nuts and Political Fanatics: U2 in Theological Perspective* (Eugene, OR: Cascade Books, 2005), 23-26.

69. Vagacs, 35.

70. Vagacs.

71. www.sweetslyrics.com/455291.JillSobule-JesusWasaDreidelSpinner.html.

72. http://artists.letssingit.com/doobie-brothers-lyrics-jesus-is-just-alright-j3hvsmj (last visited on January 28, 2008).

73. See www.stlyrics.com/lyrics/rememberthetitans/spiritinthesky.htm.

74. http://artists.letssingit.com/carrie-underwood-lyrics-jesus-take-the-wheel-8cdwsz1 (last visited on January 28, 2008).

75. http://artists.letssingit.com/mariah-carey-lyrics-jesus-oh-what-a-wonderful-child-gw88z11 (last visited on January 28, 2008).

76. http://artists.letssingit.com/bon-jovi-lyrics-i-talk-to-jesus-nxsj84f (last visited on January 28, 2008).

77. Robert K. Johnston, *Reel Spirituality: Theology and Film in Dialogue,* vol. 2 (Grand Rapids, MI: Baker Academic, c. 2000, 2006), 41-42.

78. Johnston, 43.

79. Johnston, 44.

80. Johnston, 44-45.

81. The movie was based on a novel by General Lew Wallace (1827–1905), which was published in 1880.

82. Matthew 28:19-20; Mark 16:15.

83. www.allmovie.com/cg/avg.dll?p=avg&sql=1:93405 (last visited on January 28, 2008).

84. www.allmovie.com.

85. Christopher Deacy, *Screen Christologies* (Cardiff, UK: University of Wales Press, 2001), 104-5.

86. http://store.aetv.com/html/product/index.jhtml?id=71943 (last visited on February 15, 2008).

87. http://store.aetv.com/html/product/index.jhtml?id=71399 (last visited on February 15, 2008).

88. From the Discovery Channel website: http://dhd.discovery.com/tv-schedules/special.html?paid=66.12344.81552.0.0.

89. Seen at http://dsc.discovery.com/convergence/tomb/about/about.html (last visited on January 30, 2008).

90. Tim McGirk, "Jesus 'Tomb' Controversy Reopened," *Time* magazine (online version), January 16, 2008.

91. Cindy Crosby, "Interview with a Penitent," *Christianity Today,* December 2005. Seen at www.christianitytoday.com/ct/2005/december/11.50.html?start=1.

92. Fox, 384-85.

93. www.whatwouldjesusdrive.org/. This website claims it is "A Discussion Initiated by the Evangelical Environmental Network & Creation Care Magazine, because transportation is a moral issue."

94. Dan Kimball, "I Like Jesus…Not the Church," *Outreach,* March/April 2007, www.outreachmagazine.com/library/features/ma07ftrilikejesusnotthechurch.asp (last visited May 2, 2008).

95. Kimball.

96. Kimball says the reason for this perception is that Christians live in a bubble with their own subculture, and if they would just reach out, people would change their view of the church. Kimball has parlayed his research into two books: *They Like Jesus But Not the Church* and *I Like Jesus But Not the Church.*

97. http://jasonclark.ws/2007/02/22/they-like-jesus-but-not-the-church/.

Chapter 13—Who Is the Real Jesus?

1. David Cooper, cited in Arnold F. Fruchtenbaum, *Rabbinic Quotations of the Old Testament and How it Relates to Joel 2 and Acts 2* (Tustin, CA: Ariel Ministries: Electronic version), 7.

2. Literal interpretation does not mean that a given statement has no figurative elements but that the statement should be understood in a normal way without resorting to deeper meanings not obvious in the text, such as spiritualization or allegorization.

3. Arnold Fruchtenbaum, *Messianic Christology* (Tustin, CA: Ariel Ministries, 1998), 146. "Other prophecies that fall into this category include Psalm 22; 110:1; Isaiah 7:14; 40:3; 52:13–53:12; 61:1-2a; Zechariah 9:9; 11:4-14; Malachi 3:1."

4. Fruchtenbaum, *Messianic Christology,* 148. "Other examples include: Isaiah 29:13 quoted in Matthew 15:7-9; Isaiah 6:10 quoted in John 12:39-40; Psalm 118:22-23

quoted in Matthew 21:42; Exodus 12:46 quoted in John 19:36. Many of the references to the books of Exodus, Leviticus, and Numbers in the Book of Hebrews fall into this category."

5. Fruchtenbaum, *Messianic Christology*, 149-50. "Other examples are the quotation of Isaiah 53:4 in Matthew 8:17; the quotation of Isaiah 6:9-10 in Matthew 13:14-15; the quotation of Psalm 78:2 in Matthew 13:35."

6. Fruchtenbaum, *Messianic Christology*, 151. Another example of this category is James 4:5.

7. Fruchtenbaum, *Messianic Christology*, 151.

8. Fruchtenbaum, *Messianic Christology*, 151.

9. Alexander, Bishop of the Russian Orthodox Church Abroad, *The Old Testament Regarding the Messiah: The Fulfillment of the Prophecies about the Messiah*, tr. Nicholas Semyanko and Donald Shufran, www.orthodoxphotos.com/readings/messiah/fulfillment.shtml (last visited May 4, 2008).

10. Alexander.

11. Michael Green, *Evangelism in the Early Church* (London: Hodder and Stoughton, 1970), 88, quoted in Richard V. Peace, *Conversion in the New Testament: Paul and the Twelve* (Grand Rapids, MI: Wm. B. Eerdmans Publishing Co., 1999), 191.

12. Alexander.

13. Peace, 191-92.

14. Peace, 192.

15. For a thorough defense of Isaiah 7:14 being a prophecy of the coming Messiah rather than a reference to someone born in the days of Ahaz, see Fruchtenbaum, *Messianic Christology*, 32-37; and Edward J. Young, *The Book of Isaiah*, vol. 1 (Grand Rapids, MI: Eerdmans, 1983), 283-292.

16. This quote is in the context of proving that Jesus came to offer Himself as a sacrifice, and that "we have been sanctified through the offering of the body of Jesus Christ once *for all*" (Hebrews 10:10).

17. Millard J. Erickson, *Christian Theology* (Grand Rapids, MI: Baker Book House, 1992), 684.

18. Craig A. Evans, *Jesus and His Contemporaries* (Boston: Brill Academic Publishers, Inc., 2001), 407-8.

19. Darrell L. Bock, *Blasphemy and Exaltation in Judaism: The Charge Against Jesus in Mark 14:53-65* (Grand Rapids, MI: Baker Books, 2000), 234.

20. Evans, 412-13.

21. Erickson, 706.

The Conclusion of the Matter

1. Some translations have wrongly translated *anathema* in Galatians 1:8-9 as "eternally condemned." This is a mistaken understanding of the Greek word for "curse," reflected in the Jewish view of "blessing and cursing" from the Hebrew Scriptures. Blessing is based on proper belief and obedience while cursing comes from disbelief and dis-

obedience (Deuteronomy 11:26-28). Nothing in this passage would indicate eternal damnation is in view.

Select Bibliography

❖

BOOKS OR ARTICLES ABOUT JESUS YOU MAY WANT TO READ

Anderson, Hugh. *Jesus and Christian Origins*. New York: Oxford, 1964.

Bainton, Roland H. *Behold the Christ, A Portrayal in Words and Pictures*. New York: Harper and Row, 1976.

Bennett, Clinton. *In Search of Jesus: Insider and Outsider Images*. London: Continuum, 2001.

Bock, Darrell L. *Blasphemy and Exaltation in Judaism: The Charge against Jesus in Mark 14:53-65*. Grand Rapids, MI: Baker Books, 2000.

—————. *Studying the Historical Jesus: A Guide to Sources and Methods*. Grand Rapids: Baker Book House, 2002.

Bock, Darrell L., and Daniel B. Wallace. *Dethroning Jesus: Exposing Popular Culture's Quest to Unseat the Biblical Christ*. Nashville: Thomas Nelson, 2007.

Bray, Gerald. *Creeds, Council and Christ: Did the Early Christians Misinterpret Jesus?* Geanies House, Fearn, Ross-shire, Great Britain: Mentor, 1997.

Clifton, James. *The Body of Christ in the Art of Europe and Spain: 1150-1800*. New York: Prestel, 1997.

Edersheim, Alfred. *The Life and Times of Jesus the Messiah,* updated ed. Peabody, MA: Hendrickson Publishers, 1993.

Evans, Craig A. *Fabricating Jesus*. Downers Grove, IL: InterVarsity, 2006.

————. *The Historical Jesus: Critical Concepts in Religious Studies*. New York: Routledge, 2004.

Fox, Richard W. *Jesus in America: Personal Savior, Cultural Hero, Natural Obsession*. San Francisco: Harper San Francisco, 2004.

Fruchtenbaum, Arnold. *Messianic Christology*. Tustin, CA: Ariel Ministries, 1998.

Groothuis, Douglas. *Searching for the Real Jesus in an Age of Controversy*. Eugene, OR: Harvest House Publishers, 1996.

Habermas, Gary. *The Historical Jesus: Ancient Evidence for the Life of Christ*. Joplin, MO: College Press, 1999.

Hurtado, Larry W. *How on Earth Did Jesus Become a God?: Historical Questions About Earliest Devotion to Jesus*. Grand Rapids, MI: Wm. B. Eerdmans Publishing Co., 2005.

Kennedy, D. James, and Jerry Newcombe. *What If Jesus Had Never Been Born?* Nashville: Thomas Nelson Publishers, 1994.

Kimball, Dan. *They Like Jesus but Not the Church*. Grand Rapids, MI: Zondervan, 2007.

Mayhew, Eugene. "A Common Jewish Argument on Messianism," Appendix two: *Encyclopedia of Messianic Candidates*.

Pelikan, Jaroslav. *Jesus Through the Centuries: His Place in the History of Culture*. New Haven: Yale University Press, 1985.

Price, Christopher "Did Josephus Refer to Jesus? A Thorough Review of the *Testimonium Flavianum*." 2004, 2007. www.bede.org.uk/josephus.htm.

Schlatter, Adolf. *The History of the Christ: The Foundation of New Testament Theology*, trans. Andreas J. Köstenberger, *Die Geschichte des Christus*. Grand Rapids: Baker Books, 1997.

Witherington, Ben, III. *The Jesus Quest: The Third Search for the Jew of Nazareth*. Downers Grove, IL: InterVarsity Press, 1997.

Wright, N.T. *Who Was Jesus?* Grand Rapids, MI: William B. Eerdmans Publishing Co., 1992.

Yamauchi, Edwin M. "Jesus, Zoroaster, Buddha, Socrates, and Muhammad: The Life, Death, and Teachings of Jesus Compared with Other Great Religious Figures." *Christianity Today*, October 22, 1971.

INDEX OF SCRIPTURES AND OTHER ANCIENT WRITINGS

SCRIPTURES

OLD TESTAMENT

Genesis
3:15 .... 50, 52, 107, 223, 224
34 ....265n6
41:51-52...............................163

Exodus.....................240, 298n4
3:15 ....159, 240
7:3 83
12:46 ....298n4

Leviticus...........................298n4

Numbers 298n4
24:17 .... 85, 275n13, 275n16

Deuteronomy
4:34 83
6:4 159
11:26-28..............................299n1
18:15-18.............................224
18:15-19.............................232
21:22-23 231
32:39 166

1 Samuel
10:1 48
24:7 ....283n55
24:11...............................283n55
26:9 ....283n55
26:11...............................283n55
26:16...............................283n55
26:23...............................283n55

2 Samuel
1:14...............................283n55
1:16...............................283n55
7:14..................................238
19:22...............................283n55
22:51...............................283n55
23:1...............................283n55

1 Kings
1:26 ....265n7
1:31......................................48
17:1-2.....................................23
17:3-6 ....262n25
17:14-16.................................23
17:17-24.................................23

1 Chronicles
17:10-14.............................232

Nehemiah
2:3 48
8:9 ....266n11
9:10......................................83

Psalms 123, 235
2 224
2:7 ....187, 238
2:7-8 187
22 ....50, 298n3
22:8 49
22:1-21 232
33:6 248
36 80
37 80
40:6-8 50
40:7 235
69:25 38
78:2 ....299n5
82:6 238
90:2 160
95:3-7 159
99:6-8 159
100:3 159
109:8 38
110:1 ....298n3
110:4.............................224, 232
118:22-23 ....298n4

Proverbs
30:4 38

Isaiah 23, 49, 88, 224, 225,
.................................233, 277n15,
6:9-10 ....299n5
6:10 ....298n4
7:14.......28, 233, 298n3, 299n15
9:6 167
9:6f 107
29:13 ....298n4
40:3 ....298n3
40:3-5.................................233
43:10 166
43:13 166
44:9-20.................................225
44:28 225
45:1 225
45:13...................................225
48:12 166
52:13..................................298
52:13-53:12 .... 49, 89, 224, 232,
                                   298n3
53:4 ....299n5
61 229
61:1-2.........................224, 229,
61:1-2a.......................233, 298n3
61:2b-7..............................229
78:2 ....299n5

Jeremiah 22, 226
1:16......................................24
7:1-15.....................................24
7:28 159
10:10....................................159
31:9......................................162
31:15.................................226
32:20-21 83

Ezekiel
13:3 38
18:31................................38
36:26................................38

Daniel 225
2:4 48
3:9 48
7:13-14 107
9:24-27 81
9:25 128
9:25-26........................283n55
9:25-27 81

Hosea
11:1..................................226

Micah
5:2 ....160, 226, 234

Zechariah
9:9 .... 298n3
11:4-14 .... 298n3

Malachi
2:10.................................167
3:1 .... 298n3
4:5 .... 22, 23, 224

NEW TESTAMENT

Matthew 16, 28, 41, 42, 44,
46, 47, 81, 92, 118,
138, 139, 147, 173,
225, 226, 249,
1:1-17......................................250
1:18..................................249
1:18-20 160
1:18-25 233
1:19.................................233
1:22.................................233
1:21......................49, 131, 166
1:21-23 28
1:24-25 28
2:5-6................................226
2:14-15 226
2:17-18 226
2:23.................................227
3:1-3................................233
3:7 44
3:7-10...............................32
3:15-17.............................244
4:2 251
4:11 .... 262n25
4:23.................................250
5:39-42a..........................175
5:10-12 123
5:16.................................125
5:17.................................224
5:44a................................176
5:44-45 118

6:9 176
7:28 42
7:29 46

8:1-3 243
8:4 47
8:5-13 251
8:10.................................251
8:11.................................251
8:17...............................299n5
8:22.................................118
9 237
9:2 237
9:6 ....45, 237
9:10-11 45
9:14...................................45
9:33...................................42
9:34...................................45
9:36.................................251
10:4...................................38
10:34...............................124
11:2-6 33
11:14.................................32
11:20-24 24
12:1-7 .... 266n13
12:6 .... 266n14
12:15-21 251
12:38.................................44
13:35..............................299n5
13:53-58 41
13:55.................................30
13:10-17 21
13:14-15 ....299n5
13:55.............................264n1
14-28 ....275n22
14:1-2 22
14:1-28:20 ....262n27
14:14-21 33
14:22-33.........................243
15:1-2 ....45, 46
15:7-9 .... 298n4
15:21-28 244
15:29-38 23
16 24
16:1...................................44
16:6...................................44
16:11-12............................44
16:13-17 ....21, 25
16:16............129, 166, 262n21
16:16-17 34
16:16-20 ....289n33
16:17...............................133
16:21 ......49, 266n12, 266n13
16:21-22 35
16:21-23 35
16:24...............................124
17:1-8 244
17:1-9 33
17:10-12 23
20:1-15 176
20:20-28 35
20:28...............................128
21:1-7 33
21:10-13 24
21:11.................................24
21:12...............................250
21:15.......................47, 266n13

21:23 .... 266n13
21:45-46 .... 266n13
21:42 .... 298n4
21:45-46 ....43, 266n13
22:15-22 46
22:21c..............................175
22:35 .... 266n12
22:45...............................129
23 32
23:3...................................45
23:13-29............................45
23:14.................................45
23:21-36............................44
23:23-24............................45
24 ....82, 225, 273n1, 273n2
24:1-25:46 80
24:3 ....81, 84
24:4-14 .... 273n2
24:14...............................251
24:15.......................81, 273n2
24:15-25 81
24:15-28 .... 273n2
24:15-31 .... 273n2
24:22 .... 273n2
24:23.................................82
24:21 .... 273n2
24:22 .... 273n2
24:24 ....79, 83, 274n6
24:27 83,
25:31-46 237
26-27 .... 266n13
26:3 .... 266n12
26:17-19 33
26:18...............................250
26:25.................................38
26:36-38 33
26:63...............................129
26:63-65 165
27:17.................................53
27:22.................................53
27:19.................................53
27:39-43............................47
27:40.................................49
27:42.........................49, 50
27:43.................................49
27:57-60............................38
28:7...................................32
28:10.................................32
28:19-20 ....207n82

Mark...........16, 41, 42, 46, 47,
49, 173, 185, 285n17
1:1 ....129, 138, 139, 140, 147,
1:11.................................244
1:21.................................250
1:44...................................47
2:15-16 ....45, 251
2:23-24 45
2:23-27 .... 266n13
3:6 ....44, 46,
3:17...................................35
3:19...................................38
3:22-29...............................45

5:26 122
5:35-43 129
6:1-6 41
6:4 31
6:30-44 129
7:1 44
7:5 44
7:24-37 251
8:27 20
8:29 25
8:31 .... 49, 266n13
8:31-32 123
9:13 32
10:45 .... 49, 128, 131, 266n14
11:11 250
11:15-18 47
11:27 ....266n13
12:17 175
12:24-27 45
12:37 ....21, 42
13 82
13:1-37 80
13:2 80
13:3 80
13:4 81
13:14 81
13:22 ....274n6
13:32 .... 104, 163, 251,
                        288n15
14:10 38
14:36 50
14:43 ....266n12
14:53 ....266n12
14:48 ....267n18
14:60-62 49
14:61 238
14:61-64 165
14:62 ....83, 238
15:2 ....53, 165
15:7 ....267n18
15:29-32 47
16:15 ....251, 297n82

Luke................16, 28, 29, 38, 47,
                        81, 101, 138, 140,
                        147, 173, 185, 212,
                        225, 228, 258,
                        264n4, 278n34
1:1-4 185
1:17 32
1:26-33 249
1:26-38 160
1:30-35 28
1:31-33 234
1:35 250
1:36 32
1:38 28
1:46-55 28
2:6-7 251
2:11 164
2:19 31
2:21 250
2:22 28

2:22-24 250
2:25 ....116, 281n25
2:25-35 ....115, 164
2:29-32 29
2:33-35 29
2:40 ....250, 251
2:52 251
2:41 29
2:41-42 250
2:46 ....266n12
2:49-50 30
2:51 ....30, 31
3:21-22 121
3:22 ....184, 186, 187
3:23 ....184, 187
4:16-22 234
4:17-21 224
4:18 129
4:18-19 229
4:21 ....165, 234
4:24-26 ....262n26
4:41 129
5:14 47
5:17 ....266n11
5:21 44
6:1-5 ....266n13

6:6 250
6:6-7 45
6:16 38
6:20-21 176
6:27b 176
6:29 175
6:30a 176
7:11-17 ....23, 129
7:28 32
7:36-50 ....243, 263n8
8:2 37
8:40-56 33
9:22 ....266n13
9:28-36 244
9:29 245
10:1 33
10:17 33
10:21 129
10:30-35 176
10:38-42 36
10:39-40 37
11:31-32 129
11:37 251
13:1 122
13:1-2 52
13:20b-21 176
16:1-8a 176
16:16 32
16:19-31 50
17:14 47
19:41 251
19:47 250
19:47-48 ....266n13
20:1 ....266n13
20:21-22 ....266n18
20:21-24 51

20:23 51
20:25b 175
21:5-36 80
21:7 81
21:20 81
21:24 81
22:36 124
22:42 ....164, 288n15
22:43 185
22:44 185
22:66 ....266n12
chapter 22 185
23:2 53
23:6-7 52
23:12 52
23:13-16 53
23:21 20
23:33 251
23:35 47
23:46 251
23:50-51 38
23:53 250
24:1-3 251
24:25-27 236
24:27 223
24:30 250
24:33-49 245
24:36-43 251
24:44-47 ....123, 235
24:52-53 245

John 16, 36, 37, 38, 69,
                        130, 140, 147, 156,
                        163, 172, 173, 178,
                        236, 237, 247, 248,
                        263n6, 290n20
1:1 .... 157, 160, 163, 178, 247
1:1-4 247
1:1-5 168
1:1-18 128
1:3 ....162, 163
1:14 ....75, 98, 248
1:18 35
1:29 131
1:29-36 32
1:40-44 228
1:45 ....34, 235
1:47-49 34
1:50-51 34
2:1-12 30
2:4 31
2:13 250
2:13-17 251
2:14-16 47
2:19 49
2:19 ....266n14
2:21-22 49
3 37
3:5 38
3:5 ....263n10
3:13 38
3:14-21 38
3:16 232

3:20 43
4:4-42 24
4:6 251
4:21-26 165
5 237
5:17-18 163
5:24 255
5:25-27 237
5:36 245
6:42 31
6:44 ....45, 125
6:60-66 33
6:65 133
7:2 250
7:2-6 31
7:5 31
7:14 250
7:25-52 47
7:32 ....266n13
7:45 ....266n13
7:50-52 38
8:3 44
8:21-24 21
8:24 166
8:28 166
8:51 239
8:54-55 129
8:58 ....104, 163, 178
8:58-59 239
9:1-41 244
9:35-38 244
10:17-18 49
10:22-23 250
10:22-39 241
10:30 ....163, 167
10:34-36 ....163, 288n15
10:41 22
11:8 ....263n7
11:16 ....263n7
11:16 36
11:25-27 166
11:27 129
11:32 37
11:33-35 251
11:35-36 ....263n7
11:38-44 129
11:45-53 ....263n7
11:45-57 ....47, 266n15
11:47 ....266n13
11:47-48 ....266n15
11:53 ....266n15
12:1-2 36
12:3-8 37
12:6 38
12:9-11 47
12:10 ....266n13
12:10-11 ....263n7
12:27 251
12:34 ....48, 231
12:39-40 ....298n4
14:1 ....281n31
14:1-11 240
14:3 ....281n30

14:6 ....134, 283n60
14:9 ....35, 95, 241, 167
14:26 ....113, 175, 290n19
14:26-27 130
15:18-19 43
15:25 ....283n60
15:26 ....130, 245
16:5-16 113
16:7 ....283n61
16:12-15 134
17:5 242
17:12 38
18:2 39
18:5 38
18:11 50
18:19 ....266n13
18:20 ....266n12
18:20 ....267n18
18:22 ....266n13
18:24 ....266n13
18:33-38 53
18:35 ....266n13
18:40 ....267n18
19:1 251
19:3 251
19:10-11 49
19:12 53
19:15 ....266n13
19:18 251
19:25-27 31
19:26 30
19:30 251
19:36 ....298n4
19:38 38
19:39 38
20:11-18 37
20:19 36
20:19-25 36
20:25 242
20:28 36
20:28 ....272n49
20:30-31 ....129, 255
20:31 ....36, 129, 289n33
21:20-24 35

Acts 258, 264n4, 289n2
1:8 113
1:14 ....30, 32
1:15-16 32
1:16 38
2:19 83
2:22-38 245
2:32 ....288n15
2:36 ....289n33
2:42-47 58
3:19-26 224
4:1 46
4:5 ....266n12
5:17 46
5:35-39 84
5:36 85
5:37 85
8 99

9:20 246
9:22 ....246, 289n33
10:39 64
12:17 ....263n2
15 93
15:12-23 ....263n2
17:3 ....289n33
18:2 ....268n6
18:5 ....289n33
21:37-39 84
21:38 85
23:6 46
23:8 46

Romans 118, 178
1:3 246
1:4 246
2:11 118
5:18 247
5:19 247
8:35 247
9:5 178

1 Corinthians
2:2 246
2:8 104
11:3 ....288n15
11:23 246
15 172
15:7 32
15:12-19 120
15:44 ....279n6
15:50-54 132
15:28 ....288n15

2 Corinthians
1:19 246
4:4 133
5:21 247
8:9 247
10:1 247
11:4 254

Galatians 254
1:8-9 ....299n1
1:19 ....263n2
2:9 ....263n2
3:13 64
4:4-5 246

Ephesians
5:22f 164

Philippians
2:6-9 247
2:6-11 166

Colossians 70, 162, 247
1:15-17 162
1:15-20 247
1:16 163
1:17 ....160, 163
2:9 166
2:14 50

1 Thessalonians
1:10 132

4:14..................................247
4:15-17............................132

2 Thessalonians
2:1-12 ....274n3
2:3 81
3:5..................................247

2 Timothy
2:8..................................247

Hebrews ... 50, 101, 235, 266n14,
....298n4
10:5-10 50
10:7..................................235

10:10................................299n16
13:8 163

James
4:5 ....299n6

1 John
1:1-2.....................................36
1:1-3 ....27, 262n23
1:2 163
2:18...............................81, 274n3
2:22..................................274n3
2:22-23.............................165
4:2-3....................................97
4:3 ....274n3

5:6-9.......................................99

2 John
7 ....81, 274n3

Revelation....................115, 274n5
13:1-10 ....
13:1-18 ....274n5
13-14 82
13:20 82
17:3..................................274n5
17:7-17..............................274n5
19:11-20:6 132
22:7-13 132

OTHER ANCIENT WRITINGS

APOCRYPHA

2 Maccabees
15:12-16 23

2 Esdras
2:18-19 23

DEAD SEA SCROLLS.... 9, 149, 178,
                                234, 291n29

4Q 246 f1ii:1 234

PATRISTIC LITERATURE

Archelaus
*Acts of the Disputation with the
 Heresiarch Manes*
36 (*ANF* 6.209) 275n21

Athenagoras...............................69
A Plea for the Christians 69
10 (*ANF* 2.133)................... 271n22
12 (*ANF* 2.134) 271n23
24 (*ANF* 2.141) 271n24

Augustine.............. 102, 114, 216,
                                280n16
Confessions
3.6-10 .... 279n40
Retractions
I.xiii.3................................ 280n16

Clement of Alexandria 69
Exhortation to the Heathen.........69
1 (*ANF* 2.173)................... 271n25
10 (*ANF* 2.201) 271n26
12 (*ANF* 2.205) 291n33
The Instructor
1.5, 6 (*ANF* 2.215, 216).... 271n27
(*ANF* 2.296)...................... 271n28

Clement of Rome
*First Epistle of Clement to the Corin-
 thians*..................................67

1, 16, 20, 24, 36 (*ANF* 1.5, 9, 11,
   14)................................... 270n2

Cyprian......................................71
Treatise XII
2.8 (*ANF* 5.515)................ 271n43
*The Seventh Council of Carthage
 Under Cyprian* 271n45
Prooemium (*ANF* 567).... 271n44
Didache 67
7   67
16:1-8 .... 275n22

Epiphanius of Salamis 92, 93,
   276n4, 277n15,
                                277n17
Panarion......................................92
2.15.3....................277n11, 277n17
18 ....276n6
19 ....276n6
29 ....276n6
30 ....276n6
53 ....276n6

Eusebius of Nicomedia............94

Eusebius 52, 92, 94, 114,
   270n19, 278n25,
                                280n16
Church History
Book 4............................... 280n16
I.iv.15................................. 280n16
2.7 (*NPNF* 2.1:110)...........267n25
3.27 (*NPNF* 2.7.158)...........276n5
3.27.1-6 (*NPNF* 2.1.158-159)
   ....276n1
3.27.4 (*NPNF* 2.1.158) 277n9
3.28.2 (*ANF* 1.160) 278n25
4.8.4 (*NPNF* 2.1.181).........275n18

Hippolytus...............................71
*Treatise on Christ and the
 AntiChrist* 71
4 (*ANF* 5.204) 271n40

26 (*ANF* 5.206).................271n41
67 (*ANF* 5.219)................. 271n42

Ignatius......................................68
Epistle of Ignatius to the Ephesians .
   68, 97, 178
7 (*ANF* 1.96) 270n3
19 (*ANF* 2.205) 291n31
Epistle to the Philadelphians
6 (ANF 1.82).........................276n1

Irenaeus.....69, 71, 92, 97, 99, 100
Against Heresies
1.10.1 (*ANF* 1.330)............271n13
1.26.1 (*ANF* 1.352) 278n29
1.26.2 (*ANF* 1.351) 276n1
2.23.4 (*ANF* 1.391) 271n14
3.3.4 (*ANF* 1.416) 278n24
(*ANF* 1.418)......................271n15
(*ANF* 1.421)......................271n16
(*ANF* 1.427)......................271n17
(*ANF* 1.440) 271n18
(*ANF* 1.556)......................271n19
3.11.9 (*ANF* 1.429).............278n31,
                                278n32

Jerome 62, 103, 277n15
Letter
112, 4, 13 ....277n10

Justin Martyr 68, 86, 178
First Apology..............................68
31(*ANF* 1.173)
17, 4, 23 (*ANF* 1.168, 1.164, 1.170)
   270n7
43 (*ANF* 1.184) 291n32
63 (*ANF* 1.184)....................270n8
Dialogue with Trypho 68
36 (*ANF* 1.212) 270n9
48 (*ANF* 1.219)..................277n14
56 (*ANF* 1.223) 271n10
58 (*ANF* 1.225) 271n12
61 (*ANF* 1.227) 271n11

72 (*ANF* 1.260) 292n70

Mathetes 68
The Epistle of Mathetes to Diognetus 68
7 (*ANF* 1.27) 270n5
7.9.10 (*ANF* 1.27) 270n6

Novatian 71
A Treatise Concerning the Trinity 71
10 (*ANF* 5.619) 271n46
12 (*ANF* 5.621) 272n48
21 (*ANF* 5.632) 272n47
30 (*ANF* 5.642) 272n49

Origen 65, 70, 85
*Commentary on the
   Gospel of John* 70
1.11 (*ANF* 10.303) 271n37
2.6 (*ANF* 10.328) 271n38
11.12 (*ANF* 10.440) 276n1
Contra Celsus
1.28 65
4.14 65
6.78 65
De Principiis
4, 1.2.10
   (*ANF* 4.240, 250).........271n35
1.3.4 (*ANF* 4.252) 271n36
In Luc. Hom
25 85

Polycarp 69, 278n24
Polycarp to the Philippians..........68
2, 12 (*ANF* 1.33, 35) 270n4

Tertullian............. 56, 70, 95, 100
Against the Valentinians
4 (*ANF* 3.505) 278n30
Apology
2.5.7 .... 268n4
1.31.6..................................275n18
*On Prescription against
   Heretics*................................70
13 (*ANF* 3.249) 271n30
(*ANF* 3.652)..................... 278n32
*The Five Books against
   Marcion*...............................70
Book III 70
Book IV 70
Book V 70
3(*ANF* 3.328) 271n34
3.20 (*ANF* 3.338) 271n32
4 (*ANF* 3.345-423) 271n33,
                                         271n34
Against Praxeas
2 (*ANF* 3.598)..................... 271n29

Theophilus of Antioch 69
To Autolycus
2.15 (*ANF* 2.100)............... 271n20
2.22 (*ANF* 2.103) 271n21

Qur'an 16, 114, 126, 127,
                          128, 129, 130, 131,
                     132, 282n48, 282n51,

Sura
3:42 128
3:45-47................................261n8
3:47 128
3:48 129
3:55 ....261n8
3:144 ....261n9
4:46 129
4:159 131
4:169 129
5:110....................................261n8
5:112-114.............................129
6:34 130
10:64 130
18:110..................................261n9
19:18-19..............................261n8
19:31....................................129, 261n8
21:91 128
23:50 ....114, 128
43:61 ....131, 261n8
43:64 131
61:6:.....................................129
66:12 128
Al 'Imran: The Family of Amran
3:18......................................127
3:46......................................127
3:49......................................127
3:66......................................126
3.84......................................127
Al Baqarah: The Cow
2:135....................................126
2:87......................................127
Al An'am
6:85-87................................126
Al Ma'idah
5.46......................................127
5:110....................................127
An Nisa
4:171....................................127
Al-Saff 129
61:6:.....................................127
Maryam
19:22....................................127
19:30....................................127

Eastern Literature
Bhagavad-Gita..........115, 116, 118
2:11......................................118
2:72 ....281n23, 281n26
8:17......................................282n35
9:29 118
10:20 ....281n22
10:12-13 ....281n23, 281n25
Bhavishya Maha Puranan
3.3.17-31 ....280n9
Bhagavata Purana 118
Harivamsa Purana 118
Four Noble Truths 122, 123
Eightfold Path...........122, 123-125

**Ancient Greek and Roman
   Literature**
Josephus................. 51, 52, 59-60,
     61, 62, 64, 84, 85, 238, 263n2,
     264n3, ...264n4, 5, 267n18,
     270n19, 270n20, 270n21
Antiquities......................61, 264n3
13.5.9................................... 264n5
18   61
18.1.6......................................85
18.16.............................. 266n12
18.33 60
18.63 ....270n21
Book 20...................................61
20.5.1 85
20.8.6.......................................85
20.97 84
20.200.....................................61
*Jewish Wars
   (Bellum Judaicum [BJ])*
2.4 84
2.8.1 85
2.13.4 85
2.13.5 85
2.118......................................84
2.261-263.............................84
2.8.14 ....264n5
7.11.1 84
20.97 84
Testimonium Flavianum 60, 61,
                    62, 270n19, 270n20

Mara bar Serapion......57, 269n9,
                     269n10, 269n11
Letter
ANF 8.737 .... 269n8

Pliny the Younger 56, 58, 62,
                                      268n4
Epistle to Trajan...... 268n2, 268n3
10.96 .... 267-268n1

Suetonius 56, 268n7
Life of Claudius
25.4 56

Tacitus.............................55, 62
Annals of Imperial Rome.............55
15.47......................................55
15.44 .... 267n24

Rabbinic Literature
Babylonian Talmud
Tractate Sanhedrin 43a 63-65,
                                      270n22
Tractate 29a, 30b 264n2
Abot de-Rabbi Natan
37.4......................................265n6
Mishnah Aboth
2.2 .... 264n2

······························· ✠ ·······························

INDEX OF NAMES

Abel...44
Abraham.................126, 129, 153,
        239, 247, 280n16
Abu-Isa 88,
Adam........ 161, 249, 250, 280n16
Agrippa II...................................84
Ahab..23
Ahmad, Mirza Ghulam
Alacoque, Margaret Mary (see
        Alacoque, Saint Margaret Mary)
Alacoque, Saint Margaret Mary
        ....194, 199, 206, 294n10
Aland, Kurt.............. 183, 292n68
Albright, William F....22, 262n21
Alexander, Bishop of the Russian
        Orthodox Church Abroad
        ....227-28, 230
Alroy, David 88
Ambrose......................................62
Ananus.................................. 263n2
Anderson, Charles.... 144, 286n23
Anderson, Hugh.......................141
Andrew 34, 228
Anna..228
Antiochus Epiphanes
        .... 82, 266n11
Apollinaris
        ....103, 272n55, 279n44
Arius...................72, 73, 94, 160,
        179, 259, 272n53
Athanasius 73, 103, 160
Augustus 106, 234
Baez, Joan 208
Bahat, Dan...............................215
Bahrdt, C.F.....137, 284n4, 284n5
Bar Ba'ayan, Yehonatan.............86
Bar Shimon, Masabala 86
Barth, Karl
        Epistle to the Romans,
        significance of 142

quest for historical Jesus
        unnecessary....................143
Bauckham, Richard...........277n15
Beckmann, Max..............201, 202
Blomberg, Craig 216
Bock, Darrell 136, 183, 239
Bon Jovi, Jon............................209
Bono...209
Booth, Herbert 210
Borg, Marcus ....
        dangers of Christianity...... 110
        historical importance
        of Jesus.............................25
        Jesus and Buddha.............109
        Jesus Seminar 18, 170
        perspective on Jesus..... 286n35
        postmodern thinking of
        ....279n5
        skepticism............................18
Bornkamm, Gunther 145
Bright, Bill 212
Bromiley, Geoffrey 84
Brown, Dan ....
        critique of 178-80, 189
        Da Vinci Code 176-77
        Dead Sea Scrolls, misuse
        of...............................291n29
        documentary 215
        Jesus and Mary, relationship
        between 261n1, 291n37
        Jesus Seminar 290n27
        Jesus' divinity 67, 177-78,
        188
Browne, Jackson 208
Bruce, F.F..................................46
        Ahmad's teachings
        on...............................280n11
Buddha
        Christianity incompatible
        with Buddhism 122-25

equal with Jesus..................109
identified with Jesus 112-13
irrelevance to
        Buddhism156, 253
Jesus not Buddha 121
Mani aligned with 102
similarities of Jesus to
        Buddha.................... 120-21
symposium on Jesus and
        Buddha.............................134
Bultmann, Rudolf 142, 143
Caesar Augustus ...(See Augustus)
Calvin, John..............................196
Carey, Mariah...........................209
Carson, D.A...................22, 216
Catherine of Siena193, 194, 293n7
Celsus...65
Cerinthus
        Gnostic heresy of 98-101,
        278n28
        millenarian errors........ 278n25
        view of *logos* 257
Chagall, Marc...202, 203, 295n40
Charlesworth, James 146
Chilton, Bruce 146
Claudius......................... 56, 268n6
Clementz, Hermann 200
Constantine 17, 179
Cook, Rabbi Michael J........63-64
Cooper, David 226
Cranach, Lucas 196, 197
Crossan, John Dominic...170, 286
David 28, 48, 65, 80, 88,
        126, 132, 153, 230,
        232, 249, 265n7
Decius (Emperor) 269n16
De Lacey, D.R. 264n4
Dead Kennedys 208
DeMille, Cecil B. 210
Doobie Brothers 209

Dürer, Albrecht 196, 294n16
Dylan, Bob 207-8
Dyrness, William 204
Ebion....................................92
Eddy, Mary Baker 165
Edersheim, Alfred.............84, 138
Ehrman, Bart
   critical of Dan Brown 177
   critique of 182-89
   Lost Christianities..........96, 181
   Misquoting Jesus.............181-82
   personal history............. 180-81
Elijah..21, 22, 23, 32, 33, 84, 224,
   245, 254, 262n25
Elizabeth.......................... 28, 228
Ell, Michael 203
Enoch....................................84
Ephraim.................................162
Erickson, Millard 236, 249
Eusebius of Nicomedia.............94
Eutyches................................91
Evans, Craig...........................238
Fee, Steve 206
Feinberg, C.L. 266n11
Ferreiro, Alberto 273n1
Fruchtenbaum, Arnold..... 226-27,
   298n1-n4, 299n5-n8, 299n15
Funk, Robert
   Jesus Seminar, founder
      of.......................10, 290n22
   popularity............................ 170
   Jesus as Wisdom
      Sage 286n35
   Jesus of history vs. Christ of faith
      .... 290n12
Gaius
   Emperor...............................52
   third century
      theologian 278n25
Gamaliel 264
Gardener, James.................. 204-5
Geisler, Norman145, 148-149, 150,
   274n9
Gibson, Mel 212
Graves, Kersey ... 115, 117, 280n16
Green, Michael.......................230
Greenbaum, Norman.............209
Grudem, Wayne................272n53
Gundry, Robert 279n6
Habermas, Gary 57
Hadrian.............................56, 86
Hagner, Donald.......................24
Hällström, Gunnar af 278n25
Hanh, Thich Nhat.................109
Harnack, Adolf........................58
Hengel, Martin.... 51, 149, 267n18
Herod
   Antipas 22, 33, 52
   the Great............................226
Hilary...................................187
Hitler....................................203
Holtzmann, H.J.....................138
Hooker, Morna 145

Hubbard, D.A. 266n13
Hughes, T.P. 283n57
Indyke, Amy M. 293n7
Isaiah.............................23, 88
Jacob............234, 275n13, 275n16
James
   brother of Jesus
      .... 30, 61, 263n2
   son of Zebedee...........33, 35,
      244, 263n6
Jeremiah............21, 22, 23, 23-24,
   226, 254
Jesus Christ
   consubstantial with God
      .... 74, 272n55, 272n56
   divine nature of............73, 107
   documentaries about..... 214-15
   hypostatic union
      ....103-6, 248, 249-50, 272n55
   Immanuel
      ....28, 233
   in art 192-205
   in film 210-14
   in music
      ....205-9, 296n54, 296n60
   Iesou-s (Greek, "Yahweh
      is salvation") 128
   pop-culture....................216-19
   virgin birth
      .... 117, 137, 148, 171, 235, 249
   Yeshua' (Hebrew, "Yahweh is
      salvation")........28, 63, 64, 128
John
   disciple of Jesus........33, 35, 61,
      82, 97, 98, 99, 114,
      173, 244, 248, 263n6,
      278n24, 278n25
   the Baptist 21, 22-23,
      32-33, 61, 62, 102,
      103, 126, 161, 174,
      213, 223, 244, 245, 254
Jones, Beth................206, 296n54
Jones, Jim 82, 156
Joseph
   brother of Jesus....................30
   husband of Mary...........28, 29,
      31, 70, 99, 137,
      209, 217, 233, 294n23
   of Arimathea 33, 37, 38,
      45, 284n4, 284n5
   Old Testament 126
Judas
   brother of Jesus (Jude)..........30
   Iscariot.................... 38-39, 113
   the Galilean....................84, 85
Kahler, Martin.........139, 285n16
Käsemann, Ernst.............143-145
Kempe, Margery.................... 194
Kennedy, Robert E................. 109
Kimball, Dan.....218, 219, 298n96
Koch, E.................................203
Kohler, Kaufmann 264n5
Koresh, David.........................82

Krishna 114-20
Lazarus.........................33, 36, 165
Lenin, V.I.......................201, 202
Lennon, John.........................209
Lewis, C.S. 148, 252
Lloyd Webber, Andrew 213
Lucian 57-58
Lucifer (See Satan)......................
Luther, Martin 196
Maccabaeus, Judas............23, 84
Machiavelli 43
Mahatma Gandhi..............119-20
Manasseh 162
Manet, Edouard 200
Manes...................................87
Mani....................................102
Marcion
   ...70, 72, 100-01, 258, 278n34
Marshall, I. Howard 146
Martha.........................33, 36, 165
Mary
   mother of Jesus....... 28, 29, 30,
      31, 70, 99, 106, 114,
      127, 128, 159, 160, 209,
      228, 250, 294n23
   of Magdala 15, 25, 33, 35,
      37, 150, 197, 210,
      263n8, 291n37
   sister of Lazarus...... 33, 36, 37
Masabala bar Shimon................86
Mason, Steve....................... 60-61
Mayhew, Eugene 274n10
McConkie, Bruce 159, 287n5
McDowell, Josh 60
McKinsey, Dennis....................64
Melchizedek.....................84, 232
Menahem ben Judah 84
Menander...............................97
Meyer, Ben.......................... 146
Michael (Archangel)................ 161
Miesel, Sandra 177, 263n8
Monty Python 214
Morgan, G. Campbell........ 273n2
Moses 33, 84, 126, 232,
      239, 247, 280n16
Moshe of Crete 88
Muhammad..
   Allah, pagan deity.............126
   coming predicted by
      Jesus........................... 129-31
   Holy Spirit identified
      with 130, 283n60
   irrelevance of 156, 253
   Jesus second to 127-28
   Jesus' coming and 132
   Scripture and 127, 282n50,
      282n51
   view of Christ................. 16-17
Nathaniel.......................... 34, 228
Nero...............................55, 56
Nestorius........... 106, 259, 272n55
Nicodemus............. 33, 37-38, 45,
      284n4, 284n5

Noah 126, 284n57
Noetus.......................................95
Ochs, Phil 208
Pagels, Elaine....................277n21
Papias 114
Patai, Raphael...........................88
Paul (Apostle) 16, 52, 70, 71,
                   87, 93, 101, 113,
                   246-7, 248, 254,
                   264n4, 277n15
Paulus, Heinrich......................137
Pelikan, Jaroslav........................ 19
Peter   20, 25, 33, 34-35,
                   243, 254, 282n35
Philip...........................34, 35, 241
Philo 51, 52
Picasso, Pablo..........................201
Pierre, Jean-Baptist Marie 199
Pius IX 195
Plato 98, 269n8
Plummer, Alfred 273n2
Pontius Pilate 51-53, 60,
                   62-63, 84, 122,
                   170, 201-2, 267n18
Praxeas 95
Pressley, Elvis 209
Price, Christopher 61
Proteus 57, 269n12
Pythagoras 268n8, 269n8
Quirinius 84
Rabbi Aquiba 238
Rabow, Jerry 89
Reimarus, Hermann Samuel
                  136-137
Rembrandt........ 197, 198, 295n24
Renan, Ernest 93, 276-77n8,
                   277n12
Reuveni, David 88

Rice, Anne 216-17
Rimes, LeAnn 207
Rivera, Diego...................... 202-3
Robinson, John A.T................ 216
Roth, Conrad................. 285n22
Rouault, Georges....................202
Rubens, Peter Paul.................. 198
Sabellius 95
Salvador Dali 50
Sanders, E.P. 146, 286
Satan (Lucifer) 102, 128, 158,
                  159, 160, 170,
                  214, 258, 274n5
Saturninus................................97
Schlatter, Adolf......................138
Schneerson, Menachem 88
Schurer, Emil........................226
Schweitzer, Albert.....12, 137, 139,
                140, 141, 286n24
Scorsese, Martin 213-14
Serrano, Andres 204, 205
Shalivahan, king of Paithan 112
Sheldon, Garrett 216
Shem 284n57
Siddhartha Gautama.......112, 120
Simeon 115, 228
Simon
     bar Kochba ...79, 82, 85-86, 87
     ben Kosiba........................238
     brother of Jesus 30
     Pharisee 243
     the magician (Magus)
     .... 85, 99, 278n26
     the Servant 84
Skarsaune, Oskar..276n3, 278n28
Smith
     Joseph 157
     Joseph Fielding.................. 159

Sobule, Jill...............................209
Socrates 268n8, 269n8
Solomon..................................126
Stevens, Ray............................208
Strauss, David F.............. 137, 141
Telford, W.R....................285n17
Tennant, Agnieszka........206, 207,
                  296n52
Theudas............................84, 85
Thiering, Barbara 149
Thomas 35-36, 112, 242
Tiberius...............................52, 56
Tom Ring the Younger, Ludger
                  197
Trajan........................... 56, 268n4
Uhde, Fritz von.......................200
Underwood, Carrie 209
Vagacs, Robert.........................208
Valentinus...............................100
Van Hoogstraten, Nicholas..... 198
Van Eck, Stephen 115
Venturini, K.H. 137, 284n5
Vermes, Géza................. 146, 286
Wallace, Daniel 182, 183
Weiss, Johannes...............138, 139
Wesley, Charles.......................205
West, Richard..........................203
Witherington, Ben III....170, 172,
                  176, 290n23
Wrede, William .. 139-40, 286n23
Wright, N.T. 146, 151, 161n13,
                  286n24, 287n36
Yehonatan bar Ba'ayan 86
Young, Brigham 157
Zevi, Shabbatai 88
Zoroaster.................................102
Zschech, Darlene....................207

INDEX OF SUBJECTS

A Course in Miracles................164
Abba (Aramaic, "papa, daddy")...............................117
Adoptionist.................92, 99, 186
Aeons........................100, 101, 252
Agnosticism......181, 183, 184, 188
Ahmad...............129, 130, 283n60
Alexandria.....72, 94, 259, 292n68
Alexandrinus (codex).......282n50
Allah
  Jesus and.............113, 127, 131
  New Testament inspired
    by....................................130
  pagan deity...................16, 126
Al-Masih...................................128
Anathema....................254, 299n1
Antichrist..............79, 81, 87, 165, 196, 274n3, 274n4, 274n5, 274n6
Anti-Semitism........100, 200, 203
Apocalyptic...............81, 139, 227, 286n35
Apocrypha...................30, 96, 99, 129, 270n19
Apollinarianism..........74, 91, 103, 155, 259
Apostles' Creed....................72, 73
Arabic.................60, 62, 127, 128
Aramaic.................9, 10, 102, 127, 275n13, 283n56
Archangel...............97, 161, 277n8
Arianism........74, 94-95, 155, 259
Athanasian Creed..........72, 73-74
Attributes........104, 118, 163, 205
Avatars.................16, 115, 281n33
Babylonian exile
  (captivity)...............46, 226
Babylonian Talmud..................63
Babylonians..............................80
Baha'ism..................................115

Baikuntha (in Hinduism, "kingdom of God")..............................116
Basiliea tou theou (Greek, "kingdom of God")..............................116
Ben-Hur (film)........................211
Bethabara..................................22
Book of Enoch.............................48
Brahma/Brahman 261n6, 282n35
Buddhism
  Christianity incompatible
    with.........122-25, 156, 253
  Eightfold Path...............122, 123, 124, 125
  Four Noble Truths..........122, 123
  Jesus and...................109, 110-15, 120-22, 276n8
  Mani influenced by.................102
Byzantine..........130, 191, 285n16, 293n1
Caesar.......45, 51, 53, 58, 266n18
Caesarea Philippi..........20, 21, 49, 266n13
Cana............................30, 31, 150
Cerinthianism...................98, 257
Chalcedon................................74
Chalcedonian Creed
  ....72, 74, 104
Chalcedonian Definition
  ....106, 161, 168, 272n55
Christian.......11, 15, 17, 20, 51, 57
Christian Science....................164
Christianity . 11, 16, 17, 56, 57, 58
Christians.......16, 48, 55, 56, 57, 58, 59, 60, 61, 62, 63, 64, 65, 66, 67, 68, 71, 72, 74, 75, 83, 86, 91, 93, 94, 95, 96, 97, 99, 101, 102, 103, 104, 105, 106, 109, 110, 114, 115, 117, 119, 120, 122, 125, 126, 127,

128, 129, 131, 132, 134, 135, 138, 139, 142, 143, 144, 145, 147, 149, 150, 155, 156-59, 160, 161, 169, 172, 177, 181, 193, 195, 200, 205, 206, 207, 208-9, 213, 216, 218, 223, 231, 232, 248, 252, 253, 264n4, 267n1, 268n2, 268n4, 269n12, 269n16, 272n53, 277n12, 279n5, 280n16
Christology70, 72, 73, 160, 285n16
Christos (Greek, "anointed one")
  25, 56, 262n21
Church Fathers.......67, 71, 74, 87, 92, 93, 94, 96, 98, 99, 100, 112, 114, 186, 187, 273n1, 276n1, 278n26
Codices (sing., *codex*)........96, 187, 282n50, 291n29
  Alexandrinus (fifth century)
    ....282n50
  Bezae Cantabrigiensis
    ....292n68
  Coptic Scrolls........96, 291n29
  Sinaiticus (fourth century)
    ....282n50
  Vaticanus (fourth century)
    ....282n50
Co-eternality/Eternal.........73, 74, 95, 96, 115, 158, 159, 160, 164, 165, 166, 167, 179, 239, 242, 250, 281n25, 287n5
Constantinople..................74, 106
Coptic (*see also* Codices)......39, 96
Coptic Scrolls (*see also* Codices)
 178
Coptic Gospel of Truth..............100

Coptic Scrolls............................ 178
Council of Ephesus.................. 106
Council of Jerusalem.... 93, 263n2
Council of Nicaea................36, 94
Creed of Nicaea (See Nicene Creed)
Creeds 71-75, 105, 106,
           156, 168, 170, 172,
           173, 179, 279n6
  Battle Creeds...................72-75
  Eastern...................................72
  Western...................................72
Da Vinci Code 11, 37, 67, 96,
           169, 176-77, 290n26
Day of Atonement 93
Day of Pentecost................. 32, 245
Dead Sea 227
Dead Sea Scrolls 9, 178, 149,
           234, 291n29
Deity, concepts of .. 16, 17, 20, 25,
  67, 68, 69, 70, 71, 74, 91, 92, 94,
  95, 101, 103, 104, 105, 107, 115,
  118, 121, 126, 141, ...
  155, 157, 161, 163, 167, 178, 179,
  188, 236, 242, . 244, 247, 248,
  249, 272n53
Demiurge...................98, 100, 101
Demythologization 142
Diaspora...................... 88, 266n11
Disciples   20, 22, 23, 25, 30, 32,
           33, 34, 35, 36, 37, 38,
           39, 45, 49, 57, 63, 79,
           80, 81, 83, 111, 112, 118,
           122, 123, 131, 136, 137,
           171, 174, 212, 213, 223,
           230, 231, 235, 236, 240,
           241, 242, 243, 244, 245,
           251, 252, 254, 266n12,
           283n57, 285n17, 291n37
Diocaesarea.............................. 103
Discovery Channel.................. 215
Divorce............................ 149, 150
Docetic...................97, 98, 99, 144
Docetism............................ 97, 155
Docetists....................................72
Dome of the Rock 17
Drash (Hebrew, "exposition") 226
Dualism 97
Dynamic Monarchianism168, 259
Eastern Orthodox....... 192, 293n2
Ebionism...............92, 94, 99, 155,
           257, 276n1, 276n3,
           276n4, 277n15, 278n28
Ebionites 16, 72, 91, 93
Egypt.........28, 65, 72, 85, 94, 96,
           151, 226, 240, 292n68
Elohim 158, 159, 160, 287n5
Emanation 98, 100, 258
Enlightenment
  Buddhism...................120, 121
  Gnostic idea................100, 258
  Hinduism...............116, 261n6
  Period of 17, 135, 199
Ephesus......................................98

Epistle of the Apostles.................. 99
Essence 69, 73, 94, 96, 101,
           105, 160, 167, 168, 180,
           241, 259, 272n53, 272n56
Essenes 46, 88, 227, 264n5,
           284n4, 284n5
Eternal............ 120, 121, 124, 134,
           157, 160, 178, 252,
           254, 255, 299n1
Eutychianism.............. 74, 91, 155,
           259, 272n55
Existentialism 141, 142, 204,
           217, 223
Firstborn 153, 161, 162, 247
Form criticism 143, 145
Fragments 136
Galilee........22, 23, 32, 37, 42, 43,
           174, 243, 266n12, 266n18
Gaulonites.................................. 85
Germany... 83, 196, 197, 203, 295
Gnosis 96, 97
Gnostic.............. 37, 72, 110, 147,
           164, 177, 258, 277n8,
           277n21, 278n28, 291n29
Gnosticism............. 16, 91, 96-102,
           151, 180, 257
Gnostics 16, 72, 96, 98,
           101, 180, 223, 262n22
Godspell.................................. 213
Golan 22
Gospel of Judas, The 39, 151
Gospel of Philip, The ... 151, 291n37
Gospel of Pseudo-Matthew... 263n3
Gospel of Thomas 96, 147, 151,
           150, 172, 277n21
Gospel to the Hebrews.............. 92
Gospels...........9, 10, 12, 15, 17, 27,
           29, 30, 32, 34, 39, 44,
           45, 46, 48, 51, 61, 63,
           65, 70, 80, 92, 93, 96,
           107, 111, 112, 117, 135,
           136, 137, 138, 139, 140,
           141, 142, 144, 145, 146,
           147, 148, 149, 150, 151,
           152, 153-54, 170, 171,
           172, 173, 174, 175, 176,
           178, 179, 180, 185, 192,
           211, 212, 215, 216, 223,
           225, 234, 236, 237, 246,
           247, 251, 252. 254,
           262n21, 263n3, 264n4,
           277n21, 285n22, 287n36,
           291n29, 291n37
Greek
  cosmology 248
  manuscripts.........61, 183, 184,
           186, 187
  paganism 174
  philosophy...................74, 104
Ha-mashiach 128
Herodians 43, 44, 46
Hinduism.......... 12, 110, 111, 112,

           114, 115, 116, 117, 118,
           119, 261n6, 282n35
Historical criticism.................. 145
Historical Jesus.(See Quest for the
           Historical Jesus)
Holy Spirit   28, 67, 70, 71, 73,
           74, 91, 95, 100, 130,
           131, 134, 160, 161, 166,
           167, 192, 212, 227,
           259, 287n6
Homoiousios (Greek, "of a similar
           nature") 73, 95, 160,
           272n53
Homoousios... (Greek, "of the same
           essence")..............73, 95, 160,
           272n53
Hypostasis.... (from Greek, "being")
          75
Hypostatic union...75, 103-4, 248
Infancy Gospel of Thomas..... 263n3
Injil (Arabic, "gospel") ... 127, 129,
           283n51
Iota...................................272n53
'Isa (name for Jesus in Islam)
           .... 126, 127, 128, 283n52
'Isa Masih(Arabic, "Jesus the
           Messiah") 112, 283n52,
           283n56
Islam
  Jesus according to........... 16-17,
           125-32
  Jesus postcrucifixion and
          113-14
  moon god 16
  Muhammad irrelevant to
           .... 156, 253
Jehovah's Witnesses........... 160-64
Jerusalem   29, 36, 42, 43, 52,
           80, 81, 84, 85, 86, 87,
           88, 93, 112, 123, 215,
           225, 228, 230, 235, 245,
           250, 261n3 263n2, 273n2,
           277n12, 278n25
Jerusalem Council (*see* Council of
           Jerusalem)
Jerusalem Talmud 275n16
Jesus Seminar   10, 11, 18, 96,
           136, 146-47, 169-76,
           185, 188, 189, 289n2,
           290n22, 290n23
  Five Gospels, The 147
  Seven pillars of scholarly
           wisdom 172
  Westar Institute..... 169, 289n2
Jewish
  Christianity....................16, 97
  views of Jesus...................41-50
Judaism   44, 46, 47, 51, 56, 79,
           80, 86, 97, 101, 102, 110,
           125, 126, 131, 136, 144,
           146, 151, 203, 223, 239,
           277n21
Judgment 16, 74, 80, 81, 118,

161, 174, 197, 214, 224, 229, 237, 242

Kerygma (Greek, "proclamation") 141, 143, 144, 272n51

Kingdom.....10, 27, 35, 38, 51, 88, 102, 116, 123, 139, 140, 153, 174, 211, 229, 278n25

Kreitton (Greek, "better")........ 163

Law 101, 111, 223, 224, 225, 276n8, 277n8, 277n14
  of Christ 207
  of logic 133
  of Moses.......................93, 123
  of nature 137
  of Talmud......................264n2
  Oral 266n12

Literary criticism 143

Logos.................. 99, 103, 157, 248, 249, 257, 259

Maccabean........................ 43, 230

Manda......................................102

Mandaeanism................100, 101-2

Manichaean 102

Marcionism...... 91, 98, 100-1, 258

Marriage 194, 197, 217

Mashiach (Hebrew, "anointed one") 25, 128

Meizon (Greek, "greater")........ 163

Messiah
  distorted notions about
  228-32
  Ebionites' view of
  .... 16, 92-93, 257, 276n8
  false messiahs 79, 80, 82, 83, 84, 85, 86, 87, 88, 89, 91, 273n3
  Jewish and other religions' view of 110, 111
  New Testament view of
  232-36
  promise of.....................223-28
  Qur'an on 127,

Mind Science 164-66

Miracles 16, 17, 23, 65, 87, 127, 129, 137, 142, 148, 171, 237, 276n8, 284n4, 284n5

Modalism............... 91, 95-96, 166

Modalistic Monarchianism
  ....95, 259

Monarchianism 259

Monophysitism............74, 272n55

Mormon...............37, 112, 157-60

Myth, mythology, mythological
  .... 137, 141, 142, 147, 148, 149, 160, 170, 171, 182, 285n22, 286n35, 290n12

Nag Hammadi............96, 98, 147, 151, 178, 179, 291n29

Nestorianism 74, 259

New Age 16, 164

New quest (*see* Second Quest)

Nicaea (*see* Council of Nicaea)

Nicene Creed 71, 72-73, 168, 179, 272n52

Old Roman Creed 72, 272n51

Orthodoxy 254

Pagan...................16, 74, 126, 147, 153, 157, 174, 193, 195, 272n53, 280n16, 281n33

Palestine........... 57, 152, 214, 230, 269n12

Parables 117, 143, 170, 174, 213, 266n13

Parakletos, paracletos (Greek, "advocate, counselor")......... 283n60

Patripassianism.......................166

Periklutos (Greek, "famous, renown") 130

Person 73, 74, 75, 91, 94, 103, 104, 105, 106, 155, 159, 161, 166, 167, 168, 249, 259, 272n55, 287n5, 288n15

Pharisees 43, 44-45, 46, 264n3, 264n4, 264n5, 264n6, 265n6

Pleroma 100

Priests....................................46-47

Postmodernism............... 191, 199, 204-5, 217, 279n15

Protoktistos (Greek, "first created")
 162

Prototokos .. (Greek, "preeminent")
 162

Pseudepigrapha........................60

Pshat...... (Hebrew, meaning literal interpretation) 226

Q (from German *Quelle*, "source")
  ....138, 173

Quest for the Historical Jesus, The
  First Quest 136-43, 286n24
  Second Quest 143-45, 146, 149, 218
  Third quest 17, 136, 146-47, 150, 151, 154, 287n36

Qumran ...57, 88, 149, 227, 262n1

Redaction criticism..................143

Remez .... (Hebrew, meaning "suggestion") 226

Resurrection 15, 17, 22, 25, 37, 46, 57, 74, 101, 107, 111, 112, 131, 148,

.... 161, 171, 188, 245, ...251, 261n13

Roman Catholicism
  Anne Rice and 217
  art and Christ 198-99
  film and Christ..................213
  Franciscans 199
  orthodox view of Christ.......75
  Reformation and 135, 196
  Sacred Heart 195, 199, 294n10
  Sacred Heart of
  Jesus......................... 194-95
  use of images 192-95, 196

Sadducees.... 45-46, 164n5, 265n7

Salvation ....28, 89, 93, 96, 101, 102, 106, 116, 117, 120, 128, ...133, 154, 254

Scribes......................................46

Sinaiticus (codex)............. 282n50

Sod..... (Hebrew, "mystery, secret")
  226

Son of Man .... 1, 10, 21, 48-49, ...71, 80-83, 123, 166, ... 231, 237-238, ...244, 266n14

Source Criticism 143

Substance 272n56

Synoptic (from Greek "to see together") 137-38

Syriac......................................62

Temple Mount.................... 17, 80

Theotokos (Greek, "mother of God") 106, 136

Trinity............. 69, 70, 71, 72, 73, 74, 93, 105, 117, 119, 166, 169, 179, 205, 272n53

Unitarians 168

United Pentecostal Church
  (UPC)..........................166-67

Unity School of Christianity... 165

Unum patrem incognitum (Latin, "one unknown father") 97

Valentinianism 100-1, 258

Vaticanus (codex) 282n50

Vishnu....................................115

Worldview.............110, 138, 139, 148, 153

Yahweh............. 28, 101, 126, 128, 158, 159, 223, 224, 239

Zealot..................... 50-51, 53, 84, 227, 266n18

Zoroastrianism 96

H. Wayne House is Distinguished Research Professor of Biblical and Theological Studies at Faith Evangelical Seminary in Tacoma, Washington. He was Associate Professor of Systematic Theology at Dallas Theological Seminary and Professor of Theology and Culture at Trinity Graduate School, Trinity International University, and Professor of Law at Trinity Law School. He has a Juris Doctorate from Regent University School of Law, a Doctor of Theology from Concordia Seminary, St. Louis, a Master of Arts in Patristic Greek from Abilene Christian University, a Master of Theology and Master of Divinity from Western Seminary, and a Bachelor of Arts in Classical and Hellenistic Greek from Hardin-Simmons University. He teaches as adjunct or visiting professor at a number of seminaries in the United States and the South Pacific.

He has been author, coauthor, or editor of over 30 books, author of more than 70 journal and magazine publications, and a contributor to several books, dictionaries, and encyclopedias. Among his many books are *The Nelson Study Bible* (NT editor); *Nelson's Illustrated Bible Commentary* (NT editor); *The Battle for God; Charts on Open Theism and Orthodoxy; Charts of Apologetics and Christian Evidences; Charts of World Religions; Charts of Cults, Sects, and Religious Movements; A Christian View of Law; Restoring the Constitution; Israel: the Land and the People; God's Message, Your Sermon: How to Discover, Develop, and Deliver What God Meant by What He Said; Intelligent Design 101.*

Dr. House serves on the board of numerous organizations, including the Council on Biblical Manhood and Womanhood (of which he was founding president); Intelligent Design and Evolution Awareness (IDEA Center); and Evangelical Ministries to New Religions; and he served as president of the Evangelical Theological Society (1991). He leads study tours to Israel every year, and on alternate years to Jordan and Egypt, and Turkey and Greece.

He has been married to Leta Frances McConnell for 40 years and has two grown children, Carrie and Nathan, and five grandchildren.

He may be contacted at tours@hwhouse.com for interest in travel to biblical lands. His website is www.hwhouse.com.

SEARCHING FOR THE ORIGINAL BIBLE

Who Wrote It and Why? • *Is It Reliable?* • *Has the Text Changed over Time?*

RANDALL PRICE

Lost...destroyed...hidden...forgotten. For many centuries, no one has seen any of the original biblical documents. How can you know whether today's Bible is true to them?

Researcher and archaeologist Randall Price brings his expert knowledge of the Bible to tackle crucial questions:

What happened to the original Bible text? If we don't have it, what *do* we have?

How was the text handed down to our time? Can you trust that process?

What about the Bible's claim to be inspired and inerrant?

Current evidence upholds the Bible's claim to be the authoritative record of God's revelation—a Book you can build your life and faith on.

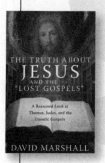

THE TRUTH ABOUT JESUS AND THE "LOST GOSPELS"

A Reasoned Look at Thomas, Judas, and the Gnostic Gospels

DAVID MARSHALL

Do the "Lost Gospels" unveil a side of Jesus we never knew?

Recent headlines, bestselling books, and even a blockbuster movie have called a lot of attention to the "Lost Gospels"—ancient documents that portray a Jesus far different from the one found in the Bible.

What are the "Lost Gospels," and where did they come from?

Are these writings trustworthy? Are they on par with the Bible?

Have we had wrong perceptions about Jesus all along?

A careful comparison of the "Lost Gospels" to the Bible itself reveals discrepancies that are cause for concern. This eye-opening resource will enable you to take a well-informed and well-reasoned stand on an ongoing and crucial controversy.

To read a sample chapter of these or other Harvest House books, go to www.harvesthousepublishers.com

HARVEST HOUSE PUBLISHERS

EUGENE, OREGON